D0164373

e-Retailing

Most experts agree that the advent of Internet retailing has transformed the market-place, but students of the subject have until now had to search far and wide for comprehensive up-to-date analysis of the new business landscape. Coverage of the recent dot.com boom and bust obscured the fact that e-retailing is now firmly established in global business, promising growth rates that will continue to rise globally to over £1 billion in 2004.

This much needed book provides readers with a guide to the implementation and operation of a successful e-retailing business, and has been written for students, entrepreneurs and researchers at all levels. By identifying and explaining the underlying principles of e-retailing and its relationship with conventional retail methods, this research-based book leads readers through this exciting and emerging subject.

Case studies include:

- iPod
- Nike
- Amazon
- eBay
- McDonald's
- Nokia.

With accessibly written features such as Key Learning Points, Questions, Think Points and Further Reading, *e-Retailing* is core reading for anyone using, studying or researching the Internet or e-retailing.

Charles Dennis is a Chartered Marketer and Senior Lecturer in Marketing and Retail Management at Brunel University Business School, UK. **Tino Fenech** is Senior Lecturer in Marketing, Specialist in e-Commerce, at Griffith University, Australia. **Bill Merrilees** is Professor and Head of the Marketing Department at Griffith Business School, Griffith University, Australia.

Routledge e-Business series

Routledge e-Business is a bold new series examining key aspects of the e-Business world, designed to provide students and academics with a more structured learning resource. Introducing issues of marketing, Human Resource Management, ethics, operations management, law, design, computing and the e-Business environment, it offers a broad overview of key e-Business issues from both managerial and technical perspectives.

Marketing the e-Business
Lisa Harris and Charles Dennis

e-Business Fundamentals
Edited by Paul Jackson

e-Retailing
Charles Dennis, Tino Fenech and Bill Merrilees

e-Economy: Rhetoric or Business Reality?
Edited by Leslie Budd and Lisa Harris

e-Retailing

Charles Dennis,
Tino Fenech and
Bill Merrilees

LONDON AND NEW YORK

First published 2004
by Routledge
2 Park Square, Milton Park, Abingdon,
Oxon OX14 4RN

Simultaneously published in the USA and Canada
by Routledge
270 Madison Ave, New York, NY 10016

Routledge is an imprint of the Taylor & Francis Group

Typeset in Perpetua and Bell Gothic by
Florence Production Ltd, Stoodleigh, Devon
Printed and bound in Great Britain by
The Cromwell Press, Trowbridge, Wiltshire

British Library Cataloguing in Publication Data
A catalogue record for this book is available from the British Library

Library of Congress Cataloging in Publication Data
Dennis, Charles E.
E-retailing/by Charles Dennis, Tino Fenech, and Bill Merrilees. – 1st ed.
p. cm.
Includes bibliographical references.
1. Internet marketing. 2. Electronic commerce. 3. Retail trade –Computer network resources. 4. Teleshopping. I. Fenech, Tino. II. Merrilees, Bill. III. Title.
HF5415.1265.E467 2004
658.8′72–dc22 2004003128

ISBN 0–415–31141–1 (hbk)
ISBN 0–415–31142–X (pbk)

Charles Dennis: To my wife Mary who endured the deprivation while I wrote late into the nights; to my daughters Trish and Juliet; to my mother Joan; and to Ross and Janine.

Tino Fenech: Dedicated to my patient and ever present cheer leader: my wife Clara; and to my great parents, who had more faith in me than I did.

Bill Merrilees: My contribution is dedicated to integrity as the core capability that helps you get through all sorts of crises; and to Dale as my integrity partner in life.

Contents

Illustrations

FIGURES

TABLES

Contributors

Authors' note: Charles Dennis, Tino Fenech and Bill Merrilees contributed equally to the content of this book.

DR CHARLES DENNIS is a Chartered Marketer and a Senior Lecturer in Marketing and Retail Management at Brunel University, London, UK, where he heads up the Marketing pathway of the University's BSc Business and Management degree. Originally a Chartered Chemical Engineer, he spent some years in engineering and technical posts, latterly with a marketing emphasis. This was followed by seven years with Marketing Methods as an Institute of Marketing approved consultant. Charles has been full-time in this current post since 1993. He has published internationally on consumer shopping behaviour, e-shopping and e-retailing. The textbook *Marketing the e-Business* (Harris and Dennis) was published by Routledge in 2002.

DR TINO FENECH has worked for many years in retailing and the services sectors as a marketer and has taught courses at a number of universities since 1984. He holds Bachelor of Business and Masters of Commerce degrees, both in marketing, and earned one of the first Ph.D.s in electronic commerce. Based upon his experience, Tino has acted as consultant to the fast food, health services, automotive, entertainment, direct marketing and telecommunications industries in Australia, Southeast Asia and the Middle East. As a specialist in direct marketing and e-commerce, Tino has often been called upon by the media, textbook publishers and academic journals for his opinions and reviews on current Internet issues. Currently Senior Lecturer in Marketing (e-Commerce) at Griffith University in Australia, Tino teaches and conducts research in Services Marketing and Non-store Marketing. His findings are published in a variety of media, conferences and journals, including the *Journal of Product and Brand Management*, *International Journal of Retail and Distribution Management* and *Journal of Retailing and Consumer Services*.

PROFESSOR BILL MERRILEES is currently in the Griffith Business School as Head of the Department of Marketing, based on the Gold Coast campus. Bill is also associated with the Services Industry Research Centre. He has worked in both academia and the government. He has a Bachelor of Commerce (Hons I) from the University of Newcastle, Australia, and an MA and Ph.D. from the University of Toronto, Canada. He has acted as consultant to companies such as Shell, Westpac and Jones Lang Lasalle at the large end, down to middle-sized companies such as accountants and even very small firms such as florists. Bill particularly enjoys conducting case research as it builds a bridge to the real world. He has published more than 70 refereed journal articles or book chapters. Six of his articles have been in the e-commerce field, including the *Journal of Relationship Marketing*, the *Journal of Business Strategies*, the *Corporate Reputation Review* and *Marketing Intelligence and Planning*. This work includes innovative scale development in the areas of e-interactivity, e-branding, e-strategy and e-trust.

DR BRIAN BAINBRIDGE received a degree in physical metallurgy from the Imperial College of Science, Technology and Medicine, University of London, in 1967. In 1972 he received a Ph.D. in Materials Science from the University of Sussex after doing research in the computer modelling of solid-state crystal growth. At present he is a Senior Lecturer in the School of Computing and Mathematical Sciences at the University of Greenwich, UK. At Greenwich, he lectures in computer languages and Web application technology, and has research interests in bioinformatics. Before that he was at the School of Business and Management of Brunel University, London, UK, and was a Principal Consultant at BIS Banking Systems. He has also worked as a Principal Research Associate in the Informatics Division of the Rutherford Appleton Laboratory, Didcot, near Oxford, doing research on financial expert systems and working within the UK Government Alvey programme directorate.

MARK HENRY is a business analyst and part-time lecturer in e-commerce at Brunel University, London, UK, where he gained an MBA, and is now involved in research into online transactions and consumer behaviour. His commercial background is in software development, from small-scale systems design to heading-up global projects with large corporations such as Diageo plc and Siemens AG.

Acknowledgements

The authors thank the many people who have helped bring this book to completion. In particular, we are grateful to Lisa Harris whose input has gone far beyond the duty of series editing; to Rachel Crookes and Jacqueline Curthoys of Routledge for patient support; to Mark Henry and Brian Bainbridge for contributing chapters; and to the many colleagues and students who have contributed cases and other material, including Jennifer Brown, Omar Chaudhry, Mehtap Durmus, Wayne Godfrey, John Honey, Chantima Kitipattarapumikul, Vijay Sisoda, Numan Tahir and Mnisha Talwar.

Introduction

AIM

The aim of this book is to demonstrate the success factors of e-retailing efficiency and effectiveness. It should be useful to readers, e-retailers and researchers seeking an understanding of, or studying, e-retail and related marketing at various levels, and should enhance their selling of a product or service to consumers (rather than businesses) via the Internet or other electronic channels. A key feature of the book is that it taps into the latest research studies and in some cases introduces new research findings. This aspect helps to ensure that the book is the most up-to-date possible and has the sharpest edge in guiding best practice e-retailing.

RATIONALE

> Rarely has the retail and consumer services sector been faced with a strategic challenge of such significant complexity and uncertainty which has grown in terms of that significance so rapidly.
>
> (Reynolds, 2000)

Reynolds reviewed e-commerce at the time of a fall in Internet stock values from previous unrealistically high expectations (the 'dot.com crash'). However, e-retail has not crept away, but rather, since that time, has progressed in acceptability to consumers and in market share. UK shoppers in particular love e-shopping, with 12 million e-shoppers, including many spending £3,000 plus per year online on products ranging from digital cameras to underwear (see Chapter 1 for more details). Reynolds also wrote that 'rarely has the academic world . . . lagged so significantly behind the world of practice'. Research has started to catch up, but we contend that a modernization of teaching and training in retail and marketing is overdue.

This is not just an academic issue. When the *Sunday Times* (UK) asked readers for their experiences of shopping online, they received an 'avalanche of complaint' about poorly designed sites, delivery, payment and many other problems (*Sunday Times* (UK) Doors, 9 February 2003). This book attempts to address some of the problems by providing research material and resources on the essential issues and success factors in e-retailing for researchers, lecturers, trainers, students and practitioners.

KEY ISSUES AND SUCCESS FACTORS IN E-RETAILING

	For a detailed discussion, see Chapter:
What is the mix of tools and techniques that e-retailers can use to provide value for customers?	1
What are the latest practices and trends in the e-retailing of the main product categories?	2
How can e-retailing be integrated into an organization?	3
How can e-retailers understand and communicate with e-consumers?	4
How can satisfying consumers' needs for information increase sales?	5
How should the e-store be designed so as to make it easy and enjoyable to move around the site?	6
How can e-shopper loyalty be encouraged?	6
How can consumers' needs and wants for good service be better satisfied?	7
How can e-retail brands be developed and integrated with high street brands?	8
What are the benefits and problems for e-retailers of 'locating' under a single 'roof' or e-mall?	9
How can the suitability of products for e-retailing be assessed?	10
What are the problems and opportunities of retailing via mobile communication devices?	11
What are the likely issues and technologies facing future e-retailing developments?	12

In Chapter 1 the advantages and disadvantages of e-retailing for retailers will be outlined along with an introduction to some of the basic tools and techniques of e-retailing (the e-retail mix).

Mini case study I.1
LIVING THE DOT.COM LIFE

E-shopping is taken for granted these days, but there can still be problems.

(Matthew Wall*, summarized and adapted from the *Sunday Times* (UK), 21 September 2003)

I've been living online for seven days – shopping, banking and playing. I can see live pictures from space, but can I get milk before tomorrow?

Since 2000, e-retailing has quietly changed from a niche for nerds to an essential for everyone – but it's still poor for impulse or emergency buying. You can get information in seconds, but not chocolate or nappies.

First, I tried a supermarket (not the market leader). It took an age and I still couldn't get products that are in the local shop. The system froze so I had to start again – three times! And no same-day delivery. Others were better. For example, photo paper from Viking Direct (www.viking-direct.co.uk), wine from Laithwaites (www.laithwaites.com) and flowers from Interflora (www.interflora.co.uk) all came on the same day.

Banking is a dream with First Direct (www.firstdirect.com). I can see statements and make transfers – and they'll text (SMS) to warn before I go overdrawn. It's great to set regular payments so that I never miss a deadline. Travel insurance was a doddle with Direct Travel (www.direct-travel.co.uk).

But what of fun? The Web has a long way to go to rival cinema, TV and radio for entertainment. The WWITV (www.wwitv.com) directory is useful but conventional TV is streets ahead. I did listen to the Test Match (cricket) on the radio, but even with only reasonable audio quality there were still breaks in the soundtrack.

Music lovers with broadband are well catered for, with scores of broadcasts at much better audio quality. There is lots of choice through Radio Locator (www.radio-locator.com) and I found gems such as the Cocteau Twins back catalogue from Emusic (www.emusic.com). I spent leisure hours booking tickets for the National Maritime Museum (www.nmm.org.uk) and checking out Roald Dahl (www.roalddahl.com) with the kids. A pizza from Domino's (www.dominos.co.uk) arrived in 25 minutes and, because I'd paid by credit card, I didn't have to fumble for change at the door.

So living online is nearly possible and the Internet is coming of age. How will it transform our lives in the next 20 years? One thing is certain – like David Blaine (45 days in a box without food), I need to get out more.

Note: *Matthew Wall is author of *The Sunday Times Guide to the Internet*

REFERENCE

Reynolds, J. (2000) 'e-Commerce: a critical review', *International Journal of Retail and Distribution Management*, 28 (10): 417–444.

Chapter 1

The world of e-retailing

LINKS TO OTHER CHAPTERS

- Chapter 4 – Understanding and communicating with the e-consumer
- Chapter 6 – e-Store design: navigability, interactivity and web atmospherics
- Chapter 7 – e-Service
- Chapter 8 – Branding on the Web

KEY LEARNING POINTS

After completing this chapter you will have an understanding of:

- What e-retail is, advantages and disadvantages for retailers
- The (e-)retail mix
- e-Retailing trends

ORDERED LIST OF SUB-TOPICS

- What is e-retail?
- Disadvantages of e-retailing for retailers
- Advantages of e-retailing for retailers
- The (e-)retail mix: sale the 7Cs
- Growth and prospects for e-retailing
- Conclusions
- Chapter summary
- ❖ Case study

WHAT IS E-RETAIL?

The business of *e-retail* has been defined as the sale of goods and services via Internet or other electronic channels, for personal or household use by consumers (Harris and Dennis, 2002). This definition includes all e-commerce activities that result in transactions with end consumers (rather than business customers), i.e. *B2C* rather than *B2B*. Some e-marketing activities that do not directly involve transactions, such as providing (free) information or promoting brands and image, are considered to be part of B2C but are not normally considered as being within the scope of e-retail.

Despite the *dot.com crash* of 2000, e-retailing has been growing, particularly for the 'top eight' categories that account for three-quarters of all European sales. These major growth areas comprise: books, music and *DVD* movies, groceries, sex products, games and software, electronic and computer equipment, travel, and clothes.

DISADVANTAGES OF E-RETAILING FOR RETAILERS

Retailers have been slow to take up e-retailing. This is to some extent understandable in the light of many disadvantages and problems. Retailers, for example, may lack the technical know-how, the substantial investment required or the order fulfilment capabilities. Set-up costs start from around £20,000 for a small site and up to £500,000 for a large operation ($A53,000 to $A1.4 million). And set-up costs are only the start – Datamonitor estimates that high street retailers are spending more on ongoing costs than on setting up new sites. A continuous cost will be fulfilment and logistics. Successful e-retailers such as Next (www.next.co.uk) and Land's End (www.landsend.com) have had the advantage of already operating profitable mail-order catalogues.

There can be legal problems. For example, if purchaser and supplier are in different countries, there may be conflict between the laws and taxation of the two countries. In Europe, the *VAT (Value Added Tax)* position is still unclear, but Richard Branson's Virgin group's e-retail operation (www.virgin.co.uk) is registered in Madeira, the country with the lowest VAT rate in the European Union (EU).

A further disadvantage is that e-selling is less powerful than face-to-face selling (it is easier to say 'no' to a computer). This viewpoint is linked to a concern of traditional high street retailers that e-retailing offers a diminished role for their expertise. For example, there are obvious difficulties with products sold by 'atmosphere' – touch, feel, smell – and impulse purchases. In addition, consumers have a perception of lower prices online. This puts pressure on margins for e-retailing, and can lead to shoppers expecting consistent low prices in-store. Finally, aftercare can be difficult, especially if the shopper is overseas.

Box 1.1:
DISADVANTAGES OF E-RETAILING FOR RETAILERS

- May lack know-how and technology
- Substantial set-up, investment and ongoing costs
- Complex logistics of fulfilment
- e-Selling less powerful than face-to-face – uptake slow for goods selected by taste or smell
- Fewer impulse purchases
- Legal problems
- Lesser role for traditional high street retail expertise
- Pressure on margins and prices in-store
- After-sales care difficulties

ADVANTAGES OF E-RETAILING FOR RETAILERS

On the other hand, there are a number of advantages for retailers. First, location is unimportant. According to some textbooks, adapting an old saying, the three most important elements in *retail* are 'location, location and location'. The best high street locations are therefore expensive. The e-retailer, though, can sell equally well to anywhere in the country and even overseas. Second, size does not matter – small e-retailers can compete on equal terms to large ones, can reach a larger audience than the high street and can be open 24 hours a day. For example, the independent, northern UK-based Botham's of Whitby has been a pioneer of e-retailing.

There are many other advantages. The socio-demographic profile of e-shoppers is attractive to many retailers, with higher-than-average education, employment and disposable income levels. In theory at least, online selling saves on the wages costs of face-to-face sales people and the costs of premises. The savings may be less than expected, though, as there are still costs in Internet customer contact, and packaging and delivery can be more expensive to provide. Perhaps a more substantial advantage is the ease with which e-retailing integrates with *customer relationship management (CRM)* and micro-marketing systems – identifying and treating the customer as an individual. This, together with the easier provision of product information, leads to greater opportunities for cross-selling and selling up. Finally, the late entrants into e-retailing are largely being driven by 'if we don't, our competitors will'.

Box 1.2:
ADVANTAGES OF E-RETAILING FOR RETAILERS

- Location is unimportant
- Size does not matter
- Saves on the wages and premises costs
- Reaches a larger audience
- Higher disposable income profile than average
- Accepts orders 24 hours a day
- More opportunities for CRM, micro-marketing, cross- and up-selling
- If we don't, our competitors will

Other retailers, though, are put off e-retailing by what they perceive as consumer resistance. According to e-research company Forrester, nearly 40 per cent of UK homes are now connected to the Internet, but estimates vary from only 12 per cent (Verdict) up to 20 per cent (Forrester) of UK adults shopping online. This contrasts with the faster take-up of e-business for B2B, with 25 per cent of businesses ordering online (Chartered Institute of Marketing, 2000). See Chapter 3 for more on why and how 'bricks and mortar' retailers integrate e-retailing into their operations.

THE (E-)RETAIL MIX: SALE THE 7CS

The (e-)retail mix is a shorthand term for the blend of tools and techniques that (e-)retailers use to provide value for customers. It is a development of the well-known marketing mix, more specific to retail and e-retail. As far back as the first half of the twentieth century, the job of the marketer was described as a 'mixer of ingredients' (Culliton, 1948). Marketers devise strategies and tactics aimed at providing satisfaction and adding value for customers. The various elements are blended into a 'marketing mix' – a phrase first coined by Neil Borden (1964) of Harvard Business School.

The marketing mix is most widely known as E. Jerome McCarthy's (1960) '4Ps': Place, Product, Price and Promotion. 'Place' is not quite self-explanatory, but refers to the routes that organizations take to get the benefits of the product or service to the intended customers – channels of distribution. 'Product' means both tangible product and also 'service', and all the ways that an organization adds value. 'Price' means not just the price charged, but also all aspects of pricing policy, including, for example, distributor margins. 'Promotion' is not just the more specialized 'sales promotion', but also every way that a product is promoted to customers – from print advertising to websites.

In recent decades there have been numerous attempts to update and revise the marketing mix. One development is particularly descriptive of the way that marketers think about the customer. The '4Cs' (Lauterborn, 1990) imply more emphasis on customer wants and concerns than do the 4Ps. The 4Cs (in the same order as the equivalent 4Ps listed above) are: Convenience for the customer; Customer value and benefits; Cost to the customer; and Communication. Reflecting the emphasis of 'new' marketing on long-term relationships with customers, we include 'Customer relationships' within the umbrella of the 'Communication' C.

C1 Convenience for the customer

'Place' (from the 4Ps), rather than implying management's methods of placing products where they want them to be, can be thought of as 'Convenience for the customer', recognizing customers' choices for buying in ways that are convenient to them.

For the retailer, 'Place' incorporates what can be the most critical decisions concerning 'location'. For the e-retailer, this is also important, as many customers prefer a multi-channel approach: browse on the Web, buy in-store or vice versa – or buy on the Web, return to the store for a refund! This perhaps goes some way towards explaining the success of *high street* and *multi-channel retailers* in e-retail, as compared to the 'pureplays'.

Physical location can also be important for the e-retailer as many customers prefer to buy from, or are more likely to trust, an e-retailer based at least in the same country, where carriage costs and maybe taxes are cheaper.

'Location' for the e-retailer also means virtual location and the ease of finding the website. This entails registration with search engines, location in e-malls and links from associates.

Convenience also includes key aspects of website design, such as navigation, layout and ease of purchase. For the '*bricks*' retailer, convenience decisions include shelf space allocation and layout. The equivalent in 'clicks' e-retail is site design and page layout – for example, whether layout follows the 'free-flow' or 'grid' type of layout, or indeed a combination such as 'free-grid' (Vrechopoulos, 2001). Virtual store layout and design is considered in more detail in Chapter 6.

C2 Customer value and benefits

'Product', rather than being something that a company has to sell, can be thought of as 'Customer value and benefits' – meaning the bundle of service and satisfactions wanted by customers. People do not buy 'products' as such, but rather solutions to problems or good feelings. Retailers and e-retailers now specify (and sometimes design) products to a much greater extent than previously, reflecting closeness to the customer and appreciation of benefits that customers want.

An essential task of retail and e-retail is selecting the range of products offered for sale – assembled for target markets from diverse sources. The wide and deep range that can be offered is one of the areas where the clicks e-retailer can score relative to the bricks retailer.

When buying online, customers are far less likely to request help than they are in the store. Rather, e-shoppers who need help in understanding a product are more likely to abandon the transaction and find an alternative supplier or even buy through a different channel. Therefore, e-businesses need to be particularly careful about describing products clearly in customer value and benefits terms.

C3 Cost to the customer

'Price' may be what companies decide to charge for their products, but 'Cost to the customer' represents the real cost that customers will pay, including, for example, in the case of bricks retail, their own transport costs. For clicks e-retail, there are also the costs of carriage and perhaps taxes to be added to the quoted prices. High carriage charges may be one reason for the high rate of carts abandoned at the checkout. Customers also need to consider the costs of Internet and telephone access.

Consumers have a perception that prices should be lower online than in-store, and this can cause problems when customers buying via other channels realise that they are paying more than online customers. For example, Screwfix (www.screwfix.com), a well-known supplier of tradesperson's supplies via paper catalogue and telesales, has a number of attractive special offers available only online. Customers who have looked up what they want online, then telephone to order, can be irritated to learn that the extra discounts are not available when ordering by phone.

C4 Communication and customer relationships

'Communication' is equivalent to the final 'P' in the 4Ps: 'Promotion'. Promotion suggests ways in which companies persuade people to buy, whereas communication is a two-way process also involving feedback from customers to suppliers. Reflecting an increasing control of elements of the retail mix by retailers rather than manufacturers, retailers spend more on advertising than manufacturers do (assisted by advertising allowances from manufacturers). Retailers are closer to the customer than are manufacturers and have more access to customer feedback.

Communication is not just advertising, though, but all the ways in which retailers communicate with their customers, including, for example, marketing research surveys, public relations (PR), direct mail, *e-mail*, Internet, marketing database and loyalty schemes. Successful e-retailers often use offline advertising such as magazines and 'click here' sections of newspapers integrated with online marketing communications. Online methods include banner ads and pop-ups (often incentivized); paid-for listings in search engines and directories; and affiliate programmes.

In addition to solving problems (see the 'Customer value and benefits' section on p. 6), there is another reason for customers buying products – to get good feelings. This is a particularly difficult area for e-retailers. The bricks retail store and the face-to-face salesperson are often much better at identifying and satisfying customers' emotional needs and wants. The physical store uses *atmospherics* in the attempt to change mood and give shoppers a pleasant emotional experience when buying. Emotional cues may be visual (decor), olfactory (perfume), tactile (smooth and cool or soft and cuddly) and aural (music).

e-Retailers can create a 'web atmosphere' using, for example, music and visuals such as 3-D displays and downloadable video clips. Such enhancements must always be a compromise, on account of the need to avoid long download times. One way of tackling the problem is to provide a 'click here for *broadband*' (for a more sophisticated, high-memory requirement version). Web atmospherics are considered in more detail in Chapter 6.

'Customer relationships' is an area that successful bricks retailers such as Tesco (www.tesco.co.uk) have used to gain a major lead over competitors. The importance of the emotional aspects of selling has already been mentioned. The sales representative selling face-to-face in the bricks retail store can use verbal and non-verbal (body language) communication to build personal relationships with customers, enhancing the emotional value of products. In trying to replicate the physical buying experience, the e-retailer is at a disadvantage. On the other hand, with transaction data ready-digitized, the e-retailer is well placed to enhance product value using CRM techniques. For example, data mining can be used to build a picture of products most likely to be wanted by individual customers. Products tailored specifically can be offered pro-actively. Amazon (www.amazon.com), for instance, uses such a system to match new books to existing customers who are likely to be interested in them.

There has been a number of suggestions for structuring a 'retail mix', equivalent to the 4Ps or 4Cs of the marketing mix, adding other aspects that may be key to retailer success. For example, McGoldrick (2002) uses a nine-element mix. In addition to those that can be incorporated into the 4Cs framework above, McGoldrick also includes factors such as 'brand image', 'logistics' and 'information'. Most versions of the retail mix are not as 'catchy' as the 4Ps or 4Cs of the marketing mix. Therefore we propose a simplified '7Cs' for the *e-retail mix*, adding Computing and category management issues; *Customer franchise*; and Customer care and service.

To some extent there is a parallel with Kearney's (2000) 7Cs for creating a rewarding customer *e-shopping* experience. In addition to Convenience, Communication and Customer care, Kearney included 'Content' and 'Customization', which we have included under 'Customer value and benefits'; 'Connectivity' (in our 'Convenience'); and 'Community' (in our 'Customer care and service'. Jones *et al.* (2001) added a further C: 'Concern' which we have again included under the 'Customer care and service' heading.

C5 Computing and category management issues

The success of retailers has been founded on supplying the products that customers want, in the right sizes and quantities, at the right time and in the right place. With the growth in consumer choice has come a proliferation of products. Superstores carry 20,000-plus branded products and department stores from 100,000, and even up to one million or more. Efficient control of this degree of complexity needs effective computer and logistics systems.

Retail logistics have been changing rapidly over recent decades. First, the growth of retailer power has involved major retailers taking more control of their supply chains. The involvement of wholesalers has been reduced, tending to give way to contract logistics (under retailer control). At the same time, supply chains have become more efficient with computer network links between suppliers and retailers – many still based on *electronic data interchange (EDI)*.

Pre-dating the Web, EDI is based on privately owned third-party computer networks. Stock levels have been reduced using techniques such as *efficient customer response (ECR* – the retailers' equivalent of *Just in Time* or *JIT*). EDI networks are expensive to install, costing at least hundreds of thousands of pounds. There is a growing trend towards the use of the Internet, particularly for smaller businesses (suppliers and customers) and smaller order quantities. Increasingly, retailers such as Tesco are allowing Internet access to their suppliers for real-time *Electronic Point of Sale (EPoS)* data. Trusted supplier partners can thus respond more quickly to changes in customer demand.

Cooperation between suppliers and retailers has been key to improving the efficiency of satisfying customers while minimizing stocks and costs. On the larger scale, this cooperative process is known as *category management (CM)*, the retailer/supplier process of managing categories as strategic business units.

High efficiency of the computer-controlled logistics systems is largely behind the success of 'bricks and clicks' retailers such as Tesco. Ironically, deficiencies in this area have been a major factor in the failure of a number of pureplay dot.coms that have concentrated on advertising and promotion at the expense of other areas of the e-retail mix. One exception is Amazon, which is founded on efficient logistics systems and customer care and service. In the UK, Amazon is using its logistics expertise to carry out distribution services on contract for bricks retailers such as WHSmith (www.whsmith.co.uk) and Toys R Us (www.toysrus.co.uk).

Apart from Amazon and the major bricks and clicks retailers, many of the e-retailers with the most efficient computer and logistics efficiency are established direct-selling businesses. For example, Quill (www.quillcorp.com) and Screwfix (www.screwfix.com), office supplies and tradesperson supplies respectively, operate established mail businesses via a paper catalogue. Dell (www.Dell.co.uk) have been pioneers in telemarketing and direct selling since the late 1980s, demonstrating that a complex product like a computer could be sold without face-to-face contact. Much of the success has been due to investment in computer-based *mass customization* systems, along with excellent customer care and service. The company was one of the first e-retailers and is the market leader worldwide for computer hardware.

Mini case study 1.1: SCREWFIX (www.screwfix.com)

Screwfix started out as a UK trade wholesale supplier, but also now sells extensively for DIY. Screwfix.com earned *Retail Week*'s 'Retailer of the Year' award for 2002. Screwfix is an example of the successful niche e-retailer and one of few to gain favourable mentions in the *Sunday Times* (UK) survey (*Sunday Times* Doors, 9 February 2003). Screwfix is owned by Kingfisher, i.e. in the same stable as the B&Q UK DIY stores. Although the branding, ordering and fulfilment are completely separate, the supply chains are integrated, resulting in economies of scale and buying power. Screwfix has 0.5 per cent of the UK repairs, maintenance and home improvement market, but a massive 20 per cent of the *direct* market for those products. Web sales are over £20 million per year (15 per cent and growing of Screwfix's total business). The (e-)retail mix is summarized below.

Convenience for the customer

Express shopping: if you have the catalogue, simply type in the quantities and catalogue number, or alternatively use 'search' to find what you want.

A freephone telephone number is available 24 hours a day, plus fax and e-mail options, offering improved personal interaction.

Customer value and benefits

Products include not only screws, bolts and nails, but also fixings, adhesives, tools, hardware, lighting, plumbing and cleaning products – the claim is 'Everything for the trade and DIY – next day', and 100 per cent stock availability of 6,000 products.

Cost to the customer

A number of special offers are always available. Most prices are significantly cheaper than in DIY retail sheds.

Communication and customer relationships

The homepage has many examples of good practice, for example: Recommend a Friend – get a reward when they order for the first time; Open a Business Account; Testimonials – 'I have just received my order and felt I must congratulate you on an excellent service. Your site is well designed. The products are well laid out and the order processing excellent.' . . . 'Your website is brilliant, the designer needs a big pat on the back. Well laid out, and to order online is so easy.'; and Register/Login – optional registration makes ordering quicker and easier. There are regular communications by mail with catalogues, 'What's new' and special offers for registered customers.

Computing and category management issues

Winner of best use of Supply Chain Management at the 2001 Internet Business Awards.

Customer franchise

Without the need for heavy advertising, Screwfix has quickly built up a reputation for cheap prices, with quick and reliable delivery based on actual performance.

Customer care and service

To test the service, we ordered a long, complex list of equipment and fittings at 4.00 p.m. on a Sunday. The complete, correct order was delivered by 8.00 a.m. on Monday.

Sources: Various, including authors' own site test and Reynolds (2002)

C6 Customer franchise

The most successful bricks retailers have invested heavily in quality and customer care and service in order to raise their standing in the assessments of customers. Some authors refer to the accumulated value of image, trust and branding as the retailer's 'customer franchise'. As we will detail in Chapters 4 and 7, consumers' lack of trust has been one of the main factors inhibiting the growth of e-retail. As McGoldrick (2002) pointed out, with greater choice consumers choose the brands that they trust.

Many bricks retailers have high-quality brands with clear personalities backed by long-term corporate promotion. These strong brands give bricks and clicks retailers a head start over 'pureplay' dot.coms. *Start-up* brands must work hard on trust. For example, one of the few pureplays to prosper, the auction site eBay (www.ebay.co.uk), includes five levels of safeguards, including fraud protection and dispute resolution.

C7 Customer care and service

According to McGoldrick (2002), retailing has traditionally been classified as a 'service industry' but, for most retailers, the preoccupation with service quality and services offered is of more recent origin. At the broadest level, most of a retailer's activities deliver a form of service to the consumer, creating assortments at competitive prices in accessible locations. These activities, therefore, all play major roles in creating customer satisfaction.

More specifically for the e-retailer, good service means, for example, reasonably fast and reliable deliveries at times convenient to the shopper; the availability of telephone help; and return and refund facilities. As we will demonstrate in Chapter 4, these are aspects in which the early e-retailers have been lamentably poor, with the big majority of e-shoppers still having a sorry tale to tell.

For the bricks retailer, even in self-service settings, store personnel play a crucial role in forming retail images and patronage intentions. The e-retailer is at a disadvantage, but elements such as *click-through* telephone help, bulletin boards and chat rooms can help to make the e-shopping experience more interactive. In general, the successful (e-)retailer sets out to make shopping more enjoyable, more convenient and/or less worrying for the customers.

When buying high-priced items and those with a high 'personal' content such as cars, shoppers particularly value personal service. Retailers such as Virgin (www.virgin.co.uk) attempt to overcome this drawback with a pop-up window with a phone number to reach a sales consultant and the working hours in which they are available.

Box 1.3:
SALE THE 7CS – THE (E-)RETAIL MIX

C1 Convenience for the customer ('Place' from the 4Ps)

- Physical location
- Multi-channel options: browse the Web, buy in-store or vice versa – or buy on the Web, return to the store for a refund
- Virtual location and ease of finding the website: registration with search engines, location in e-malls and links from associates
- Website design: connectivity, navigation, 'shelf' space allocation and ease of purchase
- Layout: 'free-flow', 'grid' or 'free-grid'

C2 Customer value and benefits ('Product')

- Satisfactions wanted by customers
- Solutions to problems or good feelings
- Specification (sometimes design) of products reflecting closeness to the customer and benefits that customers want
- Selection of the range of products offered for sale, assembled for target markets from diverse sources
- Wide and/or deep range, where the clicks e-retailer can score relative to the bricks retailer
- Content: describing a compelling offer of products clearly in customer value and benefits terms
- Customization of products to match the wants of customer segments as closely as possible

C3 Cost to the customer ('Price')

- The real cost that customers will pay, including transport, carriage and taxes
- Costs of Internet telephone access
- Customers' perceptions that prices should be cheaper online than in-store

C4 Communication and customer relationships ('Promotion')

Communication is a two-way process also involving feedback from customers to suppliers, including:

- Marketing research surveys
- Public relations (PR)
- Direct mail
- e-Mail
- Internet
- Offline advertising such as magazines and 'click here' sections of newspapers
- Online methods such as banner ads and pop-ups (often incentivized); paid-for listings in search engines and directories; and affiliate programmes
- Atmospherics and web atmospherics: visual (decor, colour management, video clips, 3-D), olfactory (perfume and samples), tactile (smooth and cool or soft and cuddly – communicated by visuals or samples) and aural (music). (But need to avoid long download times – 'click here for broadband'.)

Customer relationships

- In-store sales representatives use verbal and non-verbal (body language) communication
- Marketing database and loyalty schemes
- The e-retailer can enhance product value using Customer Relationship Management (CRM) and data mining to tailor products specifically to individual customers

C5 Computing and category management issues

- Supplying the products that customers want, in the right sizes and quantities, at the right time and in the right place
- Efficient supply chains with computer network links between suppliers and retailers
- Minimizing stocks and speed of response: Efficient Customer Response (ECR – the retailers' equivalent of Just in Time or JIT)
- Cooperation between suppliers and (e-)retailers aiming to improve the efficiency of satisfying customers while minimizing stocks and costs. On the larger scale, this is 'category management' (CM), the retailer/supplier process of managing categories as strategic business units
- Efficient logistics systems – an important component of customer care and service

C6 Customer franchise

- Image, trust and branding – long-term investment in quality, corporate communications, and customer care and service
- Safeguards, including fraud protection and dispute resolution
- Safe shopping icons, e.g. Which? Webtrader

C7 Customer care and service

- Creating assortments at competitive prices in an accessible format
- Fast and reliable deliveries at times convenient to the shopper
- Availability of help; return and refund facilities
- For the bricks retailer store personnel are crucial
- For the e-retailer click-through telephone help, bulletin boards and chat rooms make the experience more interactive and add a feeling of community
- Addressing customer concerns, particularly for credit card security, e.g. displaying the 'padlock' secure site logo

Source: The authors, developed from McCarthy's (1960) 4Ps and Lauterborn's (1990) 4Cs

The extra 3Cs of the (e-)retail mix (in addition to the 4Ps or 4Cs of the marketing mix) can therefore be seen to be particularly critical for e-retailers. The computing, category management, supply chain and delivery systems are areas in which the early e-retailers, particularly pureplay dot.coms, have been sadly lacking, affecting trust, image, and customer care and service. The stronger brands with greater customer franchise have higher sales and potentially higher profit – for example, Tesco (www.tesco.com) and Next (www.next.co.uk).

With few exceptions, it is already strongly branded bricks retailers with established computer and supply chain systems who are making the running in e-retailing. Notable exceptions include Amazon (www.amazon.co.uk) and Dell (www.dell.com), both well known for efficient systems, quality, service, communications and interaction (see Case study 2.1, pp. 46–51).

THINK POINT

If people can e-shop easily, why should anyone use the high street?

GROWTH AND PROSPECTS FOR E-RETAILING

Online shopping is growing in the UK with sales having reached £3.3 billion by 2003 (Verdict, 2003). This was only 2 per cent of all retail sales but is predicted to rise to 5 per cent within a year or two (BCSC, 2001) and to 10 per cent by 2009 (Gibson, 1999; Verdict, 2003). Other researchers estimate the market to be even larger and growing faster. For example, IMRG (2003) estimated e-retail sales to have already reached 7 per cent of all retail sales. 'Most people' will buy groceries, books, CDs and even clothes by e-shopping (RICS, 2000). Books, movies and software, high on 'factual search' (Shim *et al.*, 2001), are natural for e-retailing, but electronic products, groceries and clothing are also increasing (Doidge and Higgins, 2000; IMRG, 2003; Verdict, 2002). Ninety-four per cent will be at the expense of existing channels (half diverted from catalogues, half from the high street – BCSC, 2001) and only 6 per cent from extra growth (PreFontaine, 1999). Figures 1.1 and 1.2 indicate the growth. According to the industry body, the Interactive Media in Retail Group, there are about 4 million people in the UK who spend an average of £3,000 to £5,000 per year online (IMRG, 2003).

Shoppers have long used the Internet to browse for products before buying offline, but US e-shoppers at least are reversing that trend, with 45 per cent of e-shoppers buying online after researching in stores and catalogues, according to a survey of 1,252 e-shoppers and over 80 e-retailers (NAMNEWS, 2003). This must be a worrying trend for bricks retailers, but also helps to strengthen the competitive position of multi-channel bricks and clicks retailers.

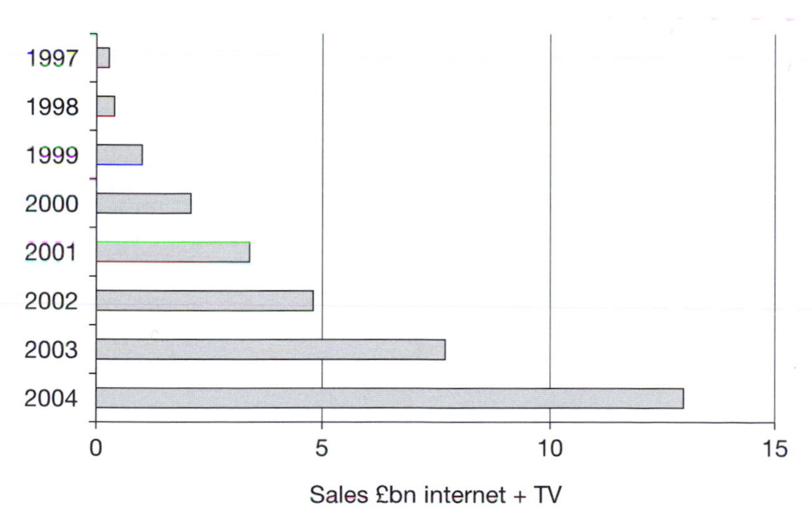

Figure 1.1 *The growth of online shopping: surveys, 1997 to 2003, forecast 2004*

Sources: IMRG (2003); Verdict (2003)

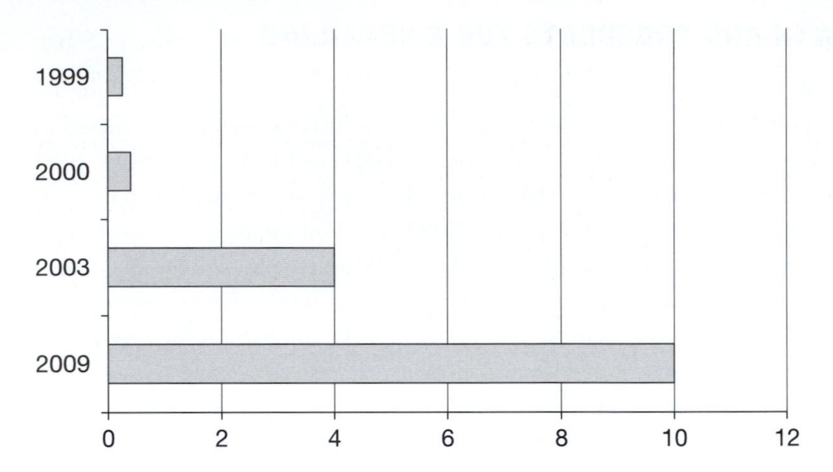

Figure 1.2 *e-Retailing as percentage of UK shopping*

Sources: IMRG (2003); Verdict (2003)

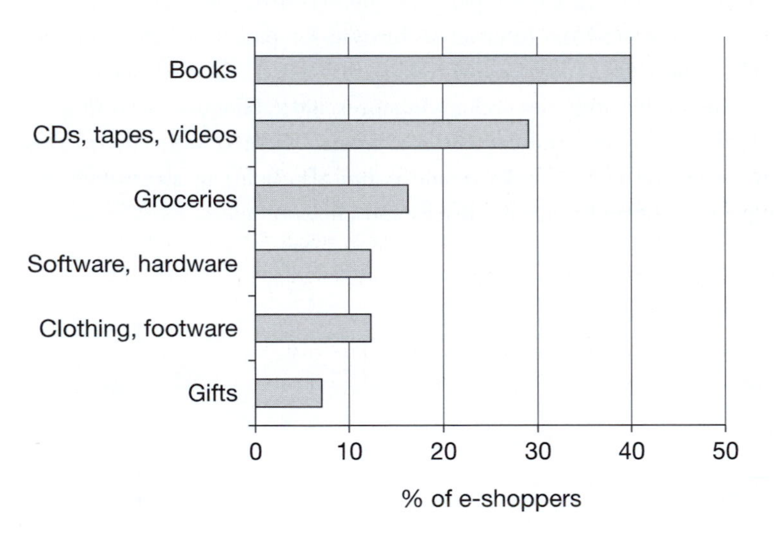

Figure 1.3 *What e-shoppers buy*

Sources: Doidge and Higgins (2000); IMRG (2003)

According to Verdict, in 2001 grocery accounted for half of all UK e-retailing – £1.3 billion – which sounds massive but represents only 5.6 per cent of groceries. The market leaders in their sectors were Amazon (books, plus CDs and DVD movies), Tesco (groceries), Dell (computers), Next (clothing) and Comet (electrical and electronic hardware). Though perhaps not actually an e-retailer, eBay is the leader for auctions and is the most visited of all UK websites.

Average spend has risen faster for men (+15 per cent) than women (+5 per cent), leading Verdict to comment that 'the proliferation of female-orientated sites . . . [has] failed to motivate women to shop significantly more'.

The proportion of e-shoppers preferring to shop from e-sites run by high street retailers rather than Internet-only is soaring (up from 22 per cent in October 2000 to 33 per cent in April 2001). The main service is travel and the main virtual product is sex (pictures, stories and video) – often absent from published statistics, but accounting for around 10 per cent of e-retailing. In the words of *The Virgin Internet Shopping Guide*: 'However much you may despise the sex industry, it has been almost solely responsible for driving forward the revolution in online shopping'.

Box 1.4:
HOW TO SHOP SAFELY ONLINE

- Always pay by credit card in order to take advantage of the safe purchasing protection (and not by debit cards such as Switch or Delta)
- Check the policy for returning unwanted goods – shipping charges can be high
- Provide payment details on secure sites only – check for the small padlock in the bottom-right corner of the screen
- Check carefully for extra charges. For example, goods from outside the EU may be subject to Customs and Excise duty and/or VAT (check out www.hmce.gov.uk)

Source: Adapted from *Sunday Times* (UK) Doors, 27 June 2002

THINK POINT

With a Boots on every high street, why shop at Boots online store?

CONCLUSIONS

While many will regret the passing of the old-fashioned high street, change is inevitable. With the technical security issues now largely resolved, consumers are overcoming reservations about e-shopping. Beyond the hype before the dot.com crash and the pessimism that followed, e-shopping has resumed growth.

Market forces in action mean that the e-retailing survivors and leaders are the strong brands who are successfully addressing the customer care and service, and fulfilment issues.

Given the unstoppable progress of e-retailing, traditionalists can at least take comfort in the current e-success of the high street multi-channel retailers – hopefully preserving at least some vibrant bricks shopping alongside the growing proportion of clicks. In the following chapters, we will compare and contrast with the successes of conventional retailing to develop the theory and practice of e-retailing, finally speculating on the shoppers of tomorrow.

THINK POINT

For each of these e-retailers – Botham's, Next, Amazon, Marks & Spencer and Boots, what do you consider to be the reasons for their success (or otherwise) as e-retailers?

CHAPTER SUMMARY

The business of e-retail is the sale of goods and services via the Internet or other electronic channels, for personal or household use by consumers.

The well-known marketing mix of the 4Ps (or 4Cs) can be extended by the addition of three more Cs to make a more catchy retail mix: 'Sale the 7Cs'. The three extra Cs are particularly relevant to e-retail success:

- Computing and category management issues
- Customer franchise, trust, image and branding
- Customer care and service.

Despite the dot.com crash, e-retail is growing and the leaders are mainly those performing well on the three extra Cs.

The next chapter will outline the latest practice and trends in e-retailing the main products.

Case study 1.1: NEXT

Next is a top name in high street fashion. The first Next store opened in February 1982 with an exclusive coordinated collection of stylish clothes, shoes and accessories for women. Next later introduced collections for men, children and furnishings for the home and now has around 330 stores in the UK and Ireland. It also franchises about 50 stores elsewhere in Europe, Asia and the Middle East.

The successful mail-order business, Next Directory, was launched in 1988 with 350 pages. The most recent catalogue now has 749 pages. Online shopping at Next began in 1999 and now the entire catalogue is available to shop from on the Internet. The mail-order expertise in order handling, fulfilment and customer care has proved invaluable, taking the business to the number one spot in UK clothing e-retailing. The entire Next Directory is available online, including formal wear, casual wear, accessories, shoes, swimwear, lingerie, men's and children's wear.

To shop online, the customer has to set up an account, which can take a day or two to arrange. There is a small charge for next-day delivery and a courier picks up returns free (or they can be returned to a high street shop). Revenue comes from its retail stores, the Next Directory catalogue, e-retailing and Ventura, which provides call centre and customer support services on contract for other firms.

The e-retail mix at Next

C1 Convenience for the customer

The website can easily be found using most search engines. The Next website is a convenient place to shop as it is well-structured and easy to navigate and buy from, pages download fast and there is general ease of access.

C2 Customer value and benefits

There is a wider product range than can be found in the high street shops, offering all the products that are available in the Next Directory.

C3 Cost to the customer

Next does not offer online customers any discount. Customers also pay a £2.95 delivery charge no matter how large the order. However, customers do save in terms of the time and travel costs of travelling to a bricks store.

C4 Communication and customer relationships

The Next website provides communication to customers via e-mail. Customers can register to receive e-mail updates of forthcoming offers and promotions, including details of the end-of-season sale. See the Web atmospherics section on p. 20 for other communications aspects of the Next website.

C5 Customer franchise

Next has a good brand name for high street and Next Directory shopping and the website has inherited this to some extent. Next claims to be attracting 700 new mail-order customers a week via the Web without pouring large amounts of cash into the online division – mainly due to the brand name. According to David Jones, Chief Executive, Next has 'spent £125,000 on [its] Internet site and will do £12m of sales'.

Next targets customers in their twenties and thirties who are looking for stylish but affordable clothes to take them through the next fashion trend. Quality, style and value for money are core brand values.

C6 Customer care and service

The Next website provides good customer care and service. If a customer wishes to return goods, they can do this with no extra charge. They can either take them back to a store, return them via a courier, or send them by post (Next provides a pre-paid label). Purchases made before 5.00 p.m. are delivered the following day, excluding Sunday deliveries.

At the time of writing, online purchases at Next can only be made between 7.00 a.m. and 11.00 p.m. This is a substantial limitation as one of the main customer benefits of buying online should be the ability to buy *24/7*.

C7 Computer and category management issues

The supply chain systems are slick and efficient, utilizing ECR techniques to provide fast delivery from minimum stocks, keeping the customer informed of progress by an automated e-mail system.

Web atmospherics

Next does not have sound on their website. Audio would not be difficult to add and could be important as, for example, music pleasure intensity can compensate for a lack of interpersonal contact (see Chapter 6).

The Next website is not very interactive; there is no chat group or message board and it does not sell any customized products. 'Extras' such as these could help to compensate for the lack of personal contact. There is separate login for customers who have bought online before, but, apart from this, no personalization or mass customization can be found on the site.

The Next website is very simple, which makes for good usability – something that many Internet retailers get wrong. The layout of the site is easy to navigate around for people who are not computer literate. Purchasing from the website is very straightforward, without too many click-through pages.

Visually, the Next site is appealing and sophisticated. Pictures of the products are downloaded reasonably fast. The quality and colour of the pictures of the products are excellent. The text on the Next website is short, yet contains all the required information.

In conclusion, the good all-round retail mix has made Next into one of the top Internet retailers. As a result, they are now looking to start sub-contract fulfilment services for other e-tailers.

As an improvement, Next could consider introducing sound to the website. This is simple to do and can help make the purchase experience more pleasant to a customer (although some customers would like the sound to have an 'off' button). Adding sound to a website will not slow down the speed much as compressed files can be used which do not take up much memory. Next will need to make sure the music is in character with their products, so needs to carry out research on what its customers would like to hear. Next could also consider using pre-recorded voice advertising on the website, as is found in many high street shops, promoting offers, new ranges, etc.

Another refinement would be to introduce a virtual changing room where items could be coordinated. This is the 'Style Builder' idea as used by Eddie Bauer (www.eddiebauer.com). A further improvement would be to implement a system for customers to see pictures of themselves wearing different garments. Records could be stored on a database for customers to refer to later. These kinds of ideas may encourage people to buy by making the experience more interactive and personal.

The colour quality of the website will be different on every customer's monitor. Next could perhaps investigate colour management systems – for example, eColour, a system that sends a *cookie* that reads the monitor's output and from this advises adjustments to the monitor settings. The Clothing and footwear section in Chapter 2 and Web atmospherics in Chapter 6 address these issues in greater detail.

Finally, but perhaps of more immediate potential benefit, the Next website needs increased working hours to provide a better service and meet customer expectations of being able to buy any time on the Internet.

Source: Kindly contributed by Mnisha Talwar

QUESTIONS

Brief feedback to these questions is included at the back of the book.

Question 1.1

What do you think would be the disadvantages of e-retailing for an independent baker like Botham's?

Question 1.2

What do you consider are the main advantages of e-retailing for a small independent baker like Botham's?

Question 1.3

Why do you think Abbey National's e-bank is separately branded as 'Cahoot'?

Question 1.4

Why do you think that the 7Cs of the e-retail mix represent a superior model to the traditional 4Ps and other versions of the retail mix?

FURTHER READING

The texts dated prior to 2002 were written before the dot.com crash, so parts of them may seem overenthusiastic now.

Collin, Simon (1999) *The Virgin Internet Shopping Guide*, London: Virgin. This is a good, concise introduction and directory for UK e-shopping.

de Kare-Silver, Michael (2001) *e-Shock: the New Rules*, Basingstoke: Palgrave. This UK book includes an in-depth analysis of the effect of e-shopping on strategies for both retailers and manufacturers.

Harris, Lisa and Dennis, Charles (2002) *Marketing the e-Business*, London: Routledge. This is one of the few introductory texts on marketing written specifically for the e-business.

Kent, Tony and Omar, Ogenyi (2002) *Retailing*, London: Palgrave. This new, up-to-date, thorough and comprehensive text on retailing includes e-retail aspects throughout as well as in a separate chapter.

Lundquist, Leslie Heeter (1998) *Selling Online For Dummies*, Foster City, CA: IDG. Written for a US general (rather than academic) reader, this is a good introduction to the basic practical aspects of e-retailing.

McGoldrick, Peter (2002) *Retail Marketing*, Maidenhead: McGraw Hill. The second edition of this classic UK text on retail marketing includes a good chapter on e-retailing.

Tiernan, Bernadette (2000) *e-Tailing*, Chicago, IL: Dearborn. This is one of the few texts on e-retailing, written for a US audience.

REFERENCES

BCSC (2001) *Future Shock or eHype?: The Impact of Online Shopping on UK Retail Property*, London: British Council of Shopping Centres/The College of Estate Management.

Borden, N.H. (1964) 'The concept of the marketing mix', *Journal of Advertising Research*, 4 (June): 2–7.

Chartered Institute of Marketing (2000) *Marketing Trends Survey*, 24 (Summer).

Culliton, J.W. (1948) *The Management of Marketing Costs*, Boston, MA: Harvard University.

Doidge, R. and Higgins, C. (2000) *The Big Dot.com Con*, London: Colliers Conrad Ritblat Erdman.

Forrester Research (2001) *The Technographics Brief*, www.forrester.com [accessed 31 July].

Gibson, B. (1999) 'Beyond shopping centres: e-commerce', *British Council of Shopping Centres Conference.*

Harris, L. and Dennis, C.E. (2002) *Marketing the e-Business*, London: Routledge.
IMRG (2003) *Internet Shopping 7% of All Retail in November*, London: Interactive Media in Retail Group/Forrester Research.
Jones, P., Clarke-Hill, C., Shears, P. and Hillier, D. (2001) 'The eighth "C" of (r)etailing: customer concern', *Management Research News*, 24 (5): 11–16.
Kearney, A.T. (2000) 'E-Business performance', Chicago, IL: A.T. Kearney.
Lauterborn, R. (1990) 'New marketing litany: 4Ps passé; 4Cs take over', *Advertising Age*, 1 October.
McCarthy, E.J. (1960) *Basic Marketing*, Homewood, IL: Irwin.
McGoldrick, P. (2002) *Retail Marketing* (2nd edn) Maidenhead: McGraw Hill.
NAMNEWS (2003) 'Shoppers browse the high street to buy online', *NAMNEWS*, www.kamcity.com/namnews [accessed 10 December].
PreFontaine, M. (1999) 'Beyond shopping centres: e-commerce', *British Council of Shopping Centres Conference*.
Reynolds, J. (2002) 'Charting the multi-channel future: retail choices and constraints', *International Journal of Retail and Distribution Management*, 30 (11): 530–535.
RICS Foundation (2000) *20:20 Visions of the Future*, London: Royal Institute of Chartered Surveyors.
Shim, S., Eastlick, M.A., Lotz, S.L. and Warrington, P. (2001) 'An online pre-purchase intentions model: the role of intention to search', *Journal of Retailing*, 77 (3): 397–416.
Verdict (2000, 2001, 2002, 2003) *Verdict on Electronic Shopping*, London: Verdict.
Vrechopoulos, A. (2001) 'Virtual store atmosphere in Internet retailing: measuring virtual retail store layout effects on consumer buying behaviour', unpublished Ph.D. thesis, Brunel University, London.

WEB LINKS

Adapted from *The Virgin Internet Shopping Guide* (2001) London: Globe Pequot.

Try these sites to taste the flavour of e-shopping

www.amazon.co.uk
Busy, friendly and informative; the market leader for books plus music and much more.

www.animail.co.uk
Masses of goodies for pets.

www.blackstar.co.uk
The top choice for videos and CDs.

www.dell.co.uk
Market leader for computer sales.

www.fao.com
Fantastic range of thousands of toys.

www.landsend.com
Simple cotton clothes in a clean and airy site.

www.softwareparadise.com
Wide range of software.

www.tesco.com
Top grocery supermarket online as well as in-store.

www.unbeatable.co.uk
Great prices on electrical goods.

www.wallpaperstore.com
Huge range of wallpaper styles.

www.winecellar.co.uk
Good range of wines.

Price-comparison sites

These sites allow comparison of the prices of the same item from different e-retailers.

www.bookbrain.co.uk
Finds the cheapest offer of any book title, after taking into account delivery costs (see Chapter 2).

www.buy.co.uk
Finds the cheapest electricity, gas or other utility; includes a *directory* of e-shops.

www.computerprices.co.uk
Finds the cheapest computer kit in the UK.

www.priceline.com
Creates a market or reverse auction. Enter the price you want to pay for a range of services such as air travel and car hire. The system searches for suppliers willing to sell at that price.

www.shopsmart.co.uk
The leading price comparison site.

Directories of UK shops

www.british-shopping.com

www.buy.co.uk

www.enterprisecity.co.uk

www.ishop.co.uk

www.lycos.co.uk

www.shopguide.co.uk

www.shoppingcity.co.uk

www.shops.imrg.org

Auctions

www.ebay.co.uk
In the US, e-auctions are the most active and popular way of e-shopping, with eBay the leader for fun (and risk?).

www.qxl.co.uk
Unlike most auction sites, the UK-based QXL sells products itself as well as allowing the public to sell in personal auctions.

More e-retail and e-mall links

pages.britishlibrary.net/~cdennis
Links to case studies and via 'Search' to e-shopping and e-malls.

www.verdict.co.uk
For links to e-retailers plus statistics and press releases concerning *Verdict on Electronic Shopping* reports.

Chapter 2

e-Retailing in practice

LINKS TO OTHER CHAPTERS

- Chapter 3 – Integration of e-retailing into an organization
- Chapter 4 – Understanding and communicating with the e-consumer
- Chapter 6 – e-Store design: navigability, interactivity and web atmospherics
- Chapter 7 – e-Service
- Chapter 10 – e-Retailing models

KEY LEARNING POINTS

After completing this chapter you will have an understanding of:

- Practice and trends in e-retailing the main tangible product categories

ORDERED LIST OF SUB-TOPICS

- What are the main e-retail product categories?
- Books
- Music
- DVD movies and videos
- Groceries
- Clothing and footwear
- Conclusions
- Chapter summary

- Case study
- Questions
- Further reading
- References
- Web links

WHAT ARE THE MAIN E-RETAIL PRODUCT CATEGORIES?

As mentioned in Chapter 1, the top categories that account for three-quarters of all European sales comprise: books, music and DVD movies, groceries, sex products, games and software, electronic and computer equipment, travel and clothes. In addition, although perhaps not a category, auctions are among the most popular UK e-retailing sites.

THINK POINT

Why do you think books, music and DVD movies head up the list of the most popular e-shopping products?

In our own study (discussed in more detail in Chapter 5) with a sample of 150 undergraduate students, the hedonic or enjoyment categories and motivations of e-shopping were indicated (Dennis and Papamatthaiou, 2003). Amazon was the most popular site. CD WOW; eBay (auctions); Ticketmaster (show tickets); and Ryanair, EasyJet and Opodo (air tickets) were also used frequently. Tesco and Sainsbury (grocery supermarkets) were also mentioned. This sample of students cannot be considered representative of all UK e-shoppers, but the results may be a useful indicator for the future as graduates have historically been found to have higher discretionary income than non-graduates.

In this chapter we look in more depth at some of the tangible products that have traditionally been mainstays of high street retailing: books, music and DVD movies, groceries and clothes. Other e-retailing categories such as computer products, travel and tickets, although important, are too diverse to cover in depth in this chapter. Auctions, though not strictly an e-retailing category, are considered as a case study in Chapter 4 (see pp. 104–105).

BOOKS

Books are by far the largest e-retailing category in the UK. Research carried out by Ernst & Young illustrates that 65 per cent of the purchases made by Web shoppers in the UK consisted of books. This is understandable in the light of books scoring highest in de Kare-Silver's (2001) ES (electronic shopping) test, detailed in Chapter 11. In de Kare-Silver's sample table, books score a total of 38 points out of a maximum of 50, ten points ahead of the next category (hotels). Books score highly on *product characteristics*, being low-touch products that are simple to deliver by post, and *familiarity and confidence*, as customers usually know exactly what they are ordering. Finally, the higher-weighted *consumer attributes* parameter is particularly favourable to books: typical book buyers and the e-shopping early majority tend to be younger, better educated and of a higher socio-economic group than the general population.

Amazon is the outstanding leader of the books e-retail category, with a market share of over 50 per cent (and is also market leader for CDs/DVDs). When readers of the *Sunday Times* (UK, 9 February 2003) were asked for their experiences of e-shopping, Amazon 'streaked ahead' of all others as the country's favourite e-retailer. This means that Amazon is the undisputed favourite on considerations such as convenience, reliability and customer service. Amazon has achieved worldwide success and brand recognition by attention to these considerations and heavy (offline) advertising, becoming one of only three dot.com brands in the Interbrand world league table (Kotler *et al.*, 2001). It is an illustration of the power of branding that Amazon is the world's top e-retailer and head-to-head with Barnes and Noble for the title of the world's biggest bookstore.

Other dot.coms such as Easy Value (www.easyvalue.com) have attempted to exploit the Web's facility for quick and easy price comparisons, claiming that 'people know the products and price is driving them'. Indeed, a price comparison site such as Book Brain (www.bookbrain.co.uk) can often find prices for identical books significantly cheaper than Amazon. These cheaper prices often come from suppliers such as Swotbooks (www.swotbooks.com) that do not have Amazon's heavy marketing costs. Nevertheless, even competitors such as Tesco (strongly branded for groceries in the UK and a number of other countries), with offers like 'the top 100 books 10 per cent cheaper than Amazon' have failed to make a substantial impact on the online books market. As Brynjolfsson and Smith (2000) put it, 'the most expensive is not always the least patronised', pointing out that Amazon.com maintained a US market share of 80 per cent while charging 10 per cent more than the cheapest. For more on Amazon, see Case study 2.1 (pp. 46–51).

Mini case study 2.1: BOOKBRAIN.CO.UK AND SWOTBOOKS.COM

BookBrain does not sell books, but is a *shopbot* that claims to provide 'the most accurate and comprehensive price search of UK online bookshops on the Web'. Fourteen sites were searched at the time of our site test.

> Once you've found your ideal read, a quick search reveals prices of postage and packing, often with significant differences. . . . The site lets you know the availability of each title, how long it takes to be delivered, and it has smart editorial reviews too. Bravo.
>
> (*The Times*, 18 November 2002)

For our site test we chose a book that might be useful for various disciplines, *Discovering SPSS for Windows: Advanced Techniques for Beginners* by Andy Field, published by Sage. The search took 13 seconds, returning a table of the cheapest eight suppliers, with links to the book on the suppliers' sites, details of how delivery charges are calculated (useful if you are considering buying more than one book), stock availability, base price, delivery charge and total price. The pricing information is particularly helpful, as, when going directly to many of the suppliers' sites, it is difficult to find the delivery costs until the very last stage at the checkout.

For this site test, the cheapest supplier was Swotbooks:

> Swotbooks is an online company based in the UK . . . trading since 2000, first of all with books and . . . now [with] CDs, DVDs, videos and computer games. [Swotbooks] does not have any shops [but] use[s] some of the UK's biggest . . . wholesalers . . . and they ship directly. . . . No messing about, no catches – just the best discounts around.
>
> (www.swotbooks.com)

In our site test, Amazon.co.uk provided the most detailed information, with a synopsis, reviews, customer review star rating and suggestions for other SPSS and research methods books.

To emphasize the benefit of using BookBrain, our testing demonstrated that there was no single cheapest supplier. When delivery costs were taken into account, two other suppliers were cheapest for our other two tests. These were: *Miss Garnet's Angel* – Blackwell's (bookshop.blackwell.co.uk) and *Harry Potter and the Order of the Phoenix* – Amazon (www.amazon.co.uk).

Sources: The authors' site tests and the websites noted

THINK POINT

The first-mover and market leader for books, Amazon, is also the market leader for CDs and DVD movies. Why do you think this is?

The Internet is not only ideal for selling new books, but also as a marketplace for second-hand books. Search results on Amazon indicate not only the new price, but also the price at which associates sell the same title second-hand. Second-hand purchases through associates are covered by Amazon's usual safety-first guarantees. It has been our experience, though, that reliability and service can fall far below Amazon's own, and guarantee claims can be very slow to settle.

The real advantage of the Internet for book enthusiasts is the ability to track unusual titles. Abebooks (www.abebooks.co.uk), for example, is a marketplace connecting those who buy books with those who sell them, and is one of the main sources used by professionals. Abebooks is the world's largest online marketplace for second-hand, rare and out-of-print books, claiming to have over 40 million available.

In summary, the strategic positioning of books e-retailers can be neatly described using the generic strategies matrix (Figure 2.1), illustrating the three feasible strategies – Cost leadership, Differentiation and Focus – of exemplar major players.

MUSIC

From the suppliers' point of view, the music industry is largely not a happy story. According to Lehman Brothers figures, music as a percentage of consumer

	Lower cost	Differentiation
Broad target	Cost leadership Swotbooks	Differentiation Amazon
Narrow target		Focus Abebooks

Figure 2.1 *Exemplar strategic positioning of books e-retailers*

Source: The authors, based on Porter (1985)

expenditure is falling and music sales in the UK dropped by 8.1 per cent in 2002. The biggest drop was in compact disc (CD) singles, which, according to British Phonographic Industry (BPI) figures, slumped by 25 per cent.

Consumers have often complained about what are alleged to be unfairly high prices for CDs. On the other hand, the major companies tend to blame piracy and illegal Internet downloads for the slump (single tracks are obviously quicker and easier to download than albums), claiming to have lost US$1 billion in revenue worldwide in 2002. In the US, the Recording Industry Association of America (RIAA) has taken legal action against hundreds of 'major offenders' alleged to have illegally distributed an average of more than 1,000 copyrighted music files. It was widely reported that a 12-year-old girl, a university professor and an elderly man who rarely uses his computer were included in the first wave of actions (*Guardian*, 10 September 2003), resulting in negative publicity for the RIAA.

e-Retailing of music can be considered under two categories: CDs and online.

CDs

There are many different formats which are used to listen to music such as tapes, CDs, records, mini discs, etc., but since the 1980s the most popular form has been CDs. According to the BPI, music buyers spend on average over £80 per year on albums, of which 92 per cent are CDs. The BPI estimates that market penetration of CD albums is 50 per cent of UK households. Many leading retailers of music products such as HMV (www.hmv.co.uk) and Tower Records (www.towerrecords.co.uk) have now begun selling CDs on the Internet but are facing huge competition from pureplays such as CD WOW (www.cd-wow.co.uk) and CDNOW (www.cdnow.com) – now owned and run in conjunction with Amazon). Indeed, CDWOW has grown hugely in the competitive CD market and was recently voted by *Net* magazine readers as number two in the world's 20 best online stores, second only to Amazon. Similarly, in the UK, *Sunday Times* Doors readers voted CDWOW the country's second-favourite e-retailer, again behind only Amazon.

Box 2.1: PRICES OF CDs

It is usually said that the Internet enables consumers to find cheaper products. This is an important consideration for CDs, as there has long been a consumer perception that CDs are overpriced in the high street. In our survey reported in Chapter 4, one of the main advantages of e-shopping vs. bricks shopping for consumers was found to be 'prices favourable'. Table 2.1 reports our comparison test, indicating a wide range of prices. The cheapest overall was CDNOW, e.g. for U2's album *Best of 1980–1990* CDNOW's price was £8, compared to CD WOW in second place selling the same CD for £13.99.

Table 2.1 *Price test results for CDs*

	HMV	*Tower Records*	*CD WOW*	*CDNOW*
U2 Best of 1980–1990	£18.99	£23.65	£13.99	£8.00
Justin Timberlake	£13.99	£12.78	£8.99	£8.50
Big Brovaz	£10.99	£13.42	n/a	£18.70
Best of David Bowie	£15.99	£15.66	£12.99	£8.00

Figure 1.3 in Chapter 1 indicates that CDs (along with tapes and videos) are among the most popular products bought online (exceeded only by books). It is natural that these are popular for e-shopping as they are low-touch products. See Box 2.2 for an analysis of the potential for e-retailing CDs.

Box 2.2:
E-RETAILING CDs – THE ES TEST

The Electronic Shopping (ES) test was developed by de Kare-Silver (2001) and is used to assess a product to evaluate the likelihood that it will be purchased online (see Chapter 10 for more details). According to de Kare-Silver, a product's potential for e-retailing can be judged by assessing three factors: 'Product characteristics', 'Familiarity and confidence' and 'Consumer attributes'. Consumer attributes are considered to carry more weight than the other two and are therefore loaded three times as highly in the model. The example of CDs follows below.

Product characteristics

A CD is a product that a consumer either wants or doesn't and is down to personal preference. The consumer gets the same product whether they buy from HMV or Tower Records. A CD does not need to be tried on, smelt or touched before it is bought. The only thing that the customer may want to do is listen to it, and they will probably have heard the music already on the radio or TV. *Score: 8 out of 10.*

Familiarity and confidence

A consumer will usually be familiar and confident when choosing a CD. They will buy a CD of their own taste, whether rock, soul, hip hop, etc. Furthermore, leading brands such as HMV sell online and CDNOW uses Amazon as a channel to sell their CDs at cheaper prices. They are well-known brands so consumers are likely to feel confident buying from them. *Score: 8 out of 10.*

Consumer attributes

The typical music buyer is younger, better educated and of a higher socio-economic group than the general population, i.e. closely fitting the profile of the typical Internet user. *Score: 22 out of 30.*

Table 2.2 *Evaluation of the e-shopping potential of CDs using the ES test*

Product	*Product characteristics (10)*	*Familiarity and confidence (10)*	*Consumer attributes (30)*	*Total*
CDs	8	8	22	38

The total score for selling a CD online was 38 out of 50. De Kare-Silver stated that if a score is above 20 then the product has good potential of being bought by consumers online. The total score therefore indicates that CDs have a high potential to be purchased on the Internet, which justifies the reason why CDs have high sales online. This can be compared to basic clothing that de Kare-Silver scored at only 19 in the ES test. This means that clothing has a lower potential for e-retailing compared with CDs.

Source: This box kindly contributed by Mehtap Durmus

Online music

Industry insiders estimate that three times as much music is downloaded on the Internet (largely for free) as is being sold on CD. A Forrester (www.forrester.com) research study found that 45 per cent of European broadband users download music and half of them saw no problem in not paying for it. Nevertheless, following a settlement between AOL Time Warner and Microsoft, legal, paid for online music now seems to be taking off.

Box 2.3: ONLINE PAID CONTENT

Online paid content from the US grew by a massive 22 per cent in 2003. According to eMarketer (2003), music is the biggest category. For example, over 17 million tracks have already been downloaded from Apple's iTunes, despite competition from free file-sharing services such as Kazaa.

Paid content is not new. Financial news and pornography (now mainly downloaded videos and 'live' webcams) have been around since the early days of the Web. What is new is the fast rate of growth of many other categories, as illustrated in Figure 2.2.

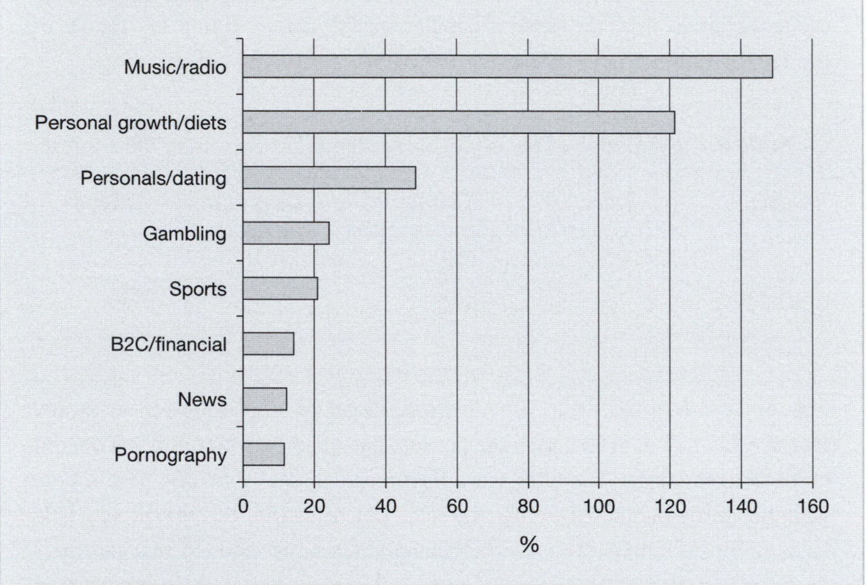

Figure 2.2 *Paid online spending growth rates for the US for 2003 – percentage increases on 2002*

Source: Adapted from e-Marketer (2002)

There are two ways of receiving music online: downloading or *streaming*. In the US one of the leaders, iTunes, launched by Apple Computers, has been successful in persuading consumers to pay 99 cents per download – 6.5 million times in the first three months. The biggest sellers included The Eagles and U2 – perhaps appealing to a more mature and affluent market than the typical pop music buyer. iTunes is also popular in Europe, with each track costing around £0.60, even though it is still only available to Apple Mac users.

Streaming means playing the track live through a computer, rather like broadcast radio. In fact, the most frequently used type of streaming is digital radio.

Interactive services where you choose your listening are gaining ground. For ex-ample, in the UK, On Demand Distribution (known as OD2 – www.ondemanddistribution.com) provides a 'music club' service for HMV and Internet service providers such as Freeserve and BT, charging a fixed monthly fee for streaming and limited downloads. But if you stop your subscription the downloads stop playing. OD2 has deals with all the big five music companies, managing the transfers to ensure that artists and record companies get paid the royalties. The company has more than 200,000 tracks by 8,500 artists. OD2's success may be partly due to the personal influence of founder Peter Gabriel (former singer with the 1970s' band Genesis). 'I have helped open doors' says Gabriel. 'We are pretty much the only player left in town' (*Sunday Times* (UK) Business, 17 August 2003).

OD2 music is also available as downloads from MSN and from Virgin, costing from around £0.60 to £0.99 per track. One incentive that OD2 uses to lure consumers to pay is offering music up to six weeks before release on CD (i.e. less likely to be available as illegal downloads). OD2 also includes exclusive versions and extra songs not available in the CD format.

For a reasonable sound quality, a broadband Internet connection is essential. Even with broadband, though, streamed sound quality is not as good as from downloaded files. A variety of systems is available to enable near hi-fi quality from the computer, either streamed or downloaded. The paid-for downloads mainly use Windows Media Audio (WMA) format, which contains controls to ensure that copyright fees are paid.

'Free' music downloads usually utilize the useful MP3 format, which is more flexible than WMA. For example, you can transfer your CDs and downloaded tracks on to a blank CD to play in-car or in a portable MP3 player such as Apple's portable iPod.

The Napster free file-swapping site has been closed down, but there are many other websites dedicated to helping users download music for free. For example, Kazaa, probably the leading site of this type, claims that its software has been downloaded 200 million times, with 2.8 million copies of its software downloaded per week. According to the *Sunday Times* (UK, 1 June 2003), when all *P2P* services are taken into account, approximately 2.6 billion files are copied per month.

Mini case study 2.2: THE IPOD – AN ICON FOR THE 00s

The iPod MP3 player weighs less than two CDs but fits 10,000 songs into your pocket. Top fashion houses have designed accessories for it, TV directors have included it in plotlines and word of mouth has made it one of the coolest gadgets. The iPod may be little more than a storage device, but it has revolutionized the way we listen to music and has become a cultural icon at the same time. Small, light and easy to use, it has helped non-technical audiences to catch on to the benefits of the personalized music library that can be enjoyed on the move.

Annual sales of 1.5 million iPods have made this one of Apple's most popular products. Its success comes from not just a stylish design, but also the ultrafast FireWire connection for transferring music from the computer. It is also an alarm clock, games console and, with optional attachments, a voice recorder and radio.

Source: Summarized and adapted from *The Times* (UK), 10 December 2003

Mini case study 2.3: KAZAA (www.download.com)

According to www.download.com, by February 2003, Kazaa had been downloaded 192, 921, 732 times! Obviously, consumers like free products. Kazaa offers searching for music, video (e.g. episodes of soaps or movies) and image files. The process is relatively simple: download the free software, agree to the terms and conditions and launch the Kazaa Media Desktop. Click 'Search', type in an artist or track title and the results are then displayed. To download, click on one of the files listed. At the time of our test, there were 4,130,879 users online sharing 810,495,758 files! Once the file has been downloaded, the user has obtained the music, initially for free, although it is the users' responsibility to pay the copyright royalties. The operators of the site state explicitly that they do not condone activities and actions that breach the rights of copyright owners: 'As a Kazaa Media Desktop user you have agreed to abide by the end user agreement and it is your responsibility to obey all laws governing copyright in each country.'

The software is free, with the costs covered through advertising revenue. Kazaa and Morpheus (a similar service) have been reported to earn US$400,000 per month from advertising. During the 20 minutes or so of download time, the user is subjected to many pop-up advertising windows. In addition, users' personal details may be used for marketing purposes (any users who have not read the terms and conditions may be unaware of this).

Apart from the advertising and the requirement to pay royalties to the copyright owner, there are other potential problems. For example, any file that is downloaded may contain a computer *virus* or *worm*. Because of the operation of the P2P system, only the owner of an infected system can delete it and stop its circulation, not Kazaa.

In order to share music with other users, the software creates a shared folder where all files can be uploaded or downloaded. The setting can be changed so that no one can obtain files from your computer, but on the default the settings can be changed by another user in such a way that your entire computer's files can be shared with everyone. In a test by HP Laboratories, a dummy file called 'creditcards.xls' was added and the computer left online for 24 hours. The file was downloaded four times (Thomas, 2002). The same report drew attention to another problem that may be worrying to parents: pornography. For example, over 70 per cent of the results obtained while searching for Britney Spears' videos on Kazaa were of pornographic content.

In our survey of 765 young people carried out in 2003, 65 per cent said that they used the Internet to download music. Eighty-eight per cent of these said that they used Kazaa or similar software, but only 12 per cent said that they used 'legal' sites (artist's web page or legal distributor). The 'legal' users also tend to be infrequent users. Respondents to our survey (of a single, West London, UK, school) have downloaded an estimated 92,000 'free' files, representing 6,600 albums. By comparison, the 'legal' downloads were only 1,000 files, equivalent to 75 albums. Worryingly, 32 per cent of the respondents were unaware of the security risks of file sharing.

Source: This mini case study was kindly contributed by Wayne Godfrey

DVD movies and videos

DVD movies and videos are mainly available from the same suppliers as are CDs (Amazon is market leader) and carry the same advantages for e-retailing (see Box 2.2, pp. 32–33). High street retailers have, of course, long supplied videos. Happily for e-retailers, the expansion in popularity of DVDs over the last couple of years has coincided with a period of rapid growth in consumers' willingness to e-shop. The main pureplays are Amazon, Bol (www.bol.com), DVD Street (www.streetsonline.co.uk) and Blackstar (www.blackstar.co.uk). The pureplays now have competition from high street retailers HMV (www.hmv.co.uk), VirginMega (www.virginmega.co.uk) and WHSmith (www.whsmith.co.uk).

DVD movie prices can vary substantially. In our test using the shopbot WebDVDGuide (www.webdvdguide.com), prices for *The Lord of the Rings – The Two Towers* 2-DVD set varied from £15.94 (www.popcorn.co.uk) up to £20.49, including delivery (compared with the 'recommended retail price' of £24.99).

Mini case study 2.4: BLACKSTAR (www.blackstar.co.uk)

Blackstar was founded in February 1998 and operates from Belfast in Northern Ireland. It began by selling a comprehensive library of 50,000 video titles. With widespread consumer support for the new DVD format that has built up over the past two years, Blackstar logically moved into the DVD movies market and now also sells games console titles as well.

Blackstar has enjoyed newsworthy successes in its short history. It has managed to attract and retain customers through its commendable level of customer service.

Typical high street video/DVD shops typically stock up to 3,000 titles, but Blackstar offers a much wider range with many otherwise-rare titles. Blackstar also offers a video/DVD hunt facility for rare or deleted titles. This service has proved to be very popular and a key factor in the company's success. However, Blackstar, like most other British e-retailers, has yet to achieve profitability. Blackstar was awarded Retail Online Success of the Year at the BVA Awards 2000.

Source: This mini case study was kindly contributed by Daniel Wells

GROCERIES

e-Grocery shopping in the UK is only around 1 per cent of total grocery shopping, but that small percentage adds up to around a billion pounds per year. The nature of groceries as non-durable necessitates delivery quickly and in such a way that quality is not lost in the delivery process. Perishable grocery deliveries can also be difficult if the recipient is not there to receive them – unlike other goods that may be popped through the letterbox or left in a lockable delivery drop. In addition, many grocery items tend to be variable in characteristics and quality and are often selected by look, feel and smell (how do you select a ripe mango online?). Compared to typical shoppers for products such as CDs, grocery shoppers tend on average to be older and less educated, and therefore less susceptible to new technology such as e-shopping. Indeed, de Kare-Silver's ES test rates groceries at 27 (out of 50), well behind Books (38) and DVD movies (39 by our estimation – see Chapter 10).

THINK POINT

If groceries are problematic for delivery and fulfilment, how does it come about that Tesco's e-grocery service is one of the largest e-retailers in the UK?

When US bookstore magnate Louis Borders founded e-grocer Webvan in 1997, he believed he could revolutionize the grocery business. The idea was deceptively simple. It was to take orders for groceries over the Internet and use highly automated centralized warehouses and computerized logistics systems controlling a local fleet of trucks to efficiently deliver groceries to a customer at a cost no greater than if the customer had gone to the supermarket themselves. The scheme was launched in San Francisco, followed by another 26 cities at an investment cost of US$35 million per city. Including marketing costs, the total investment US$1.2 billion (£840 million) was second only to Amazon in the history of e-retail start-ups. With marketing costs of 30 per cent of sales and only 50 per cent capacity utilization of the distribution centres, Webvan struggled for cash. The company folded in 2001, laying off its 2,000 employees and announcing losses of close to US$0.5 billion – the largest single e-commerce loss ever.

Tesco, the leading UK grocery supermarket, is a very different story (www.tesco.com – see Case study 3.2, pp. 72–74). Tesco's online shopping service has been one of very few grocery e-retailing successes worldwide, with 1 million users, 85,000 orders per week and profit since 2001. Tesco is the world's biggest e-grocer, and is the UK's number one by a considerable margin, with a 53 per cent share of the world's biggest online grocery market. The key has been twofold. First, Tesco had first-mover advantage, rapidly increasing its operation to cover 95 per cent of the population. By contrast, the main rival, Sainsbury's, reaches 71 per cent of UK households. Second, the initial operation (still true for most food items) employed pickers to select the goods from the shelves of local stores. This simple approach enabled Tesco to get the operation off the ground quickly and cheaply. In a warehouse, fresh food that was unsold would have to be thrown away. In addition, when e-orders are quiet, Tesco's pickers can do other work. Meanwhile, competitors have struggled. Somerfield attempted the purpose-built distribution centre approach, and retired hurt. Safeway (formerly one of the 'big three' UK supermarkets) never launched a home delivery service and has now closed down its e-retail business completely. Sainsbury's uses a combination of warehouses and in-store picking, but is still not in profit at the time of writing. Wal-Mart Asda's two dedicated warehouses have been closed. Both Sainsbury's and Wal-Mart Asda offer delivery to less than half of households across the country at the time of writing. Iceland claims 97 per cent coverage, but is reticent about its trading results.

The Tesco e-retailing model has now been introduced into the US through a deal with Safeway Inc. (not connected with the UK Safeway). Customers in Portland, Oregon, were the first to try the service, followed by San Francisco (where Webvan tried and failed). Tesco.com is also growing rapidly in the Republic of Ireland, where the service covers 70 per cent of the population, and in South Korea through a joint venture with Homeplus.

The main challenge to Tesco.com's approach in the UK may come from Ocado (www.ocado.co.uk). Ocado operates in conjunction with Waitrose, one of the UK's top six supermarkets with stores mainly in the south of England. Ocado is 40 per cent owned by department store group John Lewis Partnership, owners of Waitrose. Ocado are committed to the warehouse model with central warehouses to the north of London and in Birmingham that can each process the same amount of groceries as 20 superstores. From a pilot in Hertfordshire, the e-retailing service has been rolled out to the London area. Ocado's managing director pointed out that the company bases marketing on a low level of substitutions (claimed to be 2 per cent vs. an 'industry standard' of 15 per cent) and one-hour rather than two-hour delivery time slots (*Guardian*, 1 August 2002). The operation has a long way to go to catch Tesco, though, and even Waitrose's managing director estimated that it would take three to five years to reach profitability (*Sunday Times* (UK), 10 November 2002).

Box 2.4:
EIGHT WAYS TO CUSTOMER VALUE AND PROFITABILITY IN GROCERY E-RETAILING

(1) Customer density
(2) Loyalty
(3) Buying power
(4) Ordering efficiency and customer information
(5) Operational efficiency and customer service level
(6) Large range of products
(7) Price level
(8) Shopping convenience

Sources: 1 to 4, Tanskanen *et al.* (2002), 5 to 7, Anckar *et al.* (2002). (5 and 6 appear as similar constructs in both sources)

Tanskanen *et al.* (2002) reported on 'six lessons learned' for profitable grocery e-retailing and Anckar *et al.* (2002) identified 'four sources of customer value' – see Box 2.4. As the UK's leading supermarket, Tesco has the advantage in loyalty, buying power and range of products. Economies of scale should also give the market-leader a potential advantage in good-value selling prices. In theory, therefore, the other players need to try to gain their competitive advantage from the remaining factors: shopping convenience, operational efficiency, customer service, the ordering interface and product information. These can be addressed by, for example, making the website informative, quick and easy to use, supplying exactly (or with a minimum of substitutes) what is ordered and providing accurately timed delivery slots. See Box 2.5 for an outline of how some of the players were shaping up at the time of our site tests.

Box 2.5:
UK GROCERY RETAILERS

Tesco (www.tesco.com)

See Case study 3.2, pp. 72–74.

The Tesco website is quick and easy to use, offering a wider choice than competitors do. There is a flat delivery fee of £5, with goods delivered in agreed two-hour time slots. Tesco has the largest delivery area. Registration is quick, the site is clear and it loads quickly.

Ocado (www.ocado.com)

Delivery is free on orders over £75; otherwise it is £5, with goods delivered in one-hour slots. Delivery is available in London and surrounding areas only. The website is easy to use. Ocado claims to impose fewer substitutions than competitors do. (In conjunction with Waitrose.)

Wal-Mart Asda (www.asda.co.uk)

The site is easy to use but not as quick as its competitors. Delivery is free on orders over £99; otherwise it is £3.50, with goods delivered within two-hour time slots.

Sainsbury's (www.sainsburys.co.uk)

Sainsbury's offers a comprehensive range of products, but its site is not as easy to use and understand as Tesco's. In our test, the site was slow loading, especially when registering. There is a flat delivery charge of £5, with goods delivered in two-hour slots, although at times there can be few slots available.

Iceland (www.iceland.co.uk)

Iceland offers free delivery with a £40 minimum order to addresses within ten miles of a store. The site is self-explanatory and easy to use. Loading and registration are quick.

Source: Site tests kindly contributed by Omar Chaudhry

CLOTHING AND FOOTWEAR

Clothing is not an obvious product for e-retailing. First, of course, clothing is normally bought by look, feel and fit, all of which are difficult for the e-shopper to evaluate on the Web. Second, clothing is bought not just for warmth and modesty, but also to express our self-image. Any purchase errors in (e.g.) style, therefore, carry a particularly high perceived risk. Indeed, de Kare-Silver's ES test rates basic clothing at 19 (out of 50), well behind books (38), DVD movies (39 by our estimation – see Chapter 10) and groceries (27). (For a product to be suitable for e-retailing, de Kare-Silver recommends a minimum score of 20.) Nevertheless, clothing represents one of the major categories in UK e-retail (although worldwide it is one of the slowest-growing categories). One reason may be that clothing has historically been one of the major mail-order categories in the UK. Both shoppers and suppliers are used to home delivery channels for clothing. The clothing e-retail market leader Next (www.next.co.uk) has been supplying fashion clothing by mail order since 1988 (see Case study 1.1, pp. 19–21).

THINK POINT

If clothing does not meet the requirements for a suitable product for e-retailing, how does it happen that clothing is one of the largest categories for UK e-shoppers?

Surprisingly, lingerie and hosiery is one of the most popular product categories for e-retailing, perhaps driven by the success of the leader, Fig Leaves (www.figleaves.com), in the same way that Tesco has driven the expansion of grocery e-retailing. Fig Leaves has a winning approach both in the creative permission-based marketing and the novel online bra measuring system. In particular e-shopping for lingerie appeals to men, who may often be embarrassed to buy these products in-store.

'Look and feel' goods tend to be compared and evaluated before buying – i.e. they are high involvement purchases. For example, a survey reported in the *New Straits Times* in 2001 found that 85 per cent of respondents would not buy clothes online because they prefer to try them on before purchase. Enjoyment is often a motivation for in-store clothes shopping (and other comparison shopping). In the bricks retail store, 'atmospherics' are often used to increase enjoyment and hence sales. The effectiveness of such techniques is well known in-store, but in Chapter 6 we argue that equivalent considerations are also important for the e-retailer. Emotional aspects such as enjoyment strongly predict shoppers' attitudes towards e-shopping (Childers *et al.*, 2001). According to Chicksand and Knowles (2002), equivalent features can be identified to help in overcoming the difficulties of selling 'look and feel' goods like clothing online. The equivalent stimuli for the clicks store include: sound, personalization/customization, usability of the website, visuals and text. As we demonstrate in Chapter 6, *web atmospherics* can help compensate for the lack of sensory experience in e-shopping. Nevertheless, the indications are that shoppers' needs for enjoyment (rather than just utilitarian) benefits are not being satisfied by e-retailers (Henderson and Kunz, 2002). Even clothing market leader Next makes little attempt at the use of web atmospherics on the e-retail site.

Personalization is a key element of web atmospherics, but most clothing e-retailers personalize very little. Developments aimed at helping to overcome this drawback include the Eddie Bauer (US clothing retailer) 'virtual closet' which allows shoppers to match up items with a 'Style Builder'. With Virtual Model (www.virtualmodel.com – one of the '100 best websites' from *Internet Magazine*) you can create a 3-D virtual model of yourself online and dress yourself with clothing from top suppliers such as Lands End – claimed to increase the likelihood of a sale by 19 per cent (Lorek, 2001). These e-retailers keep a database of sizes

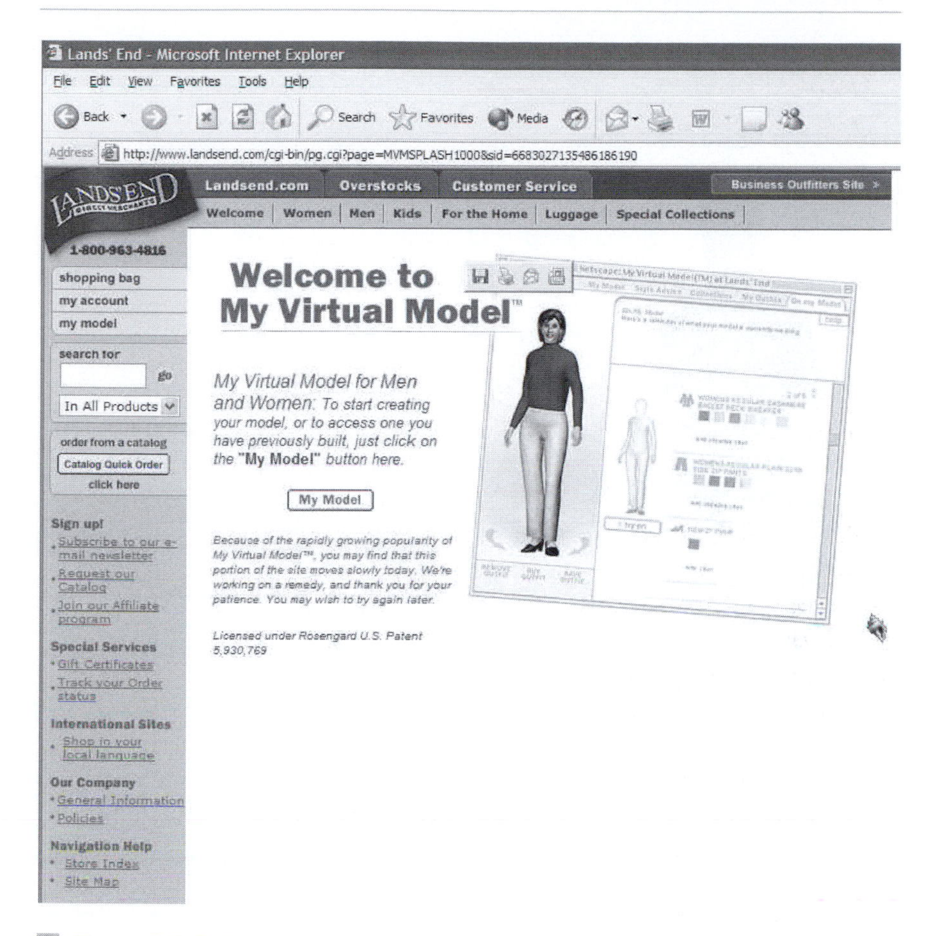

Figure 2.3 *Online systems are using computing facilities to substitute for the physical trail of merchandise*

Source: www.landsend.com

and items bought that is available on your next visit, personalizing the experience and saving purchase time.

The potential for clothing includes the body scan. For example, shoppers can visit selected Levi stores for the scan, which is then held on a database. In theory, this could then be used for e-shopping, incorporating the scan data into a 3-D virtual closet such as Virtual Model. Shoppers could be confident that the clothes would fit. Unfortunately, Levi does not actually offer the body scan data for e-retailing on the Virtual Model/Kohls (www.kohls.com) site.

Customization is another key element of web atmospherics for clothing. Mass customization refers to self-designed products. Shopper involvement in the design of the products adds considerably to the personal feel of the shopping experience. Shopper satisfaction can be enhanced by more closely matching exact needs.

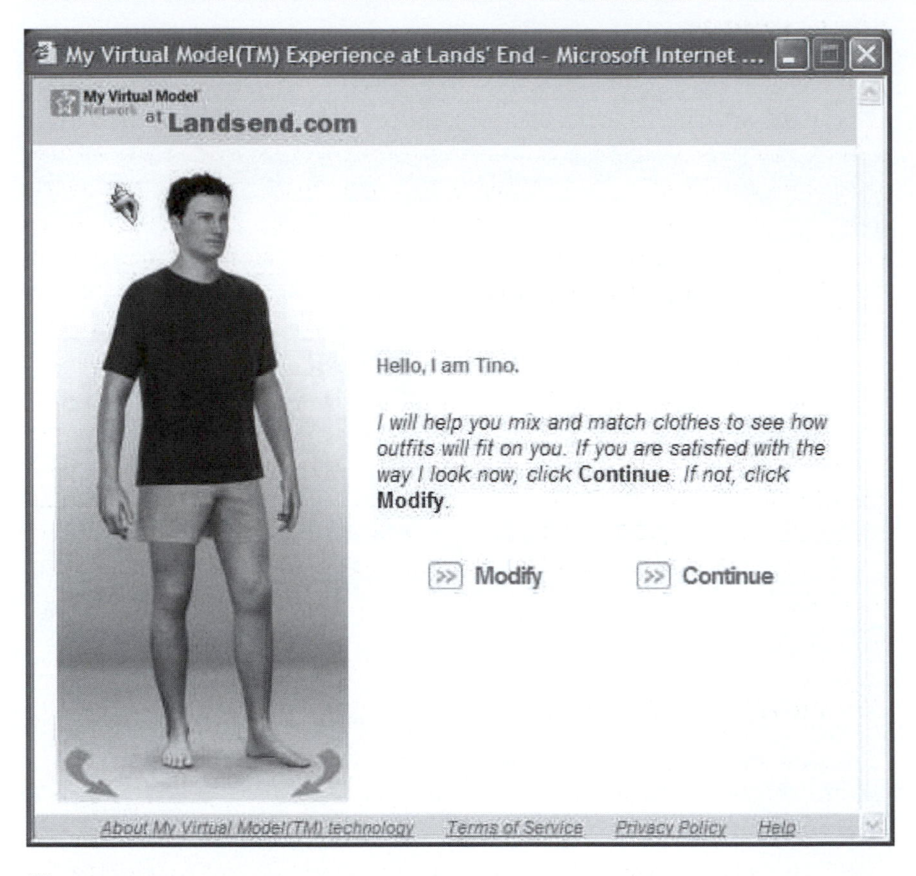

Figure 2.4 *Based on a series of online questions, the virtual model approximates the image of the Web shopper*

Source: www.landsend.com

In the case of Nike (www.nike.com), shoppers can customize shoes, not just with colours and styles, but also, for example, with a name or message. A potential drawback of this system, though, is concern over what happens if the customer wants to return the product for any reason? Fanbuzz e-retails clothes, allowing shoppers to decide their own styles, colours, graphics and sizes. These custom items are 10–20 per cent more expensive than non-custom ones, but many customers are prepared to pay more for customized products (Evans, 2001).

Although the market for e-retailing clothes is growing only slowly, if the mass-market e-retailers such as Next and Marks & Spencer (www.marksandspencer.com) were to improve web atmospherics, e.g. more attractive, interactive site design and layout, more personalization and customization incorporating features used by specialists such as Lands End and Nike, there should be considerable scope for further growth.

CONCLUSIONS

As the young adults of today become more economically active and increasing numbers of computer-literate children progress to becoming undergraduates, it is likely that e-shopping for certain key categories will increase. These include books, music and movies (despite falling high street music sales due to piracy). Grocery sales may progress more slowly as the e-shoppers are mainly an older and perhaps more conservative segment. Nevertheless, greater competition in the UK is improving levels of customer service and convenience; so, further UK market expansion of grocery e-shopping can be predicted. Tesco's successful model is being rolled out into more countries, leading to international expansion of grocery e-shopping. Clothing, like other look and feel goods, is a more questionable category. Nevertheless, with improvements to web atmospherics possible with faster broadband downloading and the diffusion of these from the specialists to the mass-market e-retailers, expansion of the clothing e-shopping market can also be predicted. Overall, it is likely that the coming years will see a growth in e-retailing of many of the traditional high street shopping products.

CHAPTER SUMMARY

Amazon is the clear market leader for the largest UK e-retailing categories of books, CDs and DVD movies. In addition to first-mover advantage and heavy conventional advertising, Amazon achieves its position by attention to convenience, customer service and reliability – in effect, branding. Similarly, customer satisfaction underlies the success of the number two in CDs: CD WOW. Despite the ease and transparency of price comparisons made possible by the availability of shopbots for these categories, the market leader is often not the cheapest.

In a similar fashion to the domination of those markets by Amazon, first-mover Tesco dominates e-groceries retailing. In addition to leveraging the brand value of the bricks stores, Tesco attributes much of the success to the store-picking model (only some non-food products such as books, CDs and DVDs are despatched from a non-store centre). Competitor Ocado is trying hard to compete on the basis of service and convenience benefits, using the custom distribution centre approach.

Next is the leader for e-retailing clothing overall, built on the existing mail order systems. Lingerie is the 'surprise' growth category, led by the highly creative dot.com, Fig Leaves.

The following chapter investigates the integration of e-retailing into an organization.

Case study 2.1: AMAZON.CO.UK

This case illustrates Amazon.co.uk's retail mix and the application of the Ansoff matrix (see also the comparison with eBay in Mini case study 8.1, pp. 178–179).

> I buy all my books at Amazon.com because I'm busy and it's convenient. They have a big selection, and they've been reliable.
>
> (Bill Gates)

Amazon has established itself worldwide as an online retail success, the world's biggest e-retailer of books and head-to-head with Barnes and Noble for the title of the world's largest bookstore, even though Amazon sells only online. From a start-up in 1995, annual sales have grown to more than US$1 billion and the company has over 2.5 million customers – but reported its first profit only in 2002. The UK site, www.amazon.co.uk, was formed in 1998 by the takeover of Bookpages, and the UK is now Amazon's biggest market outside the US. Amazon is also the clear UK market leader for CDs, DVD movies and videos and offers many other product lines, including electronics, software, games, toys, travel and auctions. According to a survey by Global Online Retailing, one in eight UK Internet users have made a purchase at Amazon.co.uk.

Amazon is the market leader in the UK for selling online books with a market share of over 50 per cent, and its main advantage is the ability to deliver low-cost

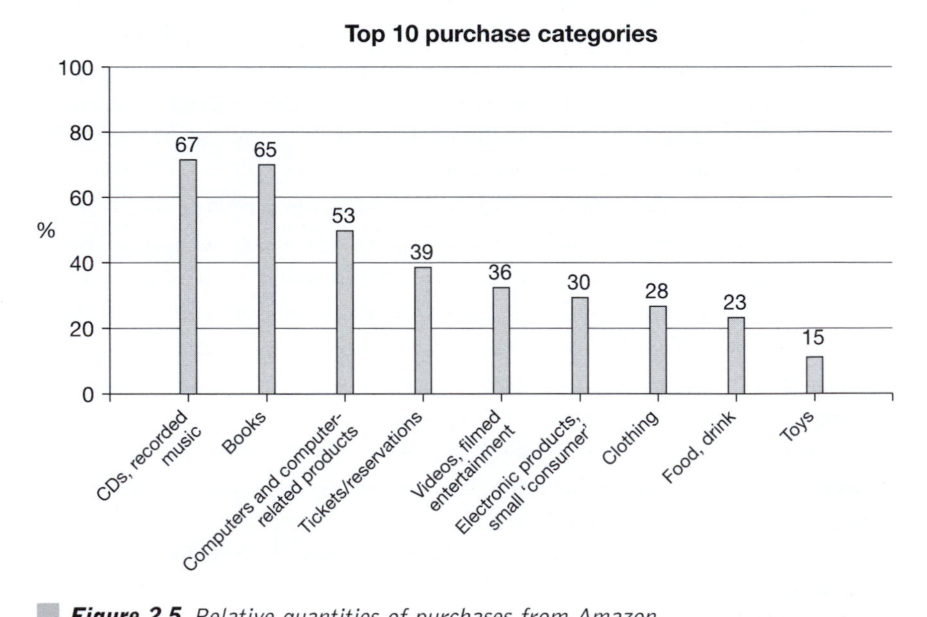

Figure 2.5 *Relative quantities of purchases from Amazon*

books by saving on store, warehouse and inventory costs. Amazon has panels of experts in all the different areas, such as music, children and technology, who write reviews from each perspective.

AMAZON'S E-RETAIL MIX

Convenience

Convenience plays an important role in gaining and maintaining new customers. There are several factors driving the level of customer convenience. First, the speed of downloading amazon.co.uk's website is fast, as it takes only three to five seconds although it is full of images of their products. Customers can quickly find the desired product, as the search facility is second to none. Once the result is located it provides value-added services such as book reviews and ratings, and displays its own price and a comparison price. Comparative pricing allows customers to see the value they are receiving from Amazon, i.e. how much they are saving. Amazon makes it easy to source and buy products and track the progress of delivery.

Amazon offers industry-leading state-of-the-art online shopping technology, the '1-click' system, which streamlines the customer buying process by storing personal information such as credit card number and shipping address, saving time and hassle. According to a survey carried out by Knowledge Systems & Research, consumers become frustrated after having to click more than six times to complete a purchase and as a result they move to other websites (e-Marketer 2002). The website offers secure socket-layer connection, which means that sensitive credit card information is transmitted in encrypted format. In some cases it even provides a guarantee that, if unauthorized transactions are made, it will reimburse the customer. All major credit and debit cards are accepted.

One of the prime factors of convenience is based on availability. If any of the titles are unavailable, Amazon will still take your order and will let you know when the title will be available. Amazon.co.uk's main aim is to maximize customers' convenience so they do not look anywhere else for their books.

The search facility is designed in such a unique way that it provides up-selling, cross-selling and down-selling. For every result of a book title search you are given the options shown in Figure 2.6.

For instance, if you are looking at a book the website will also display other books in the same category. This feature allows customers to have better choice. This is e-comparison shopping as you are comparing two books while only looking at one screen. The facility increases sales as customers can always find something that they want. Customers can view their account any time, which includes information about their past orders along with shipment details. Account information is used to make recommendations about other books that customers may like.

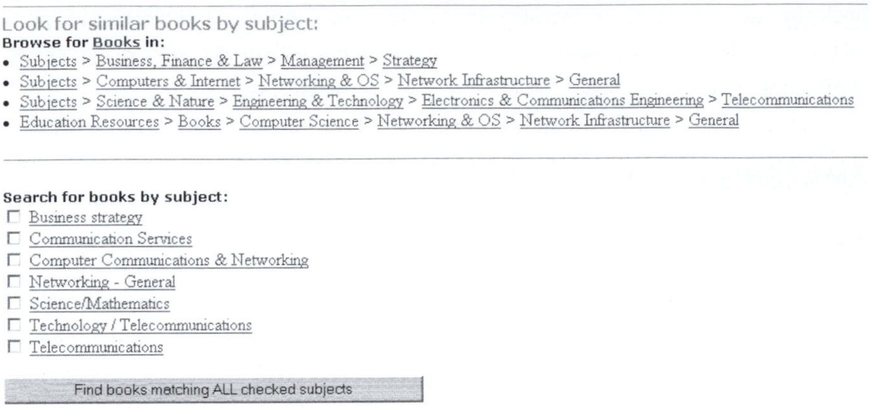

Look for similar books by subject:

Browse for Books in:

- Subjects > Business, Finance & Law > Management > Strategy
- Subjects > Computers & Internet > Networking & OS > Network Infrastructure > General
- Subjects > Science & Nature > Engineering & Technology > Electronics & Communications Engineering > Telecommunications
- Education Resources > Books > Computer Science > Networking & OS > Network Infrastructure > General

Search for books by subject:

- ☐ Business strategy
- ☐ Communication Services
- ☐ Computer Communications & Networking
- ☐ Networking - General
- ☐ Science/Mathematics
- ☐ Technology / Telecommunications
- ☐ Telecommunications

Find books matching ALL checked subjects

Figure 2.6 *Search result options to search for similar titles*

Cost

Cost is one of the features that drive customers to shop on the Web. Nevertheless, Jeff Bezos, Amazon's CEO, believed that online customers considered selection and convenience to be more important than price. This belief is probably justified as Brynjolfsson and Smith (2000) pointed out that amazon had a market share of 80 per cent while charging 10 per cent more than the cheapest (see Mini case study 2.1, p. 29, for more book-pricing examples). Therefore, Amazon did not seek to compete on price alone. Customers want to get the best price with excellent customer service. Most of the books at amazon are available at a discounted price, ranging from 1 per cent to 50 per cent off the recommended retail price. Consumers are always shown three prices: 'list price', 'our price' and 'how much you save'.

Amazon has reasonable delivery charges. There are often seasonal promotions such as free delivery if the order is over a certain amount. Different options are available, including (as an optional extra) overnight delivery.

Following a similar arrangement in the US, amazon.co.uk has a deal with Toys R Us for in-store pick up, which allows customers to collect the books at their convenience. With this option, there is no delivery charge.

Communication

Amazon has established its brand name through customer intimacy and customer relationship management. From day one their aim has been to be a customer-centric company. It welcomes returning customers with their name, e.g. 'Welcome back Charles Dennis', with the help of a cookie file stored on the user's computer. This has been referred to as the Web equivalent of customizing a storefront to suit the taste of each person walking through the door.

Customers can opt in if they wish to receive more information, for example when a new novel comes out by their favourite author. Consumers can always opt out as well if they are not interested in receiving any more information.

Amazon monitors the customer's ordering process through the Oracle database environment that feeds all the content to its website. It can track the speed and performance of each step in a transaction, including placement of an item in a cart, completion of an order and e-mail notification to the customer.

Amazon offers personalization by recommending similar books according to what other customers have bought. For example, the personalized screen will say: 'Customers who bought titles by this author also bought titles by these authors'. These features help users to make up their minds quickly and they can also read spotlight reviews by other readers. Amazon is to some extent a virtual community where users express their views about authors. Publishers and authors can also contribute.

Amazon uses an integrated marketing communications strategy that encompasses advertising, public relations, promotions and online marketing. Offline advertising includes TV commercials and billboards in train stations. Online activity includes the associates program and deals with major search engines and portal pages such as Yahoo.com and MSN.

The associates program uses other sites to promote Amazon by links that directly take users to Amazon's site. In return associates receive a small percentage commission on the total transaction value.

Computing

Amazon uses state-of-the-art technology in its back end (warehouse) and front end (website). The company has developed a customized information system and dedicated ordering system, which is linked with suppliers to automatically order books. The *search engine* employs XML and Oracle database technology, which bring up results in a matter of seconds. Once the book or an item is found, users sign in using the 1-click system and the purchase is complete. The company's software processes the orders via electronic interfaces or electronic data interchange with suppliers and all the stages in the supply chain are computerized.

Customer care

According to an internal customer research survey carried out by amazon.co.uk, 70 per cent of sales are made by repeat customers of whom 97 per cent are satisfied or very satisfied with the service – which must be one of the highest satisfaction scores among pureplay dot.coms. Its FAQs section is very informative as it explains all the main issues such as ordering process, delivery charges and returns policy.

Customer franchise

Amazon's brand relationship is like someone who knows you, understands your preferences and tells you something new every time you make contact. This builds up a strong relationship as if dealing with assistants who have come to know customers in the course of many shopping trips.

ANSOFF MATRIX

The Ansoff matrix illustrated in Figure 2.7 can be applied to Amazon.

Market penetration

Market penetration means seeking to achieve growth with existing products in their current market segments and aiming to increase their share of the market. Amazon has increased market penetration through value-added service. For example, as mentioned previously, it takes on the responsibility to order books that they do not have at present and let the users know as soon as they become available. It allows

Market \ Product	Present	New
Present	Market penetration	Product development
New	Market development	Diversification

Figure 2.7 *Ansoff matrix*
Source: Ansoff 1957

users to sell used books, and prices for used books appear alongside the selling price for a new book. The extended service and options translate into greater sales. In some cases Amazon now allows users to browse chapters within books. This gives the reader a chance to read the book before actually buying it. The more services offered, the more chances there are it will lead to a sale.

Product development

Here new product offerings are developed to market to existing customers. Amazon has added second-hand books to its product range, giving its customers the opportunity to sell their used books. Amazon also now sells e-books – readable on *Personal Digital Assistants (PDAs)*.

Market development

Market development concerns the marketing of existing products to a new audience. Amazon has extended purchasing to users of *WAP* or *3G* mobile phones.

In addition, Amazon has signed deals with bricks and mortar bookshops such as Waterstones and Borders to sell books online for them. Customers typing in www.waterstones.co.uk will be directed to a version of the Amazon website that carries Waterstone's name (although the appearance and co-branded name are still clearly Amazon). A percentage of the profit from any books they subsequently buy will go to Waterstones in a concept similar to the associates program.

Diversification

Diversification refers to entering new markets with new products. Amazon has broken into new markets by offering travel services, software, electronics and toys. This is known as unrelated diversification, as Amazon had no previous market experience in these areas. Nevertheless, having built up a successful brand name with a large number of loyal customers, the company is well placed to extend the franchise.

Conclusion

Amazon has survived the dot.com crash to become one of the world's largest booksellers. It has reached this position through careful customer focus. All of its innovations are driven by the desire to enhance customer experience. Despite not always offering the cheapest prices, Amazon has few substantial competitors – largely due to its shrewd moves to strike deals with potential competitors like Waterstones and Borders.

> The Internet store of the future should be able to guess what the customer wants to buy before the customer knows.
>
> (Jeff Bezos)

Source: This case study was kindly contributed by Numan Tahir

QUESTIONS

Brief feedback to these questions is included at the back of the book.

Question 2.1

Why are books, CDs and DVD movies particularly suitable e-shopping categories?

Question 2.2

Why is it surprising that groceries are among the biggest-selling e-retail products in the UK?

Question 2.3

Why are groceries one of the main UK e-shopping categories?

Question 2.4

How might mass-market clothing e-retailers increase business?

FURTHER READING

Harris, Lisa and Dennis, Charles (2002) *Marketing the e-Business*, London: Routledge. This is one of the few books on marketing written especially for e-commerce. See Chapter 8, The Marketing Mix, for encapsulated specific ideas on increasing e-business.

Tiernan, Bernadette (2000) *e-Tailing*, Chicago, IL: Dearborn. This is one of the few texts on e-retailing, written for a US audience.

REFERENCES

Anckar, W., Walden, P. and Jelassi, T. (2002) 'Creating customer value in online grocery shopping', *International Journal of Retail and Distribution Management*, 30 (4): 211–220.

Brynjolfsson, E. and Smith, M. (2000) 'Frictionless commerce? A comparison of Internet and conventional retailers', *Management Science*, 46 (4): 563–585.

Chicksand, L. and Knowles, R. (2002) 'Selling "look and feel goods" online', *IBM E-Business Conference*, Birmingham University.

Childers, T.L., Carr, C.L., Peck, J. and Carson, S. (2001) 'Hedonic and utilitarian motivations for online retail shopping behavior', *Journal of Retailing*, 77: 511–535.

de Kare-Silver, M. (2001) *e-Shock: The New Rules*, Basingstoke: Palgrave.

Dennis, C. and Papamatthaiou, E.-K. (2003) 'Shoppers' motivations for e-shopping', *Tenth Recent Advances in Retailing and Services Science Conference*, Portland, Oregon, 7–10 August.

e-Marketer (2002) www.marketeer.com/news [accessed July].

e-Marketer (2003) *Online Paid Content: Trends and Opportunities*, New York: eMarketer.

Evans, L. (2001) 'Fanbuzz.com launches mass customisation capability', *Sporting Good Business'*, 34 (1).

Henderson, K.V. and Kunz, M.B. (2002) 'The convergence of brick and click retail atmospherics: delivering similar worth utility online and on-land', *Ninth International Conference on Recent Advances in Retailing and Services Science*, Heidelberg, EIRASS.

Kotler, P., Armstrong, G., Saunders, J. and Wong, Y. (2001) *Principles of Marketing* (3rd European edn) London: FT Prentice Hall.

Lorek, L. (2001) 'Net-wear sells', *Interactive Week*, 8 (22).

Porter, M.E. (1985) *Competitive Advantage: Creating and Sustaining Superior Performance*, New York: Free Press.

Tanskanen, K., Yrjola, H. and Holmstrom, J. (2002) 'The way to profitable Internet grocery retailing: six lessons learned', *International Journal of Retail and Distribution Management*, 30 (4): 169–178.

Thomas, K. (2002) 'File swapping invades the home computer', *USA Today*, www.thehill.com/052202/ss_towns.shtm [accessed 1 October].

WEB LINKS

www.amazon.co.uk
Busy, friendly and informative; the market leader for books plus music, DVD movies and much more.

www.cd-wow.co.uk
A favourite site for CDs.

www.ebay.co.uk
Buy or sell anything by auction; the UK's top e-retailer measured by audience numbers (see Case study 4.1, pp. 104–105).

www.landsend.com
Simple cotton clothes in a clean and airy site. Try out the 3-D virtual model.

www.marksandspencer.com
For a good selection of mass-market clothing, underwear and much more.

www.nike.com
For customized shoes and clothing.

www.tesco.com
Top grocery supermarket online as well as in-store.

www.ukauctionhelp.co.uk
Help for buyers and sellers.

www.virtualmodel.com
See how you look in clothes from Lands End and other top suppliers.

Auctions

www.ebay.co.uk
In the US and the UK, e-auctions are the most active and popular way of e-shopping, with eBay the leader for fun (and risk?) (see Case study 4.1, pp. 104–105).

www.qxl.co.uk
Unlike most auction sites, the UK-based QXL sells products itself as well as allowing the public to sell in personal auctions.

Chapter 3

Integration of e-retailing into an organization

LINKS TO OTHER CHAPTERS

- Chapter 1 – The world of e-retailing
- Chapter 6 – e-Store design: navigability, interactivity and web atmospherics
- Chapter 8 – Branding on the Web
- Chapter 9 – e-Malls
- Chapter 10 – e-Retailing models
- Chapter 11 – m-Shopping
- Chapter 12 – Multi-channel shopping and the future of e-retailing

KEY LEARNING POINTS

After completing this chapter you will have an understanding of:

- Why traditional retailers integrate e-retail
- Strategies for e-retail integration
- Resource and change management implications

ORDERED LIST OF SUB-TOPICS

- Why traditional retailers adopt e-retail
- Strategies for integration
- Loyalty-based integration strategies
- Implementation: change management and resource implications

- Conclusions
- Chapter summary
- ❖ Case studies
- ❖ Questions
- ❖ Further reading
- ❖ References
- ❖ Web links

INTRODUCTION

During the early commercialization of the Internet, when it became clear it would provide a new channel for the sale of products and services, there was common speculation that traditional retail was dead. Investors flocked towards dot.com stocks on the premise that a new economy was emerging where established organizations, with their inherent structural rigidity and reluctance to embrace change, could not compete with more nimble dot.com start-ups, founded on embracing e-commerce.

However, this 'either/or', 'bricks vs. clicks' paradigm was short-lived. Although there are many reports of dot.com successes that became spectacular failures (see, for example, Cellan-Jones, 2003), as well as examples of dot.com survivors and outright dot.com successes such as eBay, the evolving stars have been hybrids and, most often, established retailers who have successfully integrated e-commerce.

This chapter looks at the integration of B2C e-commerce, namely e-retail, into established businesses, and begins by examining the reasons for traditional retailers to incorporate e-retail into their business model, considering some recent examples. It then goes on to review some frameworks that have been proposed to encompass strategies for integrating online and offline activities, and ends with consideration of the operational implications of such activities for the retailer.

WHY TRADITIONAL RETAILERS ADOPT E-RETAIL

The number of customers shopping online has increased markedly each year since the beginning of e-commerce in the mid-1990s. In the UK during November 2003, for example, online shopping was up 44 per cent on the previous year (ZDNet, 2003). This alone might be a reason for a traditional retailer to look at e-retail, but the influences on such decisions have varied with time and understanding of e-commerce.

Out of fashion: commerciality

Before the dot.com downturn in the spring of 2000, the word 'Internet' keyed into what seemed pervasive optimism for a new century. It meant youth, new possibilities and an opportunity to break with traditional business and create new rules. From the media and daily articles on achieved or projected *Initial Public Offering (IPO)* success, even game shows such as *The e-millionaire show*, which went out during peak viewing, to the restructuring of government and creation of new departments, such as the Office of the e-Envoy and a complement of online resources, the Internet could not be ignored. In the absence of a better reason, fashion alone was sufficient to drive most traditional businesses to consider moving into e-commerce, even if the boardroom rationale was to protect shareholder value.

However, the shakeout of 2000 left fashion with the debris of countless failed start-ups. In its place came valuable lessons across e-commerce, and evidence for incumbent retailers that factors such as having an established brand provide significant advantages in e-retail and play a part in customer loyalty and increased profit.

Advantages of being established

Analysis of dot.com failures and comparison with traditional retailers in the same industry, for example eToys (www.etoys.com), which folded in 2000 and was subsequently bought by an established toy retailer, vs. Toys R Us (www.toysrus.com), which successfully opened an e-retail channel through collaboration with Amazon (www.amazon.com), has revealed several advantages for the established retailer.

Newcomers have to attract customers, and much of their cash-burn and early debt is usually caused by brand-building and promotion. Established businesses, however, have an existing customer base and can build on brand values that are already in place. They also have existing marketing budgets usually able to furnish new online activity, and are experienced in the market they serve, unlike many start-ups. Further advantages, such as having an existing value network including suppliers, buying, fulfilment and the teams to support these functions, have been shown to be generous compensation for being late to market.

Benefits of e-retail

As discussed later, there are many strategic options for the adoption of e-retail and the level of involvement a business can choose in online activity, but clearly, as outlined in Chapter 1 (advantages and disadvantages of e-retailing for retailers, pp. 2–4), e-retail, at the very least, represents an alternative or additional channel for traditional retailers. While opening new physical retail outlets can expand the geographical reach of a business and add convenience for consumers, retailing online not only carries these benefits, but also offers further returns that are more specific to online trading. The Internet has global reach and provides the opportunity to trade internationally. Of course, this is not necessarily an advantage for a number of reasons, such as having to deal with multiple languages, currencies and even cultures, and managing far-flung logistics including returns, but, with foreign competition able to enjoy the potential of international trade online, businesses do need to consider their competitive position should they ignore e-retail.

Other broad benefits include the ability to trade 24/7 and operate with lower overheads in terms of staff and space, while more particular advantages include the ability to increase the number of customer 'touch points' and build more personalized customer experiences, products and relationships.

However, these e-retail advantages should not imply that an online presence is a recipe in itself for success; that kind of thinking was tried and failed with the dot.com boom and bust. Instead, if there is a recipe for successful integration, it is found in variants of established business practices, such as an understanding of the strengths and weaknesses of the business, for example in relation to technology awareness, which is a good indicator of e-commerce success. Most importantly, the adoption of e-retail relies on the competent formulation of an integration strategy.

STRATEGIES FOR INTEGRATION

As discussed in Chapter 1, online shopping in the UK continues to grow and is expected to comprise over 5 per cent of the retail market by 2005. Such predictions can be somewhat self-fulfilling and help fuel enthusiasm for continued research and development, providing a constantly changing environment for any integration strategy. It is necessary to keep abreast of these developments as they all impinge on strategic decisions.

Overview of current developments

While the common e-retail interface remains the Web browser running on a personal computer, many companies have investigated alternative methods of interfacing with the customer. *T-commerce*, that is e-commerce over TV or instigated by TV commercials, is an important e-retail alternative, not least because 97 per cent of UK homes have one or more televisions, and take-up of interactive TV continues to rise. During Christmas 2003, 'Freeview' (the name for the free-to-air part of digital terrestrial television in the UK) was among the top ten queries on Internet search engines. In comparison, penetration of Internet via PC has been predicted to level off at 53 per cent by 2004. Dominos Pizza had early success in T-commerce using satellite, cable and the Web to achieve

98 per cent brand recognition in multi-channel homes, and other retailers, including Dixons and WHSmith have followed. The medium has also been particularly popular with the finance industry and has attracted several banks and building societies.

Other developments that strengthen opportunities for e-retail exist in advances in mobile phone technology (considered in more detail in Chapter 11). Recent developments include 3G, with data transfer speeds up to 2Mbps that can support video-level *interactivity*, and the growing deployment of *Wi-Fi* networks couples with widespread prediction that Wi-Fi is a key growth area that will fundamentally change Internet access. For example, there is an effort under way to turn Paris into one big Wi-Fi *hotspot*, by positioning access points above and below ground at all of the city's 372 metro stations, interconnected by fibre-optic cable. The pilot phase of the project began in mid-2003, when Cisco announced that it was partnering with RATP (Régie Autonome des Transports Parisiens – the Paris public transport authority) in a proof of concept above ground at a dozen locations along the Bus 38 route. If the full project gains approval, Paris will have one of the largest Wi-Fi networks in the world.

The UK has its own significant developments, including building an advanced retail communications network at Birmingham's new Bullring shopping centre. As part of a dynamic retail environment, incorporating an intelligent buildings system and a multi-Gigabit cabling infrastructure, the 130 new shops are supplemented in the mall by 27 touch screen interactive kiosks, 25 plasma screens and 155 thin client terminals linked to one of the largest Wi-Fi networks in Europe.

Among the large traditional retailers, Argos (www.argos.co.uk), a UK catalogue company with streamlined ordering and collection at high street stores, has been prominent in developing alternative ordering and reservation methods as well as full online retail. The company has had success with in-store kiosks that provide fast track ordering and credit card payment, and was among the first to trial a text messaging 'text and take home' system for product reservation. Using the system, customers can text the catalogue number of an item to check its availability at a particular store, and then, in response to the text that confirms the item's price and stock position, can place a reservation on the product. The system reduces queuing and is part of the company's continuous innovation in ideas to increase customer convenience.

Murray Hennessy, MD of John Lewis Direct, believes that in e-retail, 'It's getting easier to be smarter' (IMRG, 2002). Software platforms for e-retail are now available off-the-shelf, and people in the industry are now more experienced. However, no matter how accessible the technology of e-retail systems becomes, or how successful the big players have already been, companies that want to adopt e-retail need to understand what it offers and pursue an integration strategy that is appropriate to their business.

Strategic options

A company's strategy towards e-retailing will be influenced by a number of factors, including its market sector and prospects for online and offline retail, in-house technical knowledge and experience of outsourcing, re-engineering and development projects, as well as its overall vision, desire and ability to operate in a very fast-changing and possibly unfamiliar commercial environment.

In order to recognize the additional complexity that e-commerce is likely to introduce, it is useful to consider the digital and physical dimensions of a business in relation to the type of product, process and delivery agent involved, as shown in Figure 3.1.

This model, developed by Choi *et al.*, maintains currency, being used in recent works such as Chen (2001) and Turban *et al.* (2002), and conveys the prospect of choices and issues for a business contemplating e-commerce from a background of traditional commerce.

For a traditional retailer, the first questions regard how readily its products and services lend themselves to e-retailing, and then the degree to which the business can exploit electronic processes. One method for approaching these questions is described by the ES test and involves consideration of product attributes in terms of the five human senses and looking at consumer type and the familiarity of the consumer in purchasing the product. This method is discussed in Chapter 10 (pp. 215–222).

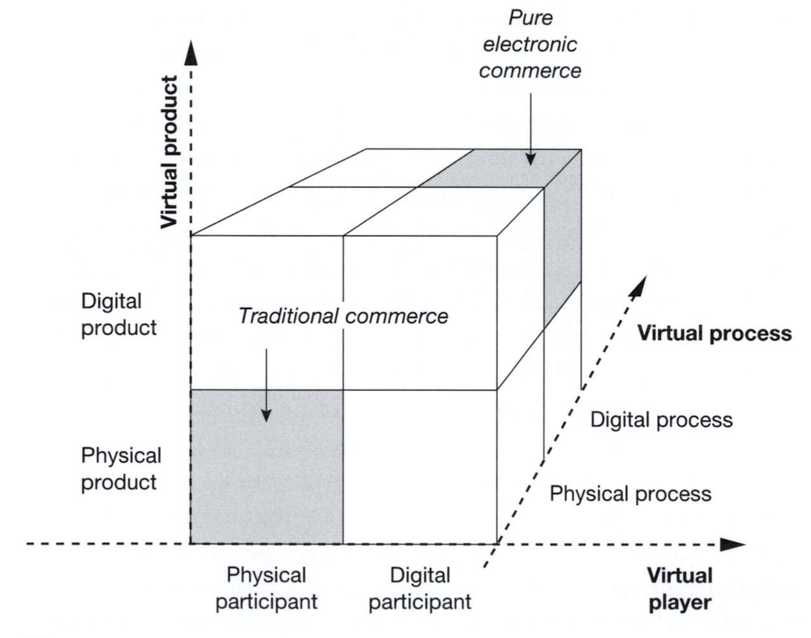

Figure 3.1 *e-Commerce digitization*

Source: Adapted from Choi *et al.* (1997)

Once a retailer has evaluated the potential of its products or services for e-retailing, it must then decide its position for e-retail adoption, and determine a course of action. De Kare-Silver (2001) lists ten options that can be arranged on a scale from 'no e-retail operations' to 'e-retail only', in order of increasing e-shopping responsiveness, paralleled with increasing commitment to e-retailing as shown in Figure 3.2.

No e-retail operations

This is the defensive option, based on revitalizing the 'experience' and social aspects of shopping based in towns and shopping centres. However, consumers now expect every organization to have at least an information website and an e-mail address.

Information only

Reluctance to tackle the disadvantages of e-retailing leads some well-known high street retailers (for example, Monsoon – www.monsoon.co.uk) to use the Internet purely as a marketing communication channel rather than for online sales.

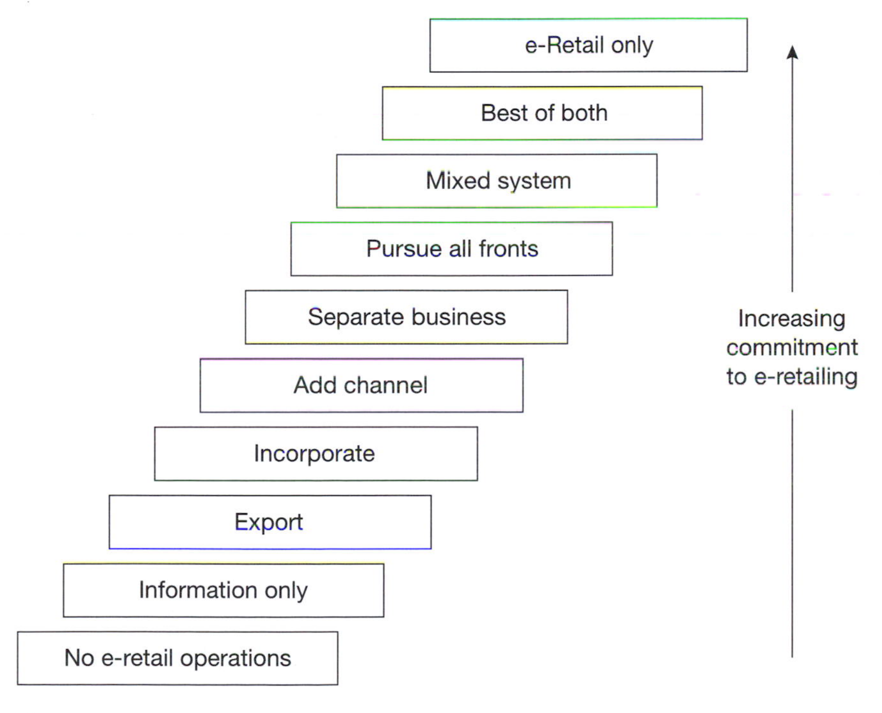

Figure 3.2 *Strategic options for retailers*

Source: Adapted from de Kare-Silver (2001)

Export

This approach is aimed at protecting the business of the high street stores while widening the potential customer base with e-channels. De Kare-Silver cites the example of bookseller Blackwells (www.bookshop.blackwell.co.uk), which has 82 outlets in university towns and campuses across the UK, but whose listing of one million specialist and academic titles is now available worldwide on the Web.

Incorporate into existing business

This option seeks to protect the existing stores by using an 'order and collect' system. The thinking is that, by coming to the store to collect the order, the shopper is more likely to think of extra purchases, or to pick up impulse buys. Safeway (www.safeway.co.uk) and Sainsburys (www.sainsburys.co.uk) tried this system but did not gain the popularity of market leader Tesco (Safeway withdrew from e-retail completely before being taken over by Morrisons, and Sainsburys introduced home delivery, initially based on warehouse picking centres rather than stores).

Add another channel

With this approach, retailers such as Next (market leader in online clothing sales, according to retail researcher Verdict) use e-retailing as an extra route to reach more of their target customers. Retailers in this category may be represented on an e-mall (see Chapter 9), saving much of the setting-up cost of a dedicated e-retailing operation.

Set up a separate business

The idea of the separate business is to offer competitive e-shopping benefits without alienating the existing customers for the high street operation, who probably pay higher prices. The separately branded direct operation has been popular for financial services – for example, Abbey National's e-bank 'Cahoot' (www.cahoot.co.uk).

Pursue all fronts

An example of this is the National Westminster Bank multi-channel system, based on making every possible channel open to the customer: high street branches, direct mail, ATMs, phone, interactive TV and Internet (www.natwest.co.uk).

Mixed system

This approach recognizes that strong brands are essential to successful e-retailing. Brand strength is showcased in flagship stores in major cities – for example, Virgin Megastore (www.virginmega.com).

Best of both worlds

Is it possible to retain all the high street operations while at the same time being state-of-the-art in e-retailing? This is probably only practicable for a clear market leader in a sector, and represents a high-investment strategy, making it more difficult for competitors to catch up – the Tesco approach.

e-Retail only

Few retailers are brave enough to close all high street outlets and operate only virtual shops. Pre-dot.com crash, though, a number of e-retail-only operations were developed, the best known and most successful being Amazon (www.amazon.com). However, even Amazon sees benefits in some 'real' presence, given its joint venture with Toys R Us (www.toysrus.co.uk). Only those operations high in e-shopping potential, such as travel, and with big budgets to build the brand (e.g. Lastminute.com – www.lastminute.com), are likely to be leaders with Internet-only operations.

THINK POINT

Would you purchase goods from an 'unknown' company on the Internet? What features of the company's website would encourage you to do so?

Of course, a chosen course of action need not prohibit changes in future strategy. By monitoring the outcome of such decisions in terms of turnover, profit, customer acquisition, satisfaction or other determinant metrics, a business can develop a dynamic strategy that best reflects the successful aspects of its e-retail adoption. It is quite possible for a business to start by adding an e-retail channel, and then find that this new addition begins to outperform the company's traditional retail business. This is especially true, say, for catalogue and mail order businesses, where their operations are already suited to selling online. For example, outdoor equipment company L L Bean has been a pioneer of mail order since the nineteenth century and is now world e-retail leader in this market (see Case study 5.2, pp. 126–127).

Mini case study 3.1: NETSHOP.CO.UK

Netshop Ltd is a privately owned company specializing in the online retail of computer networking products to end consumers. Evolving out of Homestead Electronics Ltd, a mail order electronics company founded in 1983, Netshop now forms part of a multi-business e-retail portfolio with offerings in diverse market segments.

The technology and mail order origins of the company, along with an established customer base and in-house knowledge of the networking market, assisted a smooth transition from mail order retail to e-retail, since much of the order processing and fulfilment infrastructure was already in place and the company possessed the necessary skills to develop its own transactional website and start small alongside its traditional business. Once its e-commerce systems were proven, they provided a platform for further online activities.

The company's background as a family business, coupled with its attention to success factors in the e-retail marketplace, helped it foster an appreciation of customer expectations, and the requirement to be competent at more than just the technical process behind the shopping experience.

Many new customers arrive at the Netshop website from results at search engines such as Google (www.google.co.uk), and not all of them are seasoned e-consumers. Netshop recognizes this, and works to establish trust by giving prominent space to the company's physical address, the history of the company and telephone numbers so that customers are not forced to pursue an online transaction if they do not want to. Instead, prospective customers can phone and place an order, and even arrange to collect it, obviating the need to make credit card transactions online or by phone, or disclose address details. As the company says on its website, 'Talk to a real person at Netshop. We are not just another anonymous On-Line company!' This customer-oriented approach is augmented by several features that add value, such as extensive product information, news articles on new products and aspects of networking, FAQs and support pages, manufacturers' links, and free driver downloads, providing a multi-channel presence for a company that has chosen to move most of its operation online.

LOYALTY-BASED INTEGRATION STRATEGIES

The emphasis on focusing on people rather than products, coupled with the requirement for a business to align its strategy with its ability to operate in an e-retail environment, raises the question of how to formulate strategy for e-retail integration that takes these key requisites into account.

Recent research by Cuthbertson and Bridson (2003) proposes a framework to tackle this question and how the Internet changes the traditional store-based model of marketing, by setting it in the context of customer loyalty, which has long been acknowledged as an important factor in a firm's competitive position. Successful relationship marketing is underpinned by the ability to both acquire and retain customers over the long term, and the need to customize the relationship to the individual has been shown to be a critical factor.

Modelling the online retail experience

Cuthbertson and Bridson (2003) suggest that the loyalty marketing strategy is dependent on the fundamental structure of the retailer–customer relationship, and put forward a categorization of retailer–customer relationships in an Online Retail Relationship Matrix as shown in Figure 3.3.

This matrix uses the two principal components of the retailer–customer relationship – the retailer-led channel proposition to the customer and the customer-led channel access to the retailer – and divides these based on the focus of each party.

The retailer may configure its offer as pureplay (online) or multi-channel, while the customer can choose to access the retailer directly or through a marketplace. Examples of marketplaces include those that are online, such as DealTime/Shopping.com (www.dealtime.co.uk, now relaunched as part of www.shopping.com), or an interactive TV channel.

The usefulness of the classification is that each category carries a higher likelihood of success for particular types of retailer, depending on the retailer's product/service. By mapping its type onto the matrix, a business can determine whether success is likely in a given configuration, with implications for the loyalty strategy that is most likely to succeed.

The categories comprise:

- The digital retailer–customer relationship
- The ubiquitous retailer–customer relationship
- The focal retailer–customer relationship

Figure 3.3 *The Online Retail Relationship Matrix*

Source: Cuthbertson and Bridson (2003)

Cuthbertson and Bridson (2003) outline the strengths of each category for particular retailer types.

The digital retailer–customer relationship

The digital retailer–customer relationship appears to be most applicable where:

> The service element at the point of transaction is low and the product can be distributed digitally.

This could relate to the retail of software, and financial or travel services. For example, airlines that retail tickets direct are likely to be successful by adopting a digital retailer–customer relationship.

The ubiquitous retailer–customer relationship

The ubiquitous retailer–customer relationship appears to be most applicable where:

> The retailer is selling a wide range of goods to customers where the frequency of purchase is relatively high, or selling expensive, technical products where the frequency of purchase is relatively low but a high degree of consideration is given to the purchase decision.

A grocery retailer such as Tesco, or a car retailer such as Ford, are examples of where a ubiquitous retailer–customer relationship is likely to be most successful.

The focal retailer–customer relationship

The focal retailer–customer relationship appears to be most applicable where:

> The retailer is a third party to the product/service vendor, and is providing customers with digital access to a range of goods, based on convenience.

This applies to third party convenience retailers such as Shopping.com (www.shopping.com) or to those offering customers specialist access to goods, such as eBay (www.ebay.co.uk) or online communities.

Loyalty strategies for retailers with a focal retailer–customer relationship depend on closely understanding customer requirements and providing a selection of retail opportunities to easily convert to purchases, with a mechanism for the third party to benefit from the transaction.

Using loyalty marketing strategies

Cuthbertson and Bridson (2003) expand their model to identify the relevant loyalty strategy by proposing a matrix called the Purchaser–Purveyor Loyalty Matrix, shown in Figure 3.4, with five distinct choices: pure, pull, push, purchase and purge, each appropriate for different retailers, dependent on their particular marketing mix and competitive position. The definition of each loyalty strategy is as follows:

- A *pure* loyalty strategy is based on the existing or pure relationship between the retailer and its customers, and focuses on the retailer's product and service offer.
- A *push* loyalty strategy aims to push customers towards the retailer, and focuses on the retail location and channel.
- A *pull* loyalty strategy uses retailer promotion to pull the customer to the retailer or particular products.
- A *purchase* loyalty strategy concentrates on increasing the number and value of purchase transactions, irrespective of which particular retailer benefits.
- A *purge* loyalty strategy is used where a retailer attempts to purge all unnecessary cost and aims at providing all customers with the lowest price possible.

In general, it is observed that successful digital retailers follow a purge loyalty strategy, ubiquitous retailers follow a push and pull loyalty strategy, and focal retailers pursue a purchase strategy. These findings help put forward the

Purveyor: retailer offer	Purchaser: customer perceived choice – Single retailer	Purchaser: customer perceived choice – Many retailers
Focused offer	*Pure*	*Push*
Extended offer	*Pull*	*Purchase*
Price-led offer	*Purge*	

Figure 3.4 *The Purchaser–Purveyor Loyalty Matrix*

Source: Cuthbertson and Bridson (2003)

appropriate loyalty strategy for any business attempting to integrate e-retail and, when used within the complete retailer-customer relationship model, go some way towards dealing with the complexity suggested by the e-commerce digitization view, and finding the appropriate choice among the ten strategic integration options that have been outlined in this chapter (pp. 60–63).

IMPLEMENTATION: CHANGE MANAGEMENT AND RESOURCE IMPLICATIONS

Even for businesses that develop the right e-retailing strategy with the appropriate mix of e-retail and traditional retail, and mindful of the organization's skill base, it is necessary to recognize that moving from theory to practice will have an impact across the organization, affecting resources and business processes. A fundamental re-evaluation of company strategy may lead to a radical overhaul of existing ways of doing business, with company structure and culture becoming much more customer-focused. Moving organizations towards such ways of working will have widespread consequences. Resistance at all company levels may need to be overcome, with a corresponding need to build commitment and consensus around e-retailing strategies. However, in doing this, as noted earlier, companies must also deal with a paradox. As the dot.com crash showed, there are many strengths in bricks and mortar companies, particularly their customer base and brand profile, and organizational capabilities in areas such as supply chain management. Evolving a new business model must therefore avoid throwing out the 'best of the old'. Only by recognizing and rising to these challenges and dilemmas, and devoting sufficient time, resources and expertise to them, will companies make a success of their e-retailing ventures. In other words, they have to be prepared to reorganize and restructure themselves continuously, and therefore understanding how to manage change effectively becomes essential. As Stroud (1998) notes:

> The benefits that the Internet is expected to deliver will not be realised unless a company adapts its organisational structure and methods to meet the radical new ways of working that this new technology makes possible.
>
> (p. 225)

What is surprising is the reluctance of many companies to do this. In a piece of research conducted by Jupiter Communications (2001), only 24 per cent of US CEOs regarded their Web initiatives as an integrated part of their core business. The US experience is that companies generally fall into two broad camps with their e-initiatives: being 'self-reinventing' in order to maintain market leadership, or 'change avoiding' by persevering with existing ways of doing business. The Jupiter study suggests that self-reinventors are in the minority.

The central role played by technology in e-retailing will add a layer of technical complexity to what may already be a quite dynamic situation. However, the redesign of business processes and structures is far from a simple 'technical' matter, and involves significant social redesign. Such changes are likely to be politically controversial and therefore will always be open to disturbances and threats. The interests of a wide range of stakeholders may be threatened, there may be a high degree of uncertainty regarding what to do and how to do it, objectives may be less clear than usual, and resource requirements will be less well known. In addition, it may be more difficult to create shared perceptions of goals and build and maintain necessary commitment. So, in practical terms, management will need to become change agents, spending considerable time ensuring effective communication to encourage flexibility, address perceptions and generate involvement. To illustrate the problems that can ensue in such a situation, Badham *et al*. (1997) describe Merrill Lynch's move into online trading:

> At the core of the change process was conflict at many levels within Merrill Lynch. There was conflict between the defenders of the brokers and their commissions and proponents of online investing. There was conflict between Merrill brokers who were concerned about losing customers to online brokers and Merrill brokers who were concerned about losing commissions. There was even conflict among Merrill executives between those who favoured setting up a separate online unit to compete with the brokers and those who favoured keeping the online unit under the same executive.
>
> (p. 151)

There are of course technical challenges involved in moving from a physical or bricks and mortar organization to bricks and clicks. Here, a more 'virtual' form of organization may result, mixing traditional ways of working with electronic communications. One of the key problems for existing companies here is to integrate front and back end systems while mindful that their 'legacy infrastructure' might well still be essential to other aspects of the business. While start-up companies can leapfrog these problems, established ones face some difficult challenges. This was one of the reasons why it was originally speculated that Internet pureplays would become the dominant business model in the B2C e-commerce market place. This means that, when customers interact via the Web, placing orders and purchasing goods, the stock control and financial systems need to 'speak the same language' and carry out their part of the transactions. The problem is that many such back end systems are unlikely to be based on open Internet protocols and may even have been custom-built. Nonetheless, these systems are usually critical to a company's business, and include such details as bank account data and stock rotation information. As Conway (2000) points out:

> IT managers are loath to replace them with something new and untested. They may not even fully understand how their legacies work any longer. The people who built the systems may well have left the company, leaving present IT experts reluctant to tinker.
>
> (p. 62)

Replacing such systems also takes time and requires particular IT skills and staff training – factors which may impede the developments that are critical to speedy innovation.

There is one general criticism of the change management literature: that it tends to place considerable emphasis on strategies for overcoming different barriers to change, assuming that the 'traditional' companies in question have destructive, dogmatic cultures with bureaucratic tendencies. This insinuates that, at a basic level, such companies are almost by definition 'change-phobic'. Many early writers made the rather enthusiastic presumption that Internet retailing was so revolutionary, traditional retailers would become obsolete. Traditional companies were criticized for being slow to engage and for adopting cautious 'toe in the water' strategies. For example, Windham (2000) criticized traditional retailers for not finding 'the vision, commitment and guts to proceed', and interprets caution as 'e-denial'. In fact, it now seems that those companies that exercised a careful Web integration strategy have been the ones with the most durable strategies. They have in fact not resisted change, but instead embraced it in an incremental way by creating successful and sustainable online channels as part of holistic multi-channel strategies.

THINK POINT

What is your perception of a modern company that does NOT offer multi-channel services to its customers?

CONCLUSIONS

Most businesses recognize that the minimum involvement with the Internet today is to have e-mail and an informational website. This is a step up from only a few years ago and, with the pace of change, suggests that businesses already need to consider whether it is now imperative to adopt a transactional online presence.

Many traditional retailers have already taken significant steps towards e-retail, and some of them, including larger, familiar brands such as Tesco and Argos, are setting the pace for online innovation and have e-retail integration strategies that work.

CHAPTER SUMMARY

We have seen that e-retail has matured beyond the 'must have' days of the dot.com boom, to become an additional or alternative channel with a number of serious advantages such as 24-hour availability, lower overheads, potential for mass customization and personalization of the retailer–customer relationship.

Although traditional retailers were late to market in comparison with their online start-up competitors, their e-retail efforts have often been more successful in the long term, because many important requirements are already in place. Advantages such as having an established customer base, recognized brand values and the facilities to offer customers face-to-face contact if necessary, mean that traditional businesses usually enjoy greater trust than their pureplay online competition, which often outweigh difficulties in implementing e-retail.

However, much has been learnt in recent years on how traditional businesses successfully adopt online retailing, which has led to methods for evaluating business readiness for e-retail, and the proposal of specific strategic options for e-retail integration. In particular, customer loyalty and the type of retailer–customer relationship may be used to help determine appropriate strategy when adopting e-retail.

In the following chapter we will consider how an e-retailer can start to understand and communicate with customers.

Case study 3.1: BOOTS (www.boots.com)

The case concerns the well-known bricks (and now also clicks) group, Boots the Chemist. Boots opened its first store in Nottingham in 1849, selling herbal remedies. Developing new products such as Ibuprofen (1969) and Nurofen (1983) has helped Boots become a leader in the pharmaceutical business. Boots is now in almost every high street, and is one of the largest pharmaceutical chains, selling medicines, toiletries, cosmetics, fragrances and photographic equipment. The launch of the Advantage loyalty card in 1997 helped Boots gain an insight into its customers and experience in data mining. The bricks stores, though, are approaching maturity in the retail life cycle and profits have been below expectations.

Boots has experimented with T-commerce, launching a 'Wellbeing' interactive digital TV channel in March 2001. However, due to the slow uptake, and the lack of consumer support, the service closed in December 2001. Boots still remains committed to the idea and intends to relaunch when the market is ready.

The Boots e-retailing site was launched in 2001. It is packed full of health and nutrition information content and is better stocked than most high street Boots, with 10,000 products available. As we will demonstrate in Chapter 5, providing useful information can act strongly to drive e-shopping traffic. In its first year it turned over £4.3 million in sales. Customers can track their order progress online and there is currently no charge for deliveries (except for Saturday). Returns can be posted back free. The site is renowned for customer satisfaction. According to a recent survey, 95 per cent of customers will shop at the site again. It is the only UK website authorized to sell Chanel and one of only two selling Esteé Lauder and Clinique. Boots has about one million e-shoppers, one of the largest customer bases of any UK e-retailer.

Promotion is largely via a targeted e-mail CRM/data mining system allowing personalization and offers relevant to individual consumers. Boots' experience with the loyalty card database is invaluable here. In addition, Boots uses 'link popularity engineering' (discussed in more depth in Chapter 5) to direct traffic to the site. The idea is to make the site a 'one stop shop' for health and well-being information. This makes the site popular with users and attracts links from other sites – characteristics that search engines use in determining rankings. The result is that if a surfer types 'well-being' into one of the major search engines (e.g. Google or Ask Jeeves) the first 'hits' will all be Boots – a mixture of sponsored and non-sponsored links.

The site was runner up for the 'E-business Website of the Year' at the *Computing* magazine's Awards in 2001 and won the 'Best Website' award at the 2002 *Santé* Health and Beauty awards.

Sources: Various, including *Sunday Times* (UK) Doors 'Webwatch' site test, Boots plc annual report and www.boots.com

This case study was kindly contributed by Wayne Godfrey

Case study 3.2: TESCO (www.tesco.com)

See also the Groceries section of Chapter 2 (pp. 38–41).

Tesco is one of the UK's largest e-retailers and the world's biggest e-grocer, overturning the myth that shoppers will not buy fresh products because of the 'look and feel' factor. Indeed, the opposite is the case – of the top ten selling lines, seven are fresh, with skinless chicken breasts at number one.

Tesco has been active in telesales (at pilot locations) since 1995. The initial telesales pilot, at Ealing, West London, was developed from the home delivery service to less mobile consumers, subcontracted from the Local Authority. This low-tech operation was developed in 1996 into the pilot for e-retailing (rolled out nationally in 1999) – built on the proven delivery system and hand-picking from the shelves of the grocery stores. Tesco still uses this tried and reliable system for groceries in preference to a heavy investment in warehouse picking centres, although many non-food items such as books, CDs and DVD movies are now handled from a non-store facility. While Tesco's larger stores may carry only the top 50 CDs, Tesco.com claims to offer every CD currently available in the UK. Not only leading in grocery e-retailing, Tesco is rapidly gaining share in electricals, entertainment and clothing.

Despite the low-key approach, Tesco has invested £45 million in its e-retailing operation, including £15 million for the transaction system based on the ShoppingMagic proprietary system from Unipower. Customers can purchase any of the 40,000+ product lines for next-day delivery (for orders placed by 4.00 p.m.) for UK customers within delivery distance of a store (encompassing 97 per cent of the UK population). A limited product range is available for delivery worldwide. As an alternative to shoppers composing their shopping list online, Tesco sends them a monthly CD-ROM and information on special offers by mail. Using the CD-ROM can speed up and simplify the ordering process, making it possible to save shopping lists and minimizing the effort in placing future orders. This is a significant 'convenience' benefit, since 80 per cent of grocery shopping is replenishment. Tesco follows the maxim 'make it easy for your customers to buy', accepting orders on the Web, CD-ROM, fax and telephone, and offering home delivery or collection and, of course, in-store shopping. WAP *m-shopping* was launched in 2001 followed by PDA in 2002. TV Internet had to close with the demise of ITV Digital, but at the time of writing is planned to return via BT Digital. In addition to groceries, consumers can buy books, music, clothes, PCs, and Internet and mobile phone services.

There are regular paper mailings and special offers, including non-food promotions such as 'The top 50 books 10 per cent cheaper than Amazon'. At £10 per customer, the cost of acquisition is low, compared to £50 to £100 for companies such as Amazon. Addressing the need for more social interaction, particularly for female shoppers, the Tesco site hosts the UK version of iVillage, providing information, chat rooms, travel, health and nutrition advice.

Tesco make use of the ready-digitized sales data for data mining and segmented offers. Targeted offers (for example via e-mail or SMS) are not perceived as *spam* by Tesco customers if they add value. HTML e-mails to customers achieve 10–30 per cent response rates. In one example, Tesco achieved a 28 per cent click-through to Unilever for a Dove promotion from 35,000 premium shampoo users. Tesco can use the lifestyle data from promotion responses to help plan other marketing initiatives. Running such promotions for manufacturers such as Unilever provides a valuable extra revenue stream for Tesco. In addition, there are affiliate deals with major portals based on cost-per-click or cost-per-sale.

Tesco's e-retailing joint ventures in Ireland, Korea (the country with the world's highest Internet penetration) and, particularly, the US allow the costs of development to be spread. New international markets can be entered at a fraction of the cost of starting from scratch.

Tesco has over one million registered customers, and an e-turnover of over £450 million. This success might well be attributed to Tesco's single-minded determination to provide customer satisfaction, using an easy-entry, cost-effective e-retailing system. Tesco's e-retailing operation has been in profit since 2001, with profit reaching almost £2 million by 2002. Despite the fast growth in e-retailing (6 per cent of Tesco's total growth in 2002), e-shoppers spend over 25 per cent more than Tesco's bricks shoppers, which Tesco believes is not cannibalizing in-store sales. Indeed, bricks sales have continued to increase in real terms since the launch of the e-retailing operation.

Sources: Various, Fernie and McKinnon (2003) and www.tesco.com

This case study was kindly contributed by Omar Chaudhry

QUESTIONS

Brief feedback to these questions is included at the back of the book.

Question 3.1

What do you consider to be the advantages and disadvantages that traditional retailers have in comparison with Internet pureplays, in terms of online trading?

Question 3.2

Why do you think online customers may not be loyal to a particular company?

Question 3.3

What are the dangers of multi-channel operations from a company's perspective?

FURTHER READING

Carr, Nicholas (ed.) (2001) *The Digital Enterprise: How to Reshape Your Business for a Connected World*, Boston, MA: Harvard Business School Press.

Chaffey, David (2002) *e-Business and e-Commerce Management*, Harlow: Pearson Education.

de Kare-Silver, Michael (2001) *e-Shock: The New Rules – e-Strategies for Retailers and Manufacturers*, Basingstoke: Palgrave.

Moss Kanter, Rosabeth (2001) *Evolve! Succeeding in the Digital Culture of Tomorrow*, Boston, MA: Harvard Business School Press.

Weill, Peter and Vitale, Michael (2001) *Place to Space: Migrating to eBusiness Models*, Boston, MA: Harvard Business School Press.

REFERENCES

Badham, R., Couchman, P. and McLoughlin, I.P. (1997) 'Implementing vulnerable socio technical change projects', in I.P. McLoughlin and M. Harris (eds) *Innovation, Organizational Change and Technology*, London: ITB Press.

Cellan-Jones, R. (2003) *Dot.bomb: The Strange Death of Dot.com Britain*, London: Aurum Press.

Chen, S. (2001) *Strategic Management of e-Business*, Chichester: Wiley.

Choi, S.-Y., Stahl, D.O. and Whinston, A.B. (1997) *The Economics of Electronic Commerce*, Indianapolis: MacMillan Technical Publishing.

Conway, P. (2000) 'Lasting legacy?', *eBusiness* (June) 62–64.

Cuthbertson, R. and Bridson, K. (2003) 'Online retail loyalty strategies', *IBM E-business Conference,* Surrey University.

de Kare-Silver, M. (2001) *e-Shock: The New Rules – e-Strategies for Retailers and Manufacturers*, Basingstoke: Palgrave.

Fernie, J. and McKinnon, A.C. (2003) 'The Grocery Supply Chain in the UK: Improving Efficiency in the Logistics Network', *International Review of Retail, Distribution and Consumer Research*, 13(2): 161–174.

IMRG (2002) 'Why e-retail?'*IMRG,* www.imrg.org [accessed 19 December 2003].

Stroud, D. (1998) *Internet Strategies: A Corporate Guide to Exploiting the Internet*, Basingstoke: Macmillan.

Turban, E., King, D., Lee, J., Warkentin, M. and Chung, H.M. (2002) *Electronic Commerce: A Managerial Perspective* (international edn), London: Prentice Hall.

Windham, L. (2000) 'Overcome e-business barriers', *e-Business Advisor*, 18: 10.

ZDNet (2003) 'E-marketplaces: where are they now?' *ZDNet UK*, www.insight.zdnet.co.uk [accessed 19 December].

WEB LINKS

www.imrg.org/
Information on e-retailing from many bricks and clicks high street names

Chapter 4

Understanding and communicating with the e-consumer

LINKS TO OTHER CHAPTERS

- Chapter 1 – The world of e-retailing
- Chapter 2 – e-Retailing in practice
- Chapter 5 – Information search on the Web
- Chapter 6 – e-Store design: navigability, interactivity and web atmospherics
- Chapter 11 – m-Shopping

KEY LEARNING POINTS

After completing this chapter you will have an understanding of:

- Why consumers e-shop (or do not e-shop)
- How consumers achieve satisfaction (or not) from e-shopping
- How consumer satisfaction from e-retailing compares with satisfaction from in-store shopping
- What factors are inhibiting the growth of e-shopping

ORDERED LIST OF SUB-TOPICS

- The perceived risk of e-shopping
- Introducing e-shoppers
- What does e-shopping offer the e-shopper?

- Disadvantages and advantages of e-shopping for consumers
- Social and experiential aspects of e-shopping
- Differences between male and female shopping styles
- Consumer satisfaction: bricks and clicks shopping compared
- The communications mix for the e-retailer
- Chapter summary
- Case study
- Questions
- Further reading
- References
- Web links

INTRODUCTION

> 'Do ya' feel lucky, well do ya, punk'? – Clint Eastwood's immortal character, Detective Harry Callahan, Movie *Dirty Harry*.
>
> (Fink *et al.*, 1971)

It is one of the most quoted movie lines of all time and is very descriptive of how potential consumers have felt about venturing into e-retailing. 'Do ya' feel lucky?' or, more specifically in this context, 'do you have the courage to go online and shop after all that you have seen and heard about the dangers of e-retailing and do the benefits to you outweigh the fears?' In this chapter we examine the issue of risk as it pertains to online shopping, present the evolving profile of the e-customer, and consider both the advantages and disadvantages of an e-tailing experience.

THE PERCEIVED RISK OF E-SHOPPING

Shoppers often feel apprehension or risk when considering a purchase, especially from a new vendor. Perceived risk is a function of the uncertainty when making a purchase that may have unpleasant outcomes (Forsythe and Shi, 2003). Such risk is linked to both the type of merchandise being acquired and the channel or method of acquiring that merchandise (Hisrich *et al.*, 1972). The reasons why non-store purchases fuel a shopper's perceived risk relate to the touch and accessibility issues (Gillett, 1970; Spence *et al.*, 1970; Phau and Poon, 2000), specifically:

- Not being able to touch merchandise before making a purchase.
- Barriers to returning merchandise.

Initial Internet adoption research identified risk as a significant barrier to e-retailing (GVU, 1998; Salam *et al.*, 1998) and this has continued in more recent studies (Miyazaki and Fernandez, 2001). Yet, simply identifying this phenomenon under the single concept of 'risk' is to miss the complexity of the issue. Risk is a multi-dimensional construct for e-shopping (Fenech, 2003) with the economic, social, performance, personal and privacy dimensions (Vijayasarathy and Jones, 2000). These initial risk dimensions were summarized as:

- *Economic risk* – the probability of making poor purchase decisions.
- *Social risk* – the possibility of incurring societal disapproval for engaging in shopping using a particular medium.
- *Performance risk* – the chance of product/services performing less than expected.
- *Personal risk* – the potential for theft and abuse of credit card information.
- *Privacy risk* – the danger of compromising personal information.

(Vijayasarathy and Jones, 2000)

The first three Vijayasarathy and Jones risk dimensions (economic, social and performance) were an integral component of retailing prior to the Internet. A shopper in a bricks store can make a poorly researched purchase decision or select merchandise that fails to deliver its performance promise as easily as it could be done online, whereas the remaining risk dimensions (personal and privacy) are more frequently attributed to e-shopping and receive greater media attention.

INTRODUCING E-SHOPPERS

The Internet did not create the non-store shopper or even the electronic shopper. An early characterization of the non-store shopper was by Gillett (1970) who was looking at what he described as in-home shoppers. Such buyers were reported as being:

- More willing to buy without handling items and to like shopping but not crowds.
- In greater need of convenience and product assortment.
- More price conscious and seeking a price advantage.
- Infrequent shoppers who make unplanned purchases.

Improvements in communications offered potential retail shoppers new avenues to make non-store purchases and become e-shoppers. One such facility was *videotex*. Videotex is a generic name for an interactive, mass medium that transmits text and visual information between suppliers and consumers of these services, usually through an adapted television set (Sauer *et al.*, 1989). The reason most cited by retailers for moving to videotex in the late 1960s was to achieve a competitive advantage over retailers who have not adopted videotex and allowing small businesses to compete against larger competitors. The popularity of videotex, especially in France (referred to as Minitel), came before the common home ownership of computers and allowed the first true overseas Internet commerce when linked to the US Infonet (predecessor to today's Internet) system (English, 1990).

Shim and Mahoney (1991) identified impressions and characteristics that were applicable to videotex adopters, the first true e-shoppers, to be:

- a belief that it is easy to use electronic shopping;
- less concerned with convenience for shopping;
- a tendency to be recreational shoppers;
- a tendency to be shopping innovators.

The advent of the World Wide Web and online shopping through the Internet gave rise to a consumer with similarities and contrasts from the earlier non-store shoppers. Based upon the work of Donthu and Garcia (1999), the evolving Web e-shoppers were then characterized as:

- more innovative in their shopping activities;
- convenience oriented;
- more impulsive in purchases;
- less brand conscious;
- less price conscious.

As will be described in greater detail in Chapter 11, e-retailing did not finish with the cabled (wired) versions of the Internet and World Wide Web. The latest incarnation of the e-shopper is not restricted to a desktop or notebook computer with cable-linked modem or broadband connection. Quite the opposite – the new e-shopper is mobile and may use e-retailing anywhere a wireless network is being broadcast. The mobile e-shoppers or m-shoppers share the characteristics of earlier non-store shoppers in that they are innovative shoppers likely to be impulsive in their purchases as they seek shopping convenience (Fenech, 2002). What distinguishes the m-shopper from other e-shoppers is that they look for variety in their shopping activities. The m-shopper is a consumer wanting diversity in the shopping offerings of retailers, a seeker and adopter of new retailing channels, and, if offered the right balance in the retail offering, will make an unplanned purchase because an item is attractive and is perceived to be good value.

WHAT DOES E-SHOPPING OFFER THE E-SHOPPER?

Shopper research by Tauber (1972, 1995) suggests the existence of personal and social consumer motives of shopping behaviour. Personal motives for shopping include role-playing, diversion, self-gratification, physical activity and sensory stimulation; social motives include meeting with others, peer group status and bargaining (Tauber, 1972, 1995; Midgley and Dowling, 1993). For some individuals the shopping experience is enjoyable and treated as a leisure activity or for amusement (Westbrook and Black, 1985). Work by Reynolds (1974) and Berkowitz *et al.* (1979) established that, while non-store shoppers may enjoy shopping, they have a negative attitude towards the traditional store-based shopping environment because of such issues as overcrowding and a lack of parking. Later research includes work on catalogue shopping by Gehrt and Carter (1992) and cable television shopping by Eastlick and Liu (1997). Those authors found that the shopping enjoyment motivation is a positive influence for adoption of non-store shopping environments such as e-shopping through the Internet.

Whatever the shopping motivation of an individual, the result is not inevitable *shopping enjoyment* or purchase behaviour (Fenech and O'Cass, 2001). For some individuals there is a feeling of apathy or reluctance towards shopping and this compels them to minimize the amount of time spent shopping. As part of a larger research project on multi-channel retailing, data was collected by the authors on the benefits expected from using the Web by customers of both business to consumer (B2C) and business to business (B2B) e-commerce. The results in Tables 4.1 and 4.2 show that, despite the variation in recipient profiles (personal versus business), the principal advantages sought from and given by the Web are principally the same. That is, the Web provides speedier ordering processes, faster usage, an effective search facility and up-to-date product-related information.

DISADVANTAGES AND ADVANTAGES OF E-SHOPPING FOR CONSUMERS

Disadvantages

Consumers have been slow to embrace e-shopping. Back in 1996, the UK's largest e-consultancy, Cap Gemini, carried out an employee survey. The main disadvantages for shoppers, in ranked order were: 'Availability', 'Can't be in to receive delivery', 'Premium charged for delivery' and 'Can't see or feel the merchandise'. With years' more experience, many e-retailers still do not have satisfactory answers to these problems. Typical shopper comments have included: 'They left it in the garden and didn't tell me', 'It's a 24-hour shopping service but only a 6-hour delivery service' and 'Returning unwanted products is when it all goes low-tech' consumer surveys from Vincent *et al.*, 2000). Another survey reported,

Table 4.1 *The principal benefits expected by consumers from e-shopping*

	%
Faster – direct ordering process	19
Quicker to use	13
Efficient search facility	12
Web has most up-to-date information	10
Can do at own pace anywhere with Web	6
Order accuracy – ability to check stock availability	6
Easier to compare products and prices	6
Able to seek more information	4
Saves time	4
Environmentally friendly – no paper wasted on orders, invoices or promotional material	4
Available to place orders 24 hours a day	4
Ease of use	2
Web-only specials	2
Ability to track account details or order progress	2
No paperwork to type or fill in	2
Overall convenience	2
All products in range are shown in one place	2
Able to recall previously ordered items	2
Total	100

Source: Author's soon-to-be-published study of 650 personal shoppers (B2C) on the Web

in ranked order, reasons why Internet-connected shoppers do not e-shop: 'Prefer personal shopping, seeing goods', 'Credit card worries' and 'Don't know how' (Doidge and Higgins, 2000 – see Figure 4.1). In 2001, Verdict confirmed security fears as the number one barrier to more consumers shopping online. Our own surveys (e.g. Dennis *et al.*, 2002a – discussed more fully in the following section) have indicated that sixth-form (year 12) pupils are avid e-shoppers using their parents' credit cards. This is an obvious security worry for parents, but also a nuisance for young people, restricting their e-shopping activities. Credit cards are only offered to those of 18 years of age and above, although alternative 'plastic cash' is available for children, with transactions authorized (in the example of the Solo card – www.solocard.co.uk) only up to what is in the bank account. The disadvantage is that so far these cards are accepted by only a tiny fraction of

Table 4.2 *The principal benefits expected by business customers from e-purchasing*

	%
Faster – direct ordering process	11
Quicker to use	10
Efficient search facility	9
Web has most up-to-date information	8
No paperwork to type	7
Available to place orders 24 hours a day	6
Can do at own pace anywhere with Internet	6
Saves time	5
Overall convenience	5
No catalogues to store and retrieve	5
Can seek more information	3
Environmentally friendly – no paper wasted on orders, invoices or promotional material	3
Web-only specials	3
No seller human interference with order	3
Ease of use	3
Order accuracy – ability to check stock availability	3
All products in range are shown in one place	2
Can recall previously ordered items	2
Can get a better look at the products	1
Enjoyment of using online systems	1
Can track account details or order progress	1
Easier to compare products and prices	1
Ease of changing order	1
Can minimize web page order if interrupted	1
Total	100

Source: Author's soon-to-be-published study of 978 occupation-related shoppers (B2B) on the Web

e-retailers. At the time of writing, the major credit card companies are developing a 'pay-as-you-go' system for e-shopping that should overcome these problems.

The disadvantages are typical of those that faced mail order traders a few decades ago. Given time, as sales grow, sellers work to overcome the customers' concerns, and consumers become more confident. In the US, L L Bean

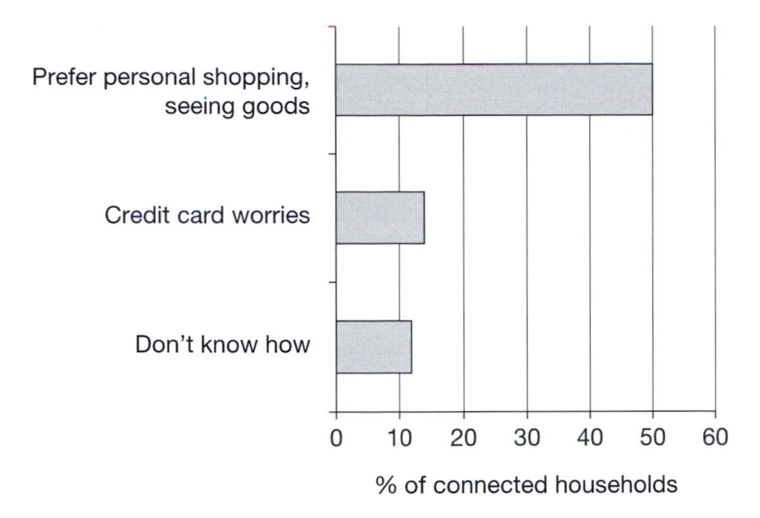

Figure 4.1 *Why Internet-connected consumers do not e-shop*

Source: Doidge and Higgins (2000)

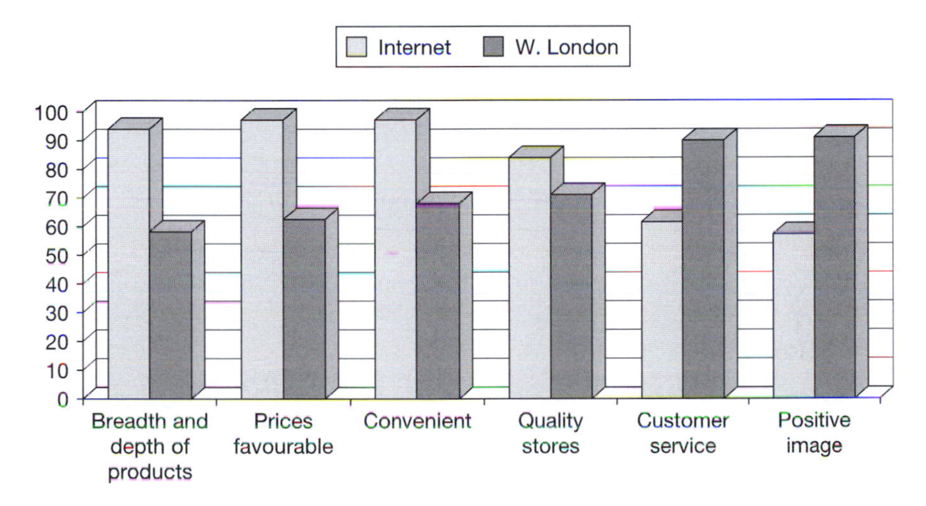

Figure 4.2 *Comparing ratings – Internet vs. West London shopping centre*

Source: Dennis *et al.* (2002a)

(www.llbean.com) could claim to be the pioneer of mail order, selling goods to rural farmers since way back in the mid-1800s. Today the company has put their reputation for customer responsiveness, helpfulness, cheerfulness and reliability to use in becoming world leader in e-retailing outdoor equipment and clothing, with an efficient, award-winning site. See Case study 5.3, pp. 126–127, for more on L L Bean.

Box 4.1:
DISADVANTAGES OF E-SHOPPING FOR CONSUMERS

- Credit card and security worries
- Lack of personal and social interaction
- Can't see or feel the merchandise
- Don't know how
- Can't be in to receive delivery
- Premium charged for delivery
- Difficulties with returning goods for refund

Advantages

Counterbalancing the disadvantages and the slow responses of many UK e-retailers to addressing them, there is a number of advantages for shoppers. First, in ranked order from the Cap Gemini survey: 'Convenient/easy', 'Saves time' and 'Fits in with other activities'. Other commonly cited advantages, typified by responses to our own survey, include: 'Breadth and depth of products', 'Prices favourable' and 'Convenient' (Dennis *et al.*, 2002a – see Figure 4.2). According to Verdict, 'cost effectiveness' (rather than just low prices) is the key reason for shoppers to buy online, followed by convenience and ease of purchase.

Box 4.2:
ADVANTAGES OF E-SHOPPING FOR CONSUMERS

- Cost effective
- Convenient
- Easy
- Saves time
- Fits in with other activities
- Breadth and depth of products
- Easy search of many alternatives
- Personalization of presentation and merchandise
- Prices favourable

SOCIAL AND EXPERIENTIAL ASPECTS OF E-SHOPPING

Research has drawn attention to the importance of the social aspects of shopping (e.g. Westbrook and Black, 1985; Shim and Eastlick, 1998; Dennis *et al.,* 1999; Dholakia, 1999; Lunt 2000; Dennis and Hilton, 2001; Dholakia and Uusitalo 2002; Dholakia and Chiang 2003). Shopping has even been found to be central to loving relationships within the family (Miller, 1998). Similarly, enjoyment and entertainment have been demonstrated to be important benefits of shopping, increased by a pleasant atmosphere and reflected in spending (e.g. Smith and Sherman, 1993; Babin *et al.*, 1994; Donovan *et al.*, 1994; Ang *et al.*, 1997; Spies *et al.*, 1997; Jones, 1999; Machleit and Mantel, 2001; Sit *et al.*, 2003).

In the case of e-shopping, social influences are also important but e-retailers have difficulty in satisfying these needs (Kolesar and Galbraith, 2000; Shim *et al.*, 2000). Rohm and Swaminathan (2003), in a study comparing a sample of e-shoppers with non-e-shoppers, found that social interaction, variety seeking and convenience were all significant motivators for e-shopping. Childers *et al.* (2001) found enjoyment was strongly correlated with attitude to e-shopping, particularly in the case of examples that the authors described as 'hedonic' or pleasure-related: e.g. Amazon (www.amazon.com) or Hot Hot Hot (sauces – www.hothothot.com). Similarly, Parsons (2002) found that social motives such as social experiences outside home; communication with others with similar interests; membership of peer groups; and status and authority were valid for e-shopping. Social and pleasure motives, important for bricks shopping, are, despite some qualification, also significant for e-shopping.

Two of our own current studies emphasize the importance of the experiential aspects of e-shopping, as outlined briefly below. These studies are reported in more detail in *e-Economy: Rhetoric or Business Reality?*, in the same series as this book (Dennis and Richardson, 2004).

Box 4.3:
MOTIVES FOR E-SHOPPING

- Socializing
- Enjoyment
- Usefulness
- Ease of use
- Convenience
- Navigation
- Knowledge and ability to make a purchase
- Influence of friends and family

Sources: Parsons (2002); Dennis and Papamatthaiou (2003)

Study 1

We have already referred to this first study (initial results in Dennis *et al.*, 2002a) in the sections above. The method used was a questionnaire survey that compared shoppers' opinions of Internet shopping versus bricks shopping centres. The 308 respondents were sixth-form (year 12) and university undergraduate students – the shoppers of tomorrow. One of the main themes from the qualitative part of the study was a preference for shopping in shopping centres as more enjoyable and sociable. Shoppers who both e-shopped and shopped in shopping centres commented typically: 'Internet shopping is not a personal experience. You cannot try and see what you're buying. . . . Shopping [should] be very sociable.'

Results from the questionnaire indicated that shoppers rated e-shopping higher than shopping centres for *favourable prices* and *convenience*. On the other hand, shopping centres were preferred for *positive image* and more emphatically for *customer service*. Figure 4.2 (p. 83) illustrates the results for the sixth-form (year 12) students, but the results for undergraduates were similar. One striking figure is that 57 per cent of the sample were e-shoppers – compared with the UK average for all adults of around 15 per cent (estimated from NetValue, 2001). The average expenditure of the Internet shoppers on e-shopping was £22 per month, compared to £86 per month on conventional shopping. Thus, over half of the student sample shopped on the Internet, spending on average over 20 per cent of their non-food shopping by Internet.

Box 4.4:
SOCIAL MOTIVES FOR E-SHOPPING

- Social experiences outside the home
- Communications with others having a similar interest
- Peer group attraction
- Status and authority – raising the standing of the shopper in the eyes of friends and colleagues
- Virtual communities

Source: Parsons (2002)

Study 2

Our second study concerned motivations for e-shopping and is discussed in more detail in Chapter 5 (preliminary results reported in Dennis and Papamatthaiou, 2003). Enjoyment, usefulness, ease of use, convenience, navigation, knowledge and ability to make a purchase, and the influence of friends and family were found to be important motivations.

Our results apply to students and are not representative of the average population. Indeed, these are people who within a few years are likely to be earning and spending significantly more than the national average. Bearing in mind this income effect and the high computer literacy of graduates, these are shoppers who will account for a disproportionately high percentage of discretionary income and comparison shopping. Our results, and those of other researchers, show a consistent picture of the importance of the social and experiential aspects of e-shopping. These motivators are being satisfied to good effect by the most successful e-retailers such as, for example, eBay – one of the most successful sites in terms of sales, time spent on the site and providing enjoyment (Reynolds, 2000; Nielsen NetRatings 2003 – see Case study 4.1, pp. 104–105).

Box 4.5:
ENJOYMENT AND E-SHOPPING

Enjoyment motives for e-shopping

- Involvement
- Not boring
- Fun for its own sake

Enjoyment and social features of e-retailing sites

- Chat rooms
- Bulletin boards
- Customer written stories
- Product reviews
- Suggestion boxes
- Personalization of offers

The most popular 'enjoyment' e-shopping sites (in ranked order)

- Amazon (www.amazon.com)
- CD WOW (www.cd-wow.co.uk)
- eBay (auction, www.ebay.co.uk)
- Ticketmaster (show tickets, www.ticketmaster.co.uk)
- Ryanair (www.ryanair.co.uk)
- EasyJet (www.easyjet.co.uk)
- Opodo (air tickets, www.opodo.co.uk)

Source: Dennis and Papamatthaiou (2003)

DIFFERENCES BETWEEN MALE AND FEMALE SHOPPING STYLES

Differences between male and female shopping styles may go back a long way. In hunter–gatherer societies, females tend to carry babies, are based around the camp and do the gathering. Males on the other hand are more likely to protect the group and do the hunting. Humans may have evolved in such a way that those best at their respective roles have been more likely to find a mate and to survive. For females, this meant excelling in gathering: finding the best food and other materials for the family. For males, it entailed being good hunters: fast, strong and decisive. Both sexes would look for those respective qualities in a potential mate, resulting in persistent traits. These differences in mate-seeking behaviour have survived into a wide cross-section of modern cultures (Buss, 1989). In Western consumer societies, gathering may have translated into comparison shopping, hunting into earning money to support the family. Even in the US, where gender equality in the workplace is greater than most countries, differences in shopping styles can be clearly observed. The female style involves searching, comparing, weighing the advantages and disadvantages of alternatives, finding the best value and taking a pride in the shopping activity (Underhill, 1999). This pride is justified as on average women make a 10 per cent better cost saving than men do, making women the 'better shoppers' (Denison, 2003). Women see the activity of shopping as a satisfying experience in itself – i.e. a leisure activity. On the other hand, men see shopping as a mission and tend to go straight for what they want in a purposeful way (Underhill, 1999). For men, the focus is on 'the kill' – the actual moment of purchase when their heart rate quickens.

Evolutionary psychology has been founded on research demonstrating consistency of mating behaviour across widely different cultures. Accordingly, our own study has sought empirical evidence for an evolutionary basis to shopping sex differences by comparing shopping styles across cultures (reported in more detail in Dennis, 2004). Thirteen 'mini focus groups' wrote shopping scenarios about the national culture(s) that they were most familiar with. Fourteen cultural nationalities were represented: five judge participants represented the UK national culture, eight Continental European and 23 Asian, i.e. 36 judge participants in total. In general, there were some differences in shopping styles between the national cultures, but the differences between males and females were much more striking, reflecting the hunter and gatherer roles and providing support for the evolutionary hypothesis.

The stereotypes are not 100 per cent accurate but in the UK have been found to apply to 80 per cent of women and 70 per cent of men (Denison, 2003). The styles have been found to be equally valid for e-shopping (Lindquist and Kaufman-Scarborough, 2000). As with bricks shopping, the stereotype reverses when the product purchased is technical and expensive (Dholakia and Chiang, 2003).

Box 4.6:
SHOPPERS IN CYBERSPACE: ARE THEY FROM VENUS OR MARS?

Female shopping style – the gatherer

- Ritual of seeking and comparing
- Imagining and envisioning the merchandise in use
- Tallying up the pros and cons
- Taking (justified) pride in ability as shoppers
- The total shopping process (not just buying) is a leisure activity
- Women like to spend longer shopping than men do
- Social interaction is an important part of shopping
- Women favour sites designed for women – e.g. iVillage (www.ivillage.co.uk) – with horoscopes, health, beauty and diet
- Women are more likely to browse online, then buy in-store

Male shopping styles – the hunter

- Men are incisive, decisive and determined shoppers
- Men's excitement with shopping is at the moment of 'kill' (purchase)
- Men try to complete the shopping activity in the shortest possible time
- Men's lack of patience means they often miss the best buy
- But the stereotype reverses when the product is technical and expensive. Men do take a pride in shopping for, for example, cars and computers (and women are purposeful for those products)
- Men's favourite sites tend to include games, gambling and pornography
- Male e-shoppers are heavier Internet users and are more likely to shop via mobile devices and PDAs

Sources: Dholakia (1999); Underhill (1999); Lindquist and Kaufman-Scarborough (2000); eTypes (2001); Lindquist *et al.* (2001); Denison (2003); Dholakia and Chiang (2003)

Box 4.7:
MALE AND FEMALE SHOPPING STEREOTYPES?

Is this cultural stereotyping? Or is there any truth in this research? BBC News (2003) ran a story on the Denison (2003) research asking readers to post their own answers to these questions. Of 64 replies posted, 19 asked further questions or made different points ('Louise [who hates shopping] – will you marry me?' *Debt-ridden husband*). Of the remainder, 22 per cent disagreed with the stereotypes and 78 per cent agreed.

Perhaps reflecting the greater attention given to the selection process, US women are 30 per cent more likely to browse online, then buy in-store (Lindquist and Kaufman-Scarborough, 2000). In the early days of the Internet, male users heavily outnumbered females, but this is now changing, with 50 per cent of US e-shoppers now female. The UK is catching up with 44 per cent in 2000 (up from 30 per cent reported by Pavitt in 1997). Countries that are less developed in terms of Internet use tend to have lower proportions of female e-shoppers.

Men tend to be major users of games sites (eTypes, 2001), gambling and pornography. Male e-shoppers form the large majority of the most sophisticated eTypes life-cycle stage 'Wired 4 life' (see Mini case study 4.1) – heavy Internet users and also heavier than average in usage of mobile Internet devices and personal digital assistants (PDAs). See Chapter 11 for more on m-shopping.

Mini case study 4.1: ETYPES.INFO

An award-winning tool for understanding online consumer behaviour, eTypes features extensive information on how consumers behave and transact online, and has been constructed by combining demographic and lifestyle datasets from profiling company CACI with data from Forrester, the leading Internet research organization. The system works by classifying consumers into seven groups denoting life stage; Internet usage levels and 23 eTypes – detailing online behaviour; and five e-shopping lifestyle stages.

The system aims to tell e-retailers about the characteristics of e-shoppers and what they use the Internet for – whether it's finding holidays, buying CDs, managing their stocks and shares or just chatting, and claims that this means e-retailers can get more from their e-shopper data – and a higher return on website investment.

Box 4.8:
E-SHOPPING LIFE CYCLE STAGES

- *Stage 1 – Virtual virgins* Only 12 per cent of these Internet users have bought online – half the average. A high proportion is female. Age tends towards the youngest and oldest
- *Stage 2 – Chatters and gamers* These are avid Internet users, spending 20 per cent more time online than the average. Twenty-five per cent are e-shoppers (the national average). This group tend to be more worried about security than average
- *Stage 3 – DotCom dabblers* Forty per cent of these Internet users are e-shoppers. They are heavy users of entertainment and scientific sites
- *Stage 4 – Surfing suits* These are heavy e-shoppers, but spend less time online – only 60 per cent of the average. They tend to be professional and financially aware
- *Stage 5 – Wired 4 life* The heaviest e-shoppers – 70 per cent have purchased online. Many are graduates or cosmopolitan. These users tend to be in the mid-range age groups

Source: www.etypes.info

Earlier in this section we drew attention to the importance of shopping as a social activity. In line with the evolutionary psychology approach, these interpersonal aspects are particularly important for female shoppers (for example, see Elliot, 1994; Dholakia, 1999). Women tend to want more interpersonal contact from e-shopping than men do, preferring chat and women's sites (eTypes, 2001). 'Women want ease of navigation and sense of personalised relationship' – helped by 'community' or 'chat' rooms (Harris, 1998). An example of the more female- and 'community'-orientated approach is the e-mall iVillage (referred to in the preceding section) for which Tesco hosts the UK site. Women tend to be later adopters of e-shopping and are more likely to be in the first of the eTypes e-shopping life-cycle stages, 'Virtual virgins' (eTypes, 2001).

CONSUMER SATISFACTION: BRICKS AND CLICKS SHOPPING COMPARED

As outlined in Chapter 1, even at modest projections, e-retail will soon take a share approaching 10 per cent of total retail sales. This may seem a small percentage, but it represents around £12 billion in sales. High street banks, other financial services and travel agents are most at risk (BCSC, 2001). Some forecasters predict the eventual disappearance from the high street of any businesses that work better as e-businesses: banks, travel agents and book, music and electronics shops. 'Clothes shops will persist because the experience of shopping for clothes is too deeply ingrained, especially in women, to be abandoned'. Also specialist, up-market retailers who require expertise and offer the consumer a specific experience will flourish. 'The high street will be freed of its ranks of the same old stores and become a more interesting place' (Bryan Appleyard, writing in the *Sunday Times* (UK) Magazine, 22 July 2001). The winners in the high street are likely to be well-branded retailers offering service and added value. Indications so far are that most e-retail success too is going to existing, well-branded retailers – likely to have efficient supply-chain and fulfilment systems (Verdict, 2001) – a trend likely to continue for several years (BCSC, 2001). According to a *Computer Weekly* survey, the three top-rated e-retailers for customer satisfaction and service are Marks & Spencer (www.marksandspencer.com), Littlewoods (www.littlewoods.co.uk) and Iceland (www.iceland.co.uk).

Researchers attempting to answer why people e-shop have tended to look to various components of the 'image' of e-retailing and specific e-retailers, in a similar way to measurements of the image of a bricks store (Wolfinbarger and Gilly, 2002). This may be a valid approach for two reasons. First, 'image' is a concept used to mean our overall evaluation or rating of something in such a way as to guide our actions (Boulding, 1956). For example, we are more likely to buy from a store that we consider has a positive image on considerations that we may consider important, such as price or customer service. Second, this is an approach that has been demonstrated to work for bricks stores over many years (e.g. Berry, 1969; Lindquist, 1974) and it is largely the bricks retailers with strong images that are making the running in e-retail. According to Kimber (2001), shopper loyalty in-store and online are linked. For example, Tesco's customers using both on- and offline shopping channels spend 20 per cent more on average than customers who only use the store. Tesco is well known as having a very positive image both in-store and online, being the UK grocery market leader in both channels.

Measurements of e-retail image that have been used by commercial marketing research studies include ease of use, product selection, product information, price, on-time delivery, product representation, customer support and privacy. There is empirical support for some of these dimensions of image, for example 'product selection' and 'ease of use' (Dennis *et al.*, 2002a; Dennis and Papamatthaiou, 2003 respectively), but in general the connection between the components of image and e-shopping spending behaviour remains an under-researched area. Perhaps the most extensive investigation to date has come from Wolfinbarger and Gilly (2003), who carried out focus groups and quantitative surveys to determine the components of e-retail quality. The qualitative analysis identified four factors: (1) fulfilment/reliability, (2) website design, (3) customer service and (4) security/privacy. *Fulfilment/reliability* includes both the description of a product and efficient delivery. *Website design* includes navigation, search and ordering. *Customer service* means reactive and helpful service, and responding to customer enquiries quickly. The quantitative surveys indicated that these three factors were all significantly related to e-shoppers' understanding of e-retail quality.

Security/privacy refers to credit card payments and privacy. As mentioned earlier in this chapter, security worries have often been reported as one of the most important reasons for not e-shopping. It is surprising, therefore, that the survey did not find this factor to be significantly associated with e-retail quality. Other studies have shown that, as e-shoppers become more experienced, they tend to shop more and become less concerned about security. In the case of the Wolfinbarger and Gilly study, those e-shoppers who were satisfied with e-retailers' reliability, website design and service may well have been more confident e-shoppers and therefore suffered fewer security worries, resulting in security/privacy being swamped by the other factors in the analysis.

Box 4.9:
COMPONENTS OF E-RETAIL QUALITY

Fulfilment/reliability

- Accurate display and description of a product so that what customers receive is what they thought they ordered
- Delivery of the right product within the time frame promised

Website design – all elements of the consumer's experience at the website:

- Navigation
- Information search
- Order processing
- Personalization
- Product selection

Customer service

- Reactive, helpful and willing service that responds to customer inquiries quickly

Security/privacy

- Security of credit card payments
- Privacy of shared information

Source: Wolfinbarger and Gilly (2003)

There is a distinct geographical distribution of e-shopping in the UK, with a heavy concentration in London and the Southeast. According to Kimber (2001), this is being driven by affluence and high credit card ownership. Also, e-shoppers in that region are more confident about security. After London, the highest e-shopping areas are Reading, Cambridge, Bristol and Birmingham. Conversely, areas further away from London and less affluent areas tend to e-shop less and to be more concerned about security. Newcastle-on-Tyne has the lowest e-shopping level of any UK city, followed by Sheffield, York, Glasgow and Hull (eTypes, 2001).

The balance of the evidence available is that a wide range of image and other attributes are important in consumer satisfaction and behaviour for e-shopping. Many attributes that are important for bricks shopping are also important for e-shopping. Some e-retailers have often paid less attention to elements such as the social and enjoyment aspects of e-shopping, but the best and most successful e-retailers are deliberately and successfully satisfying e-shoppers on motivators such as these. Emphasizing the importance of addressing the overall experience of e-shopping, one survey indicated that, if the worst-rated e-grocery were to improve the online experience to match the best competitor, online sales could be improved by 480 per cent. For the average e-retailer, improved user experience could result in a 33 to 54 per cent sales increase (Meekings *et al.*, 2003).

Mini case study 4.2: CUSTOMER SERVICE FROM SCREWFIX (www.screwfix.com)

See Chapter 1, pp. 9–10.

Screwfix's approach to customer service can be illustrated by our experience with a concrete mixer. After a few weeks' use, the electrical contactor start button failed, meaning the mixer would only run if the start button was held in by hand. We informed Screwfix, explaining that the machine had already had some use, expecting to be offered a replacement electrical contactor. With such a large item of equipment, and the length of time it had been used, we did not realistically expect a replacement mixer. Nevertheless, the Screwfix help desk could not have been more helpful and did authorize the replacement mixer – asking us just to pack up the old one in the original packaging and hand it over to the delivery driver who brought the new one. The problem was that the (very bulky!) packaging had been disposed of some time ago. No problem for Screwfix: 'we'll send you the new one. Unpack it over the next few days, then dismantle the old one and put it into the new packaging. We'll send another lorry to pick it up next week.'

THINK POINT

Why do you think Screwfix offered to replace the item, despite the heavy extra carriage requirements, when a simple replacement of the contactor would have been acceptable?

Mini case study 4.3: CUSTOMER SERVICE FROM MCWILLIES (not its real name!)

A contrasting approach to that of Mini case study 4.2 can be illustrated by our customer service experience from McWillies. We used the shopbot Kelcoo to identify the best deal for a photo printer – which turned out to be from McWillies. Not only was McWillies cheapest for the printer but also there was a special offer including a free pack of photo print paper. McWillies sent an e-mail confirmation showing the price and the two items, printer and paper. The printer arrived within a few days, but without the paper. Some weeks later, despite an (unanswered) e-mail, the paper had still not arrived, so we phoned the 'customer service' line. Here is a summarized extract from the conversation:

McWillies (M): The paper was sent with the printer.
Customer (C): But we didn't receive it.

M: You must have received it because it was sent in the same box.

C: There was only one box, the original packaging, and it was completely full with the printer.

M: Well we sent it.

C: Well we haven't received it [and so on for a few minutes], until:

C: Can I speak to a supervisor?

M: The supervisor's busy.

C: Well, can I speak to someone at head office?

M: I'll speak to head office, please hold. [Long wait.]

M: I've checked with head office and they say it's too late to do anything about it now.

C: I would still like to speak to a supervisor [audible click in mid-sentence]:

M: Supervisor speaking. We can PROVE that we sent the paper, because we weigh all the parcels, so all we have to do is to check the weight on the docket and we'll prove that we sent it.

C: That's great! What a good idea. Could you check it now, please, as it will prove that the paper wasn't in the box.

M: *NO!* We will not be doing that because *YOU* should've sent us an e-mail to let us know that the paper had not arrived.

C: As I've already explained, we did send an e-mail.

M: Well we have no record of it so the matter ends here.

C: Can you check with head office before you refuse to confirm the weight of the parcel as that will prove that we didn't receive the paper?

M: *NO!* We can't check the weight and I'm not going to discuss this any further.

(Line went dead.)

Postscript: We still have not received the paper and have given up trying to get it.

THINK POINT

Why do you think McWillies suggested checking the package weights, but decided against this course of action when the customer said it was a good idea?

THE COMMUNICATIONS MIX FOR THE E-RETAILER

All elements of the e-retail mix can actually form part of the communications mix. For example, *Convenience* can include the ease of finding the site, say by paid links from other sites or search engines communicating the existence of the site to the potential customer. *Customer value and benefit* can be reflected in the width and depth of product offered and ease of navigating around this large range, communicating a benefit of buying online rather than in-store. *Cost to the customer* can communicate price positioning in the case of a cost leadership strategy. Alternatively, high prices with 'round' figures can communicate quality and prestige. *Computing and category management* can communicate added value from the availability of a wide range of products on short delivery times. *Customer franchise* is largely a communications and branding issue. For example, improving the information value of an e-retailing site can improve image and branding. Similarly, *Customer care and service* can communicate a positive image. Although many of the critical aspects of service are not visible until the order is fulfilled, a generous returns policy can act as a proxy in communicating an image of good service. Finally, *Communication and customer relationships* describes the communications mix proper, which can have a huge variety of elements from marketing research surveys to e-mail, and from advertising to sponsorship. Rather than try to cover everything (which would need another book), we will illustrate the elements outlined in Chapter 1 with some examples.

Mini case study 4.4: THE E-RETAIL MIX COMMUNICATES WITH THE CUSTOMER

Compass 24 boat chandlery and accessories (www.compass24.com)

Compass 24 is Europe's largest direct sales boating equipment company. A brief illustration of how the Compass 24 e-retail mix is utilized to communicate positively with customers follows below.

Convenience

Entering 'boating equipment uk' in the Google search engine (www.google.co.uk) brings up Boatz.co.uk (www.boatz.co.uk) close to the top of the non-sponsored links. This is because many boating information sites are linked *to* the Boatz site. Many boat equipment sites are linked by paid links *from* Boatz.co.uk precisely because it is near the top of the Google (unpaid link) search results. There is a link to Compass 24 (www.compass24.co.uk) in the 'Chandlers' section. Links from Boatz and other popular sites related to the product category represent added convenience for the customer and greatly increase exposure to surfers interested in the specific product types.

Customer value and benefit

The huge range of 8,000 products is clearly available and easy to find. Navigation is by a close approach to 'free grid' (Vrechopoulos, 2001). This is a combination of a grid hierarchical tree structure with a free-flow navigation capability. Shoppers can either move through the e-store in a logical progression through departments or obtain direct access to end-products using a search engine. Product categories are displayed in a 'left-frame'. The ease of finding products and the huge amount of boating equipment that can be supplied communicate the site's ability to satisfy wide-ranging customer requirements.

Cost to the customer

The Compass online shop page does not offer 'bargain' positioning but, rather, promises 'good value'. With a separate search facility for 'brands', there is an emphasis on differentiation rather than price leadership. The pricing therefore communicates value, for example 'Magellan [a top brand] GPS 320 top value offer'. Nevertheless, the value pricing is strongly emphasized by using 'psychological pricing'. For example the GPS 320 is priced at £139.95, i.e. psychologically below the price point of £140 – emphasizing the communication of good value. There are often premium-based rather than price-based special offers, for example 'spend £20.00 or more and we'll give you a free vacuum flask'. Promotions such as this communicate extra value for the customer without risking damage to the customer's perceptions of quality and the price goods are worth, as can be the case with price-based promotions like '£10 off'.

Computing and category management

Compass is based on established and efficient supply-chain arrangements with suppliers. Thus, there is a huge range of products available either from stock or drop-shipped directly from suppliers on short delivery times. Compass delivers 'Just in Time': tell Compass when you want the goods (for example when you expect to return from your boating cruise), and for a small extra fee it will deliver that exact day. Supply-chain efficiency is used to communicate the site's ability and desire to satisfy customers' particular needs.

Customer franchise

The Compass site communicates established branding and image by links to bodies such as the Royal Yachting Association, weather forecasts from the Met. Office and tides data from Yachting and Boating World (www.ybw.com, Europe's top marine website). When the site was launched in the UK (it is German-based), added credibility in the form of endorsement from Sir Robin Knox-Johnston, the famous record-breaking ocean rower and yachtsman, communicated an established brand.

Customer care and service

Compass offers a 14-day 'no questions asked' return policy. Deliveries are fast and reliable. Fast and easy e-mail help is available, with the e-mail pages also showing telephone numbers. The telephone helpline is courteous, knowledgeable and helpful. Some months after we got our 'free' vacuum flask (the offer mentioned above), the top started to leak. We contacted Compass 24 to ask if we could buy a replacement top but it was unable to supply one as it was no longer selling that flask. Compass 24 quickly sent a replacement, better quality, flask – free. Such surprisingly good service communicates a commitment to putting the customer's interests first, despite the costs to the company.

Communication and customer relationships

In addition to the communication tools mentioned above, Compass 24 uses a wide range of communication mix elements, including:

Advertising – in specialist paper-based yachting magazines in addition to websites such as Boatz.
Direct mail – catalogues, mini catalogues and special offers.
Word of mouth – e.g. recommend Compass 24 to a friend and get a free tool set.
Customer relationships – customers can opt in to the e-mail newsletter for tip-offs on special offers and other news.
Web atmospherics – good illustrations and snappy animation that does not take too long to load.

Marketing research surveys

When we bought a new digital camera from Samsung, we had to register the software online. The registration process entailed uploading basic information on the use of the product that the supplier can use, for example to inform us of updates or new products that may be of interest. Other suppliers use a huge lifestyle questionnaire that gives the impression of being the guarantee registration. The lifestyle data can be used for profiling, but also may be rented for a highly selectable mailing list by other companies. To comply with data protection legislation, there is an 'opt out' box that can be checked, but the 'if you don't want this service, please tick' message is sometimes in very small print almost hidden among many pages of conditions. Most e-shoppers just click 'accept' and never even know.

Offline advertising*

The scope of offline advertising is too wide to cover in detail here. Suffice it to say that an e-retailer should naturally include the Web address not only in TV, radio and press ads, but also on all brochures, stationery, plus the label and packaging of the product (whether sold on or offline). Advertisements in specialist targeted publications are often more cost-effective than the mass media, especially for smaller niche markets. For example, for boat insurance, craftinsure (www.craftinsure.com) advertises in publications like *All at Sea*, a monthly newspaper distributed partly by subscription but mainly distributed free at boating shops and marinas. For a product of general interest to most people, like the department (e-)store John Lewis (www.johnlewis.com) e-retailers can advertise in Internet magazines such as *.Net* (www.netmag.co.uk), the biggest selling UK Internet magazine, whose readers are likely to e-shop. Another tip for the e-retailer is to advertise in the 'click here' sections of the general press (e.g. *Sunday Times*, *Daily Mail*), which are a lot cheaper and likely to be more cost-effective than large colour advertisements.

*This section is adapted from Lundquist (1998)

Public relations (PR), sponsorship and publicity

PR and publicity aim to communicate positive messages without paying directly for the media space as advertising. An example of publicity came from the conjurer David Blaine hanging in a box under Tower Bridge for weeks without food – with the www.channel4.com logo visible. Most news reports at the time mentioned Channel 4's sponsorship. PR activity also includes press releases and press conferences, which can contribute towards positive press coverage. Publicity and PR opportunities are not limited to the official sponsors of such stunts. Searching for 'david blaine' on Google (www.google.co.uk) produced many sponsored links, including ten from 'Search the Web' (www.searchtheweb.com). These included 'Magic tricks by David Blaine' – magic tricks, books, DVDs and videos for both professional and amateur magicians from Merchant of Magic (www.merchantofmagic.co.uk); David Blaine's new book and 'many items from his TV specials' from Magic Tricks (www.magictricks.co.uk); and a David Blaine video from Amazon (www.amazon.com). These were all in addition to David Blaine's official website (www.davidblaine.com).

The car e-retailer Edmunds (www.edmunds.com) illustrates PR in action. The website has a dedicated media area providing easy contact with the PR department, press releases (such as forecasts of changes in the levels of car prices) and 'Edmunds in the News'. For example: 'One of the leading online automotive resources continues to upgrade its services' – *Entrepreneur* magazine.

Direct mail

Many of the most successful e-retailers communicate regularly with customers by post. Tesco (www.tesco.com) is a well-known example, mailing news, vouchers and special offers every three months. Tesco have found that expenditure on direct and database marketing can be far more cost-effective than traditional above-the-line advertising. This cost-effectiveness also leads niche marketers in particular to use direct mail. For example, Screwfix (www.screwfix.com – trade and DIY supplies – see Chapter 1, pp. 9–10) posts regular catalogues, mini catalogues and special offers.

e-Mail permission marketing

Permission marketing via e-mail is increasing. The response rates to *opt-in* e-mail campaigns are significantly higher than to other online ads; the cost per acquisition is lower; turnaround time is faster; and results can be accurately tracked. More companies are moving greater proportions of budget from postal direct mailings and conventional advertising to e-mail. Unfortunately, spam has also increased dramatically. More aggressive spam filters have been developed but, even so, most e-mail users are experiencing unacceptably high levels of unwanted e-mail messages. Responsible marketers use opt-in or even *double-opt-in* permission marketing and also make it easy for customers who have opted in to opt out again. For example, *Web Promote* (www.webpromote.com), one of the largest Internet marketing newsletters, has over 170,000 double-opt-in subscribers.

Box 4.10:
THE PRINCIPLES OF AN E-MAIL MARKETING CAMPAIGN

- Acquire e-mail addresses (e.g. of people who have registered to receive information)
- Obtain permission to use the e-mail address for marketing. This is best done at the time of collection, e.g. registration or free samples may only be possible if the respondent checks the 'yes' box
- Select the addresses to target for the particular message
- Execute the campaign (possibly in conjunction with other communications channels)
- Respond to customer replies
- Correct and clean the e-mail list
- Track and measure the campaign performance.

Source: adapted from Harris and Dennis (2002)

Short message systems (SMSs) and multimedia messaging services (MMSs)

While mobile phones and other mobile devices can be useful for 'distress' purchases such as paying a congestion charge (to drive into a city), the growth of m-commerce has been slow, even since the introduction of 3G. Nevertheless, even though it represents a small proportion of marketing budgets, advertising via *short message systems (SMSs)* and *multimedia messaging services (MMSs)* achieves high response rates. Because of this, spending on mobile advertising has been predicted to rocket to £6 billion over the next year or two (Harris and Dennis, 2002). Mobile advertising is growing in popularity not just because of the high response, but also because mobile Web users represent an attractive demographic, with the majority being males aged 20–39 with incomes over £30,000. They are well segmented as a target for games, gambling and travel services – currently the biggest mobile advertising categories. For example, in the US, the marketing agency Mobliss has launched Snow Report (www.mysnowreport.com). Customers who have registered their interests can receive text messages detailing snow conditions at winter sports resorts. Recipients of the message can follow a link for a travel package to the resort. As with e-mail, the key to success is opt-in, with customers giving permission for these marketing activities when they register for the information service. See Chapter 11 for more on m-marketing.

Viral marketing

Viral marketing is growing as more companies use it to promote and brand their products and services. For example, the low-budget horror movie *The Blair Witch Project* owed worldwide success to a vast volume of 'word of mouse' recommendations passed around Internet chat rooms. These campaigns are becoming more sophisticated with tracking of open, click-through and success rates. A potential problem with viral marketing campaigns is that the company is reliant on each individual in the chain to have permission to send such messages to each recipient. In many cases this is not done: viral marketing spreads much spam. The responsible marketer will be using tracking systems that can be used for follow-up of sample recipients to ensure that they do not object to such communications. As an example of *opt-out* viral marketing, consider the hypothetical way that this book could be promoted. Prospects may initially receive an information-only message, for example an invitation to a marketing conference, ending with something along the lines of:

> Please forward this message to anyone else who may be interested. In the future we may want to inform you of other services and products (for example books) in which we think you may be interested. If you do not wish to receive such messages, please contact the sender to be removed from the list.

Banners, pop-ups and interstitials*

Online advertising expenditure on media such as banners and pop-ups is growing and has reached well over £150 million per year (£30 million more than cinema advertising, for example). The interstitial – a pop-up that interrupts browsing to show an ad – is a much more active form of advertising than banners. Some people using the Web for a specific purpose find these irritating, though. Online advertising company RealMedia (www.uk.realmedia.com) is using a less-intrusive system called adPointer. This generates an ad when the cursor has not moved for a specific time.

Schemes that incentivize users to look at advertisements have been around for some years, but in the UK Bananalotto.com (www.bananalotto.com) has raised the stakes by offering the chance to win one million pounds as you click the banner ad. KPE, the media and entertainment consultancy, has developed around ten games for their clients. Managing Director Paul Zwillberg says:

*This section is summarized and adapted from *Marketing Business* e-business supplement

> So much of the Internet has been characterised by repurposing things that worked well in print or TV. 'Advergaming' is . . . a new combination that's made for the medium. . . . You take one of the most popular uses of interactive content and marry it with tried and tested advertising models like brand association, trial or data capture and you get something really wonderful.

Customer relationships

The direct mail and e-mail activities described above are part of the management of customer relationships. Building on these basic communication tools, the most successful e-retailers such as Amazon (www.amazon.com) and Tesco (www.tesco.com) use various techniques of data mining, personalization and customization (explored in more detail in Chapter 2). For example, Amazon customizes the web page, making offers for new books, music or movies that are likely to be of interest based on past purchase patterns. Tesco likewise personalizes its communications and special offers almost down to the level of the individual. These e-retailers are thus able to satisfy customers more specifically and therefore are better using the customer relationship and data mining tools.

Web atmospherics

Web atmospherics is too important and complex a topic for this single section, but is explored in Chapter 6 in greater depth. Briefly, atmospherics includes *visual* (e.g. text, design, colour management, video clips, 3-D), *aural* (e.g. music or sound effects) and *olfactory* (e.g. perfume and samples) stimuli. The Edmunds (www.edmunds.com) car sales site is a good example of the use of exciting downloads of video and sound effects to illustrate cars in action. With effects like this, there is a need to avoid long download times (e.g. by having a separate 'click here for broadband' version for the larger memory effects).

Perfume is available by e-retail, although most suppliers rely on description and well-known brands, rather than offering samples, for example Perfumania (www.mydesignerperfume.com): 'Contains citron, rose, jasmine and is accented with honeysuckle, vanilla and oakmoss making Allure by Chanel perfect for romantic use'. Atmospherics, even when fairly low-tech, have much to offer in communications mix design.

Link popularity

Search engines use 'link popularity' in locating and ranking sites. Improving link popularity by persuading other sites to link to yours raises a site in search-engine rankings and is therefore a critical aspect of the communications mix. For more details, see the 'Link popularity engineering' section in Chapter 5 (pp. 123–125).

CHAPTER SUMMARY

There are disadvantages and advantages of e-shopping for consumers, but retailers and shoppers are overcoming the problems and e-shopping is growing. Shopping provides not just functional goods but also real social and enjoyment benefits. Although originally thought of only in mechanistic terms, e-shopping can also provide social interaction and enjoyment. Even though, in some aspects such as recreation, e-shopping trails behind bricks shopping, it is often the e-retailers who are good at satisfying these non-tangible benefits who are having most success. Although the stereotypes cannot be generalized with certainty, there are differences between the sexes in shopping styles. Men tend to be more purposeful and faster shoppers. Women take more care, and want more social interaction than men do. In the past, e-shopping has been more suited to the male style, but women are becoming heavy users of female-orientated sites. For technical products such as cars and computers, the gender stereotypes tend to be reversed.

There is a wide range of potential communications channels available to the e-retailer. Many successful e-retailers use a broad, integrated range of offline and online communications, but there is a trend towards the use of more permission and database marketing techniques.

In the following chapter we will explore the relevance to e-retailing of consumers' needs for information.

Case study 4.1: EBAY.CO.UK

See also the comparison with Amazon in Mini case study 8.2, pp. 178–179.

The eBay site was founded in the US in 1995, originally under the name Auctionweb. The UK site was launched in 1999, growing after a slow start to become the UK's top e-commerce site measured by monthly audience numbers, with 6.8 million people (compared with Amazon's 6.1 million and Tesco's 2.7 million). In the year to March 2003, eBay's audience increased by 160 per cent, compared to Amazon's 28 per cent. Internet growth overall was only 7 per cent. The figures are 'a significant sign of the potential of [the most profitable and successful Internet players] to sell to consumers', according to Nielsen/NetRatings (www.nielsen-netratings.com), who supplied the figures. Cheap though most individual products may be, eBay still sells over £1 billion of them per year. If eBay were considered to be an e-retailer, this would make them number one in UK market share. While many dot.coms are mainly hype, eBay is profitable, making a quarter of a billion dollars on worldwide operations in 2001. It survived the dot.com crash relatively unscathed and the share price rose from US$18 in 1998 to US$110 by 2003.

Visitors to eBay spend an average of 1 hour and 11 minutes per month on the site – one of the longest of any UK site. Visitors return to the site to check the status of items they are bidding for or selling and ebay.co.uk is one of very few e-retailers to achieve over a billion pages views per month.

Many UK users are earning a healthy living as 'power sellers', taking advantage of the worldwide market to offer everything from sports utility vehicles (SUVs) to comics, records and oddments like garden gnomes, T-shirts and kettles. In the same way as the major bricks retailers are suffering increasing competition from charity shops and car-boot sales, so the established e-retailers face growing competition from online auctions.

Most sellers are private individuals. For example, Pat Austin makes £30,000 per year selling an assortment of bric-a-brac that she finds in charity shops, car-boot sales and physical auctions. She sells 1,000+ items per year and 99.9 per cent of her transactions have been positive. It is a full-time job, though, with correspondence and despatch taking up the mornings and sourcing goods the afternoons. Rosie English has a turnover of £100,000+ selling high-class women's fashion for prices of £100 to £1,000+. She reads the fashion press to identify what editors recommend and what celebrities are wearing, then buys from sample and factory sales or direct from designers. However, eBay is not all one-person businesses, as the 'big boys' are seeing the opportunities and joining in with companies like Dell, Dixons and Sears using eBay to shift excess stock.

It's a case of 'buyer beware', as auction sites do not take responsibility for deals that go wrong and offer only low insurance cover for losses. The way for buyers to identify the most reliable sellers is from feedback ratings – many regular sellers have hundreds of positive ratings.

Box 4.11:
HOW EBAY WORKS

- Signing up is free
- Buyers bid online and the highest wins
- Sellers and buyers rate each other
- Listing fees vary in the approximate range £0.15 to £2
- The site also charges a percentage of the sale price, between approximately 1.75 per cent and 5.25 per cent – the more valuable the item, the lower the percentage

Box 4.12:
AUCTIONS

Tips for auction sellers

- *Provide a detailed description* Include a photograph if possible. Be honest about any faults in order to avoid negative feedback
- *Choose a suitable category* The categories help bidders to find goods quickly. Fees are higher in some categories than others
- *Sell internationally* This is how to reach a bigger audience – but always get the payment cleared before sending the goods
- *Provide a 'little extra' customer service* Rosie English gift wraps everything. She has 500 positive feedback messages and 100 per cent feedback rating

Tips for auction buyers

- *Read the description carefully* Make sure that you know what you are getting. For example, one buyer bid for a rug, then found out that it was from a doll's house!
- *If in doubt, contact the seller* The relationship may be important if things go wrong
- *Think whether it is too good to be true* In-demand items like home theatre, plasma screens and digital cameras can attract the dodgy deal at very low prices
- *Check for spelling mistakes* For example, the 'Stradivarious' violin offered at a fraction of the price you would expect
- *Bid high, then stop* Research shows that the final price can be up to 30 per cent higher when bids arrive fast (Haubl and Popkowski Leszeczyc, 2003). Limit spending from the outset in order to avoid bidding frenzy

For auction advice see www.ukauctionhelp.co.uk

Sources: Adapted from *Sunday Times* (UK), 6 July 2003 and *Sunday Times (UK)* Doors, 10 August 2003, with additional material from *Marketing Business*, June 2003

QUESTIONS

Brief feedback on these questions is included at the back of the book.

Question 4.1

Why do people shop?

Question 4.2

Can e-shopping satisfy shoppers as much as bricks shopping does?

Question 4.3

How can the mechanistic process of e-shopping satisfy shoppers' social motives?

Question 4.4

What can e-retailers do to provide enjoyment and social benefits for e-shoppers?

FURTHER READING

Chaston, Ian (2001) *e-Marketing Strategy,* Maidenhead: McGraw Hill. This is a comprehensive textbook on Internet marketing.

Dennis, Charles, Harris, Lisa and Sandhu, Balraj (2002) 'From bricks to clicks: understanding the e-consumer', *Qualitative Market Research – An International Journal,* 5 (4): 281–290.

Harris, Lisa and Dennis, Charles (2002) *Marketing the e-Business,* London: Routledge. This is one of the few marketing texts written specifically for e-business. It has useful chapters for communicating with the e-consumer on relationship and multi-channel marketing.

Lundquist, Leslie Heeter (1998) *Selling On Line For Dummies,* Foster City, MI: IDG. Written for US readers, this is a simple guide to promotion and all aspects of selling online.

Tiernan, Bernadette (2000) *E-tailing,* Chicago, IL: Dearborn. This is one of the few texts on e-retailing, written for a US audience, with useful material for communicating with the e-consumer.

Wilson, Ralph *Planning Your Internet Marketing Strategy: A Doctor Ebiz Guide,* New York: John Wiley & Sons. Written for US readers, this is a practical guide to Internet marketing strategy.

REFERENCES

Ang, S.H., Leong, S.M. and Lim, J. (1997) 'The mediating influence of pleasure and arousal on layout and signage effects', *Journal of Retailing and Consumer Services,* 4 (1): 13–24.

Babin, B.J., Darden, W.R. and Griffin, M. (1994) 'Work and/or fun: measuring hedonic and utilitarian shopping value', *Journal of Consumer Research*, 20: 644–656.

BBC News (2003) *Primeval Shopping Instincts Revealed*, www.news.bbc.co.uk [updated 17 September 2003].

BCSC (2001) *Future Shock or eHype?: The Impact of Online Shopping on UK Retail Property*, London: British Council of Shopping Centres/The College of Estate Management.

Berkowitz, E.N., Walton, J.R. and Walker, O.C. (1979) 'In-home shoppers: the market for innovative distribution systems', *Journal of Retailing*, 55 (Summer): 15–33.

Berry, L.L. (1969) 'The components of department store image: a theoretical and empirical analysis', *Journal of Retailing*, 45 (1): 3–20.

Boulding, K.E. (1956) *The Image*, Ann Arbor, MI: University of Michigan.

Buss, D.N. (1989) 'Sex differences in human mate preferences: evolutionary hypotheses tested in 37 cultures', *Behavioural and Brain Sciences*, 12: 1–14.

Childers, T.L., Carr, C.L., Peck, J. and Carson, S. (2001) 'Hedonic and utilitarian motivations for online retail shopping behaviour', *Journal of Retailing*, 77: 511–535.

Denison, T. (2003) 'Men and women arguing when shopping is genetic', *News Shop*, Exeter University, www.ex.ac.uk/news/newsshop/htm [accessed 22 September 2003].

Dennis, C.E. (2004) 'The savannah hypothesis of shopping', *Eleventh International Conference on Recent Advances in Retailing and Services Science*, EIRASS, Prague.

Dennis, C.E. and Hilton, J. (2001) 'Shoppers' motivations in choices of shopping centres', *Eighth International Conference on Recent Advances in Retailing and Services Science*, EIRASS, Vancouver, Canada.

Dennis, C.E. and Papamatthaiou, E-K. (2003) 'Shoppers motivations for e-shopping', *Recent Advances in Retailing and Services Science, 6th International Conference*, EIRASS, Portland, Oregon, August 7–10.

Dennis, C.E. and Richardson, O. (2004) 'e-Retail: paradoxes for suppliers and consumers', in L. Harris and L. Budd (eds) *e-Business: Reality or Rhetoric*, London: Routledge.

Dennis, C.E., Marsland, D. and Cockett, W.A. (1999) 'Why do people shop where they do?', *Recent Advances in Retailing and Services Science, Sixth International Conference*, EIRASS, Eindhoven, The Netherlands,

Dennis, C.E., Harris, L. and Sandhu, B. (2002a) 'From bricks to clicks: understanding the e-consumer', *Qualitative Market Research – An International Journal*, 5 (4): 281–290.

Dholakia, R.R. (1999) 'Going shopping: key determinants of shopping behaviour and motivations', *International Journal of Retail and Distribution Management*, 27 (4–5): 154.

Dholakia, R.R. and Chiang, K.-P. (2003) 'Shoppers in cyberspace: are they from Venus or Mars and does it matter?', *Journal of Consumer Psychology*, 13 (1/2): 171–176.

Dholakia, R.R. and Uusitalo, O. (2002) 'Switching to electronix stores: consumer characteristics and the perception of shopping benefits', *International Journal of Retail and Distribution Management*, 30 (10): 459–469.

Doidge, R. and Higgins, C. (2000) *The Big Dot.com Con*, London: Colliers Conrad Ritblat Erdman.

Donovan, R.J., Rossiter, J.R., Marcoolyn, G. and Nesdale, A. (1994) 'Store atmosphere and purchasing behavior', *Journal of Retailing*, 70 (3): 283–294.

Donthu, N. and Garcia, A. (1999) 'The Internet shopper', *Journal of Advertising Research*, 39 (3).

Elliot, R. (1994) 'Addictive consumption: function and fragmentation in post-modernity', *Journal of Consumer Policy*, 17: 159–179.

English, W.D. (1990) 'Videotex: Pandora's Box for retailers', *Journal of Direct Marketing*, 4 (2): 7–18.

eTypes (2001) *Who's Buying Online? UK Online 2001*, London: eTypes/CACI.

Fenech, T. (2002) 'Exploratory study into WAP (Wireless Application Protocol) shopping', *International Journal of Retail and Distribution Management*, 30 (10): 482–497.

Fenech, T. (2003) 'Factors influencing intention to adopt wireless shopping', in J.E. Lewin (ed.) *Proceedings of World Marketing Congress*, Perth, Western Australia, Academy of Marketing Science, p. 729.

Fenech, T. and O'Cass, A. (2001) 'Internet users' adoption of Web retailing: user and product dimensions', *Journal of Product and Brand Management*, 10 (6): 361–381.

Fink, H.J., Fink, R.M. and Riesner, D. (1971) *Dirty Harry* (movie) (Siegel, D., ed./ producer/director), Hollywood, CA.: Warner Bros.

Forsythe, S.M. and Shi, B. (2003) 'Consumer patronage and risk perceptions in Internet shopping', *Journal of Business Research*, 56: 867–875.

Gillett, P.L. (1970) 'A profile of urban in-home shoppers', *Journal of Marketing*, 1 (34) (July): 40–45.

GVU (1998) 'Eighth user survey', *Graphic, Visualization, & Usability Center*, www. gvu.gatech.edu/user.surveys/survey_1998 [accessed 7 October 1998].

Harris, K. (1998) 'Women on the Net II: the female-friendly site', *Sporting Goods Business*, 31 (13): 16.

Harris, L. and Dennis, C.E. (2002) *Marketing the e-Business*, London,: Routledge.

Haubl, G. and Poplowski Leszczyc, P.T.L. (2003) 'Bidding frenzy and product valuation in ascending-bid auctions', *Tenth International Conference on Recent Advances in Retailing and Services Science*, EIRASS, Portland, Oregon.

Hisrich, R.D., Dornoff, R.J. and Kernan, J.B. (1972) 'Perceived risk in store selection', *Journal of Marketing Research*, 9: 435–439.

Jones, M.A. (1999) 'Entertaining shopping experiences: an exploratory investigation', *Journal of Retailing and Consumer Services*, 6: 129–139.

Jupiter Communications (2001) *Market Forecast Report*, Darien, CT.: Jupiter Communications.

Kimber, C. (2001) *Researching Online Buying's Offline Impact*, London: CACI.

Kolesar, M.B. and Galbraith, R.W. (2000) 'A services-marketing perspective on e-retailing: implications for e-retailers and directions for further research', *Internet Research: Electronic Networking Applications and Policy*, 10 (5): 424–438.

Lindquist, J.D. (1974) 'Meaning of image: a survey of empirical and hypothetical evidence', *Journal of Retailing*, 50 (4): 29–38, 116.

Lindquist, J.D. and Kaufman-Scarborough, C. (2000) 'Browsing and purchasing activity in selected non-store settings: a contrast between female and male shoppers', *Retailing 2000: Launching the New Millennium, Proceedings of the Sixth Triennial National Retailing Conference, the Academy of Marketing Science and the American Collegiate Retailing Association*, Hofstra University: Columbus, Ohio.

Lundquist, L.H. (1998) *Selling On Line For Dummies*, Foster City, MI: IDG.

Lunt, P. (2000) 'The virtual consumer', *Virtual Society? Delivering the Virtual Promise? From Access to Use in the Virtual Society,* ESRC presentation led by Brunel University, London, 19 June.

Machleit, K.A. and Mantel, S.P. (2001) 'Emotional response and shopping satisfaction: moderating effects of shopper attributions', *Journal of Business Research*, 54: 97–106.

Meekings, A., Russell, C., Fuller, M. and Hewson, W. (2003) *Profit or Pain from Your User Experience*, London: Hewson Consulting Group.

Midgley, D.F. and Dowling, G.R. (1993) 'A longitudinal study of product form innovation: the interaction between predispositions and social messages', *Journal of Consumer Research*, 19: 611–625.

Miller, D. (1998) *A Theory of Shopping*, London: Polity.

Miyazaki, A.D. and Fernandez, A. (2001) 'Consumer perceptions of privacy and security risks for online shopping', *The Journal of Consumer Affairs*, 35 (1): 27–44.

NetValue (2001) *Home Internet Use Continues to Grow in the UK*, NetValue, London, www.netvalue.com.

Nielsen NetRatings (2003) www.nielsen-netratings.com [accessed August].

Parsons, A.G. (2002) 'Non-functional motives for online shoppers: why we click', *Journal of Consumer Marketing*, 19 (5): 380–392.

Pavitt, D. (1997) 'Retailing and the high street: the future of the electronic home shopping industry', *International Journal of Retail and Distribution Management*, 25 (1): 28–43.

Phau, I. and Poon, S.M. (2000) 'Factors influencing the types of products and services purchased over the Internet', *Internet Research: Electronic Networking Applications and Policy*, 10 (2): 102–113.

Reynolds, F.D. (1974) 'An analysis of catalog buying behavior', *Journal of Marketing*, 38 (July): 47–51.

Reynolds, J. (2000) 'Pricing dynamics and European retailing: direct and indirect impacts of e-commerce', *Proceedings of the International EARCD Conference on Retail Innovation* (CD-ROM), European Association for Education and Research in Commercial Distribution, ESADE, Barcelona.

Rohm, A.J. and Swaminathan, V. (2004) 'A typology of online shoppers based on shopping motivations,' *Journal of Business Research*, 57 (7): 748–757.

Salam, A.F., Rao, H.R. and Pegels, C.C. (1998) 'An investigation of consumer-perceived risk on electronic commerce transactions: the role of institutional trust and economic incentive in a social exchange framework', *Proceedings of Conference for the Association of Information Systems (AIS)*, Baltimore, Maryland.

Sauer, P., Young, M. and Talarzyk, W.W. (1989) 'The potential impact of emerging communication technologies on distribution channel', *Journal of Direct Marketing*, 3 (4): 28–37.

Shim, S. and Eastlick, M.A. (1998) 'The hierarchical influence of personal values on mall shopping attitude and behaviour', *Journal of Retailing*, 74 (1) (Spring): 139–160.

Shim, S. and Mahoney, M.Y. (1991) 'Electronic shoppers and nonshoppers among Videotex users', *Journal of Direct Marketing*, 5 (3): 29–38.

Shim, S., Eastlick, M.A. and Lotz, S. (2000) 'Assessing the impact of Internet shopping on store shopping among mall shoppers and Internet users', *Journal of Shopping Center Research*, 7 (2).

Sit, J., Merrilees, W. and Birch, D. (2003) 'Entertainment-seeking shopping centre patrons: the missing segments', *International Journal of Retail and Distribution Management*, 31 (2): 80–94.

Smith, R.B. and Sherman, E. (1993) 'Effects of store image and mood on consumer behaviour: a theoretical and empirical analysis', *Advances in Consumer Research*, 20 (1): 631.

Spence, H.E., Engel, J.F. and Blackwell, R.D. (1970) 'Perceived risk in mail-order and retail store buying', *Journal of Marketing Research*, 7: 364–369.

Spies, K., Hesse, F. and Loesch, K. (1997) 'Store atmosphere, mood and purchasing behaviour', *International Journal of Research in Marketing*, 14: 1–17.

Tauber, E.M. (1972) 'Why do people shop?' *Journal of Marketing*, 36 (October): 46–59.

Tauber, E.M. (1995) 'Why do people shop?' *Marketing Management*, 4 (2): 58–60.

Underhill, P. (1999) *Why We Buy*, London: Orion.

Verdict (2001) *Verdict on Electronic Shopping, 2001*, London: Verdict.

Vijayasarathy, L.R. and Jones, J.M. (2000) 'Print and Internet catalog shopping: assessing attitudes and intentions', *Internet Research*, 10 (3): 191–202.

Vincent, A., Clark, H. and English, A. (2000) 'Retail distribution: a multi-channel traffic jam', *International Journal of New Product Development & Innovation Management*, 2 (2): 179–196.

Vrechopoulos, A. (2001) 'Virtual store atmosphere in Internet retailing: measuring virtual retail store layout effects on consumer buying behaviour', unpublished Ph.D. thesis, Brunel University, London.

Westbrook, R.A. and Black, W.C. (1985) 'A motivation-based shopper typology', *Journal of Retailing*, 61 (1): 78–103.

Wolfinbarger, M. and Gilly, M.C. (2002) *.comQ: Dimensionalizing, Measuring and Predicting Quality of the e-Tail Experience*, Working Paper No. 02–100, Cambridge, MA: Marketing Science Institute.

Wolfinbarger, M. and Gilly, M.C. (2003) 'eTailQ: dimensionalizing, measuring and predicting etail quality', *Journal of Retailing*, 79 (3): 183–198.

WEB LINKS

www.emarketer.com
e-Marketing statistics and reports.

www.etypes.info
Demographics, classifications and consumer e-shopping behaviour.

www.forrester.com
Internet usage data.

www.nielsen-netratings.com
Performance and viewing ratings for Internet sites and advertisers.

www.nma.co.uk
New media news items.

www.nua.com/surveys
Internet statistics.

Chapter 5

Information search on the Web

LINKS TO OTHER CHAPTERS

- Chapter 2 – e-Retailing in practice
- Chapter 3 – Integration of e-retailing into an organization
- Chapter 4 – Understanding and communicating with the e-consumer
- Chapter 8 – Branding on the Web
- Chapter 9 – e-Malls

KEY LEARNING POINTS

After completing this chapter you will have an understanding of:

- The difference between the clicks and bricks experiences
- Shoppers' search behaviour on the Web
- Search engines
- Directories
- Ways to improve your Web 'visibility' and monitor the use of your pages

ORDERED LIST OF SUB-TOPICS

- Clicks and bricks
- The background to searching the Internet and the Web
- Surveys on what people do and where people 'go' on the Web
- Searching and finding on the Web

'CLICKS AND BRICKS'

In the e-retail literature, much is made of the *similarities* between the new electronic ways (clicks) to sell goods to consumers and the traditional ways (bricks). One can talk about e-stores, e-shop fronts, e-shoppers, e-malls and so on. In this chapter, we highlight some of the *differences* between clicks and bricks. These differences arise from the totally different technologies which are used in a clicks store compared with a bricks store, and the totally different approach used by e-shoppers to find goods and services, to compare prices and to generally browse around. The essential concept is *search* – the process by which e-shoppers find information about products and services.

THE BACKGROUND TO SEARCHING THE INTERNET AND THE WEB

The Internet is a worldwide network of servers and machines, originally set up (as the ARPAnet) to facilitate information exchange between US government contractors and university researchers (Wolinsky, 1999). From the earliest days of the Internet, a major activity has been *searching* for information. As the Internet grew, a variety of tools were set up to help users perform searching to find the required information.

Nowadays, the focus of activity is the World Wide Web, which uses Internet technology with an improved user interface, making huge amounts of information available to the end-user, often a home computer user. Much of this information is about products and services for mass distribution provided by e-retailers.

The interface employed by most users is a graphical Web browser, typically Microsoft Internet Explorer or Netscape Navigator. In practice much of the information is textual in nature, with graphical layout (such as the use of lists) to provide structure and additional graphics to provide other information and 'decoration'. Although much has been made of the idea of e-malls (see Chapter 9), where a group of e-shops congregate together like a conventional shopping mall, the typical user experience involves focusing on a specific website often linked to one company's offerings.

SURVEYS ON WHAT PEOPLE DO AND WHERE PEOPLE 'GO' ON THE WEB

A computer scientist would say that what e-shoppers actually do is to use a Web browser to examine data from the Web rendered into graphical images. A typical user would say something rather different – the experience is that you explore a virtual world and that at any moment you are at one 'place' in that world. From then you might explore the place more deeply or move on to other places which are linked.

Many surveys have been done to help us understand why people use the Web. According to Rodgers and Sheldon (2002), there are four primary motives for Internet use: researching (in the most general sense), shopping, socializing and generalized surfing (for enjoyment).

Shehan (2002) carried out a cluster analysis of types of Internet sessions, finding that 'I need to find some information' was a significantly stronger motivation than all others. Visiting news sites, using search engines, searching for product information and using online databases together accounted for 34 per cent of users' online time. Searching for product information alone accounted for 7 per cent of online time, compared with only 1.7 per cent spent e-shopping. Eighty-five per cent of all Internet traffic comes from 13 major search engines (Gehan, 2003). Information search is important for consumers and it is important for e-retailers too: in a US study, the use of the Internet to search for information was the strongest predictor of e-shopping intention (Shim *et al.*, 2001). In addition, information search improved shoppers' attitudes towards e-retailing a nd helped overcome the perceived barriers to e-shopping. Similarly, Fink and Laupase (2000) carried out an experiment with 30 Australian and 30 Malaysian participants who evaluated selected websites. They found evidence of a relationship between products and services and news stories. The authors argued that the impact of products and services displayed could be maximized through the presence of news stories providing information about recent developments. In Chapter 4 we referred briefly to our study investigating shoppers' motivations in e-shopping (Dennis and Papamatthaiou, 2003; discussed in more detail in *e-Economy: Rhetoric or Business Reality?*, in the same series as this book; Dennis and Richardson, 2004). The respondents were a sample of 150 undergraduate students. Enjoyment was one of the main motivations and 'involvement' was one of the most important enjoyment dimensions. In line with previous work drawing attention to 'variety seeking' (Rohm and Swaminathan, 2004), the most popular sites were Amazon (www.amazon.co.uk), CD WOW (www.cd-wow.co.uk) and eBay (www.ebay.co.uk), i.e. 'hedonic' e-retailers (Childers *et al.*, 2001).

Amazon and eBay are the UK's top two sites in terms of audience numbers (Nielsen NetRatings (2003) – see Case studies 2.1 (pp. 46–51) and 4.1 (pp. 104–105) respectively and the comparison in Mini case study 8.1 (pp. 178–179). In fact, the worldwide success of eBay has made it the biggest e-commerce site in the world (NAMNEWS, 2003). It is particularly strong on involvement, with visitors spending on average 1 hour and 11 minutes on the site, one of the longest of UK e-retailers. Visitors return to the site frequently to check on items they are buying or selling. There is also a feedback feature on sellers that helps to build trust, and eBay is one of few UK e-retailers to achieve over one billion page views per month. Such sites enthusiastically embrace the 'involvement' aspect of enjoyment with features such as chat rooms, bulletin boards, customer written stories and product reviews, suggestion boxes and personalization of the website offers. In short, many of the features that make these sites involving, enjoyable and successful are based on satisfying shoppers' needs for information in one form or another. Some e-retailers use surfers' needs for information as a successful method of directing traffic to their sites. For example, outdoor equipment supplier L L Bean (www.llbean.com) provides information on national parks, and chemist/drugstore Boots specializes in nutrition and health information. See Case studies 5.2 (pp. 126–127) and 3.1 (pp. 71–72) respectively.

SEARCHING AND FINDING ON THE WEB

Shoppers, then, spend a lot of time *searching*, and e-retailers are, of course, most interested in what they *find* ('Seek, and ye shall find!'). They would like shoppers to find information on their products and services at their virtual store, and to find (and execute) ordering and payment processes. They thus need to understand what technologies the shoppers use, and how they use these technologies, in order to improve the chances of sales and services on the Web. Thus, e-retailers who can help satisfy surfers' wants for information have a head start in selling to those customers.

THE AVERAGE WEB SESSION

Let us consider what average users do in an average Web session:

- The users sit down and start their Web browser, often set up so that the initial screen (the home page) points to some major website, and it displays a list of links to other sites and services. For example, the home page might be set to the Yahoo! main page (www.yahoo.com). Possibly they might decide to *focus* immediately on some site they know about and type in the Web address (URL) or use 'favourites' or 'bookmarks' to access that site.

- Otherwise, they look through the home page visually and *evaluate* the list, and make some decision based on what they are interested in.
- They might then decide to access a *search engine*, for example Google, (www.google.com) and, by entering suitable search phrases and hitting the Search button, instruct the engine to produce a list of relevant web pages with a brief summary of their contents. Having got that list, it is then scanned and evaluated.
- They might decide to examine a *directory system* related to their search goals, and scan through that and evaluate items.
- The process of scanning through lists for relevant items and/or using search engines is repeated until the relevant items are found. If nothing suitable is found, the search is refocused or *abandoned* at any point, or the search goals may be refocused from information retrieved, deliberately or not (some advertisement might pop up). The users might even go directly to some site, even if it does not come up on a directory or search-engine list, if they know the Web address (URL).

Several important concepts arise from the above considerations. Let us now examine these in more detail. They are:

- focus
- directories
- search engines.

FOCUS

Suppose you want to purchase some hair conditioner. If you go down to the local town centre and locate a major shopping mall or high street area, you have expectations as to what you might find there and the ways you can quickly locate items of interest. For example, you would expect to be able to find a chain pharmacy store in a few minutes – in the United Kingdom, a branch of Boots or Superdrug. Having found such a store, you would expect to locate quickly a section with hair products and, equally quickly, a range of shampoos and conditioners. What you might also do is use some sort of directory (possibly the Yellow Pages) to locate stores of interest.

Compared with the bricks experience, an e-shopper on the Web operates in a rather different way. On the Web, a user starts up a Web browser with some initial page, perhaps that of their Internet service provider. They then start searching for the item required, following appropriate links. Almost certainly they will use some sort of Web search engine.

Obviously, we need to design web pages so that they are usable and attractive to the user. Nielsen (2000) has written extensively on website usability, and has pointed out a number of important considerations. A prime component of making sites usable is clarity and focus. If the user finds the site difficult to use, and the design messy and unfocused, they will abandon the site and turn to searching elsewhere. Neilsen suggests some standards to create user consistency, good design and relevance, leading to a unified user experience across the site. As we discuss in detail later, we also need to make automatic Web search systems (search engines) 'notice' our pages and rank them highly.

DIRECTORIES

People like lists, from the Seven Wonders of the Ancient World to the Top 20 pop songs. Directories are lists compiled around some specific topic, such as the telephone directory and trade directories. In the early days of the Web, people (editors) compiled lists of the most popular sites. As the number of sites grew, the lists became rather long. To improve accessibility, they were split into categories and sub-categories. Well-known Web directories include Yahoo! (www.yahoo.com) and MSN (www.msn.com).

Let us consider Yahoo! in a little detail. Yahoo! is compiled by human editors who also create a short description that is shown alongside the link to the Web address. The editors categorize the topics logically, in a way a search engine does not. For example, a category listed on the Yahoo! main page might be *Shopping*. This might lead to *Electronics*, which might lead to *Cell Phones*. This might point to a list of cell phone items e-shoppers might be interested in.

This hierarchical arrangement ensures that shoppers can fairly quickly get to items in which they are interested.

Improvements in search engines mean that directories are losing some value, but they are still useful for locating groups of relevant websites on a similar topic. It should be noted that directories of this nature can be very wide in scope, or they could be more focused, in the nature of a trade directory. To ensure contact with potential customers, e-retailers might consider something much more focused.

One point: note that Yahoo!, for example, is rather more than just a directory. It includes a search engine (formerly, the Google engine), and a range of services such as mail and instant messaging. Such a service, which acts as a 'port' to many other Web and Internet services, is known as a *portal*. Portal owners hope that users will use their portal as their home page and point of departure, hence making them targets for selective advertising and other delights. This does make portal sites attractive (if expensive) places to place web banners and other advertising material. The big portals are hard at work implementing a 'Search, Find and Obtain' model across information, shopping and entertainment channels. The effectiveness can be demonstrated by usage figures: MSN and Yahoo! are the most popular websites worldwide, each with 83 million users (eMarketer, 2003).

SEARCH ENGINES

Search engines on the Internet have been around some time. The first ones actually did a 'live' search of remote file systems holding documents (FTP servers), looking for filenames which matched search terms. When the Web became popular, researchers built Web search engines to try out new software and hardware on the huge amounts of data that became available. Later on, these experimental systems were commercialized. Well-known commercial search engine systems are Google (www.google.com) and AltaVista (www.altavista.com.). There are actually *two* sorts of search engine involved.

First, programs called 'crawlers' gather information about websites. This is done by starting with a list of 'well-known sites' and from there searching the sites they reference. This is an automatic process. The HTML (HyperText Markup Language) code corresponding to each web page is scanned for links to other sites. In the HTML, such a link will appear like this:

<a href='http://www.gre.ac.uk/schools/index.html'>

If this link is followed, the corresponding web page will also have links, and these too are followed. This process is continued, until millions of web pages are accessed. Each page is analysed for content. What this means is all the information in the page HTML – the title, the text of the body of the page and any additional information tagged on to the page (metainformation) – is extracted and examined for relevance, according to rules set up by the owner of the crawler. All this information is then put into a database (also called a catalogue or index). This process is repeated at regular intervals, possibly every two weeks.

The database is indexed on content, and is made available to the e-shopper via a Web interface. Given some *search term*, such as 'shampoo', the database is searched for matching terms and the corresponding page URLs are retrieved, together with the page titles and summaries of the page contents. This information is then formatted into a web page which is returned to the e-shopper. So the user inputs the word 'shampoo' and obtains a page of references to websites involving that term.

A few technical points:

- Following of links from any one page is only done to a certain 'depth', which means that it is important to put significant information on the Home Page or just a little 'below'.

- *Web crawlers* see a web page split into 'frames' as a number of pages, and therefore explore these less deeply than pages without frames.
  Frames are best avoided if you want Web crawlers to extract as much information as possible from your pages.
- Web crawlers are not clever enough to deal with databases (for example, catalogues) which might be accessed from your pages. Really significant information should be able to be accessed as plain HTML pages, rather than by using some catalogue systems. Catalogues are really meant for human users.

Note that the process of database construction is automatic, but guided by concepts such as *well-known sites* and *relevance*. It is also possible to notify a search-engine system of a site for inclusion, which again guides the crawler. Websites that meet the criteria are added to the index whether they have been submitted for inclusion or not.

Popular search engines

Google (www.google.com) is the world's most popular search site, accounting for 60 per cent of all searches (Gehan, 2003). Google compiles its catalogue of over four billion web pages very week or so. Despite being faster, larger and more efficient than competitors, even Google indexes only a fraction of the total web pages available. However, the coverage is very wide.

Although most e-shoppers use search engines, the typical user is usually not willing to spend much time formulating search terms, and often gets rather frustrated if the information they require is not returned. They might abandon the search, or perhaps try another search engine. Many systems offer Boolean searching, which means that search terms and phrases can be linked, for example:

Digital camera AND Canon AND inexpensive

Some systems also offer the option of fine-tuning the results by allowing the user to input terms used to rank (put in some order of precedence) the returned results. The average e-shopper is not usually willing to learn how to set up these more sophisticated queries. They want a reasonable set of results with as little work formulating the query as possible. Otherwise, they tend to give up and try some other method.

They might use *metacrawlers*, which bring together results from various search engines and directories. Coverage is wide but operation can be cumbersome, with little fine-tuning possible, so these are not that popular.

The most useful systems as far as many e-shoppers are concerned are systems that allow natural language, for example a query such as:

Where I can buy inexpensive Canon digital cameras?

Systems such as *AskJeeeves* (www.ask.com) specialize in such natural language queries. Observation by the authors shows that users often pose their questions in natural language whatever the system! They do this because no one has ever told them that they cannot, and because reasonable results are often returned, since many search engine systems filter *noise words* (such as 'the', 'and' and 'but') and use the remaining words as search terms and for ranking the results. Systems such as Google also make suggestions in an attempt to correct spelling results.

Growth in search engine activity

Most of the growth in e-shopping (according to the *New York Times*, 4 December 2003) is being driven by search engines like Google and other sites like the online marketplace eBay. Improved search quality, pioneered by Google, has made search engines an easy and efficient way for people to find things online – and for advertisers to find customers. At the same time, eBay, a haven for small businesses, has become the fastest-growing major shopping site, and much of Amazon's growth has come from serving as an intermediary for independent retailers. Another example is that of Visa, which noted that online sales, including travel, have increased considerably, much more than sales using Visa cards with traditional retailers.

According to eMarketer, a firm that compiles Internet research, online sales are rising by nearly 30 per cent per year, and soon 100 million people a year are expected to make online purchases. A PricewaterhouseCoopers survey indicates that:

> not only are search capabilities and product information important to online shoppers when selecting an online shopping site, but they can help e-retailers turn shoppers into buyers and make the online shopping experience more like the on-land one. Search functions are the most popular online shopping feature. The majority of online shoppers – 77 per cent – have used a search function while shopping online and most of these users are satisfied enough with search functions to use them on a regular basis. In addition to being the most popular features, survey results indicate that search capabilities and product information are most important to online shoppers when selecting an online shopping site. Search functionality and product information are ranked as the most important online shopping features by 43 per cent and 40 per cent of online shoppers, respectively.
>
> (PricewaterhouseCoopers, 2003)

Mini case study 5.1: POSTOPTICS – WEB ADVERTISING REVENUES

Postoptics is a small firm but is the UK's leading mail-order contact-lens supplier. Contact lenses by post are a niche focus market; they are used by only 6 per cent of the population, and at any one time only 3 per cent of those are looking for a new pair. Boss Trevor Rowley faced the problem of communicating with this small proportion of the population.

Rowley had tried conventional media advertising, but found that the most cost-effective results have come from 'pay-per-click' advertising with search engines such as Google, Yahoo!, Lycos and others. Pay-per-click is now the fastest growing form of Web advertising and, according to Google, generates five times as many hits as other types of online advertising. The advertising consists of listings that appear to the side of or above the list of websites generated by the search. Advertisers bid for keywords that are relevant to their businesses – the higher the bid, the higher in the listings. Bids may range from as low as £0.10 for specialist terms like 'multi-focal contact lenses' up to double figures in pounds to be highly placed for broad terms such as 'finance' or 'insurance'. This type of advertising can be ideal for small firms because it allows them to compete with larger companies on a level playing field.

The important thing for the advertiser is to find the right keywords. For example 'optical' might get many leads, but 'disposable contact lenses' would be a less expensive search term. A mix of generic and specific words is probably best. Some small companies like Postoptic bid on 20 or so terms; big companies can use 1,000 or more.

The benefit for the advertisers is that they only pay for customers who click through to their website from sponsored links. Postoptic has used listing companies such as Overture (the US pioneer) and Espotting (UK) to provide listings on sites such as MSN and eBay and also has had good results with Google. As a result, about 60 per cent of Postoptic's £5 million sales are now online. It costs an average of £12 to acquire a customer and the typical order value is £50 to £60.

Source: Summarized and adapted from *Sunday Times* (UK) Business, 9 November 2003

Mini case study 5.2: DAVID STEAD ORCHIDS (www.orchid-guide.co.uk/~davidstead)

David Stead Orchids is a small to medium-sized supplier of orchid plants and orchid-related sundries, based in Leeds, UK. Its website was created by a local Web developer.

Focus

The firm has a (fairly) memorable URL, which they quote in their advertisements in the orchid press. The site has an internal database, which the e-shopper can use to home down on what they require.

Directories

The firm appears in a number of directories, for example The Wedding Network (www.wsn-uk.co.uk/England/West_Yorkshire/Flowers), Easy Exotics (www.easyexotics.co.uk) and the Stephen H. Smith Garden Centre (www.shrubs.co.uk).

Search engines

All pages are correctly titled, and meta-information is used (description and keywords). Searches on the phrase 'David Stead Orchids' gave 39 hits on Google and 39 hits on AltaVista. Using the metacrawler Dogpile (www.dogpile.com) gave 49 hits!

The site is an example of how a small, local company can achieve international visibility by using the three main techniques mentioned.

MONITORING THE USE OF YOUR WEB PAGES

Having set up your site, you need to monitor what use is made of it. The simplest approach is to add a page counter to each major page. The information from this can be rather limited, but at least you can find out how many visits ('hits') have been made over a given period.

Every time a web page is accessed, information is recorded in a log file on the Web server. These logs can be provided to you by either your IT personnel or by the company that 'hosts' your pages (sometimes at an additional cost). The log stores information about the page URL, the time and date of access, the type of browsers used for access, (possibly) the location of the user and so on. By themselves, the logs are quite difficult to process, but there are log analysis programs which can produce useful tables and charts which summarize activity. By examining the logs, it is even possible to see what Web crawlers are accessing your system! You might get a few surprises here, and read information about visits from experimental crawlers at universities, and from Web crawlers run by institutions like the US Defense Department.

SOME PRACTICAL CONCLUSIONS

A number of things can be done to make your website more visible.

First, encourage shoppers to *focus* on your site. There are a number of aspects of the concept of focus that have arisen from the above discussion. Nielsen (2000) considers focus in the context of web-page design and suggests retaining the attention of users by building consistent style ad pages, built to good design standards, and with relevant content.

Advertisements, which can be added on to directory and Web search engine web pages are a means of changing the focus of a user's search towards your pages.

Make it easy for users to get to your site by choosing a memorable URL, for example www.gardenplants.com (not www.somesite.com/gardens/).

Advertise your website URL in your conventional advertising (magazines, flyers and so on). Winemakers have printed the URL on their bottles in order to bring the site to the attention of users.

Make shoppers want to look at your website by constantly changing the information. One way to do this is to link the site to a product catalogue database, so that shoppers can search for the latest up-to-date product information.

Ensure your website is well designed. Use a professional website designer. Do *not* use your computing staff – they can build you a site but are (probably) not professionals in human–computer interaction.

Submit your website URL to major Web directory systems. But be careful of offers you may receive to list your web page URLs in directories. Some of these are like offers to list your profile in a directory of 'World Business Leaders'. It might be that the only people who ever access these directories are the subscribers who have paid a substantial fee!

Link popularity engineering*

Ensure that your URL appears in listings relevant to your product area. This approach is sometimes called *Link popularity engineering*.

As mentioned briefly in Chapter 4, search engines use link popularity in locating and ranking sites – the term refers to both the number of other sites linking to

*This section summarized and adapted from www.webpromote.com, originally from *Internet Marketing Challenge*.

the measured site and especially the importance and relevance of the linking sites. Improving link popularity raises a site in search engine rankings. To measure your own site on Alta Vista, Google and Hotbot, visit www.linkpopularity.com. View a comparison of your site's link popularity relative to your competitors and to other well-known sites at www.marketleap.com/publinkpop. Some ideas for engineering higher link popularity ratings on search engines follow below.

Instead of a single site that covers many different keywords, separate each product or service into groupings. Use related specialist sites that all link to the 'mother site' and to each other. Each should cover its own niche based on a core theme. The sites should be about the same size, say around five pages. Ideally, locate each on a different ISP. A sample matrix can be viewed at www.marketingchallenge.com/chronicles/278/matrix.gif.

'Seed' your website Home Page with meta-information. At the beginning of a web page, it is possible to add extra information about the content of the page. This information does not get displayed, but is used by the Web crawlers to rank and index your pages. The information is basically a description of the web page and a set of key words provided to assist the indexing process.

For example, the Norwegian wood-carver's site at sherpe.com/carving/index.html has key words, which suggests a marketing function for specific products: meta name='keywords' content='ale, ale bowl, art, bowl, carving, chip, chip carving, craft, family, hand-carved, mangle board, norsk, norwegian, Norway, ole, Ostrem, sherpe, skjerpe, Tomtengson, Wang, wood'.

Isle of Man Kippers (www.isleofmankippers.com/kippers-main.htm) introduces terms such as 'cooking' and 'recipes', which implies that they are going beyond marketing into an educational function: kippers, herring, specialist food, gourmet food, fish, smoked fish, sea fish, Isle of Man, Manx, Manx kippers, Irish Sea, cooking, recipes.

Title all your pages. The title line is always used by Web crawlers for indexing. If it is missing, the page might be ignored.

Get a listing in Yahoo! It can be difficult to achieve but can be worth a paid listing: deadlock.com/promote/search-engines/yahoo.html.

Get a listing in the Excite/LookSmart paid inclusion program. As with Yahoo!, other search engine managers consider that, if you are listed in LookSmart, your site must be worth listing. A single step submits your page to both, and also supplies results to AltaVista, MSN and iWon: listings.looksmart.com/?synd=none&chan=lshomebus.

Get a listing in top directories such as the free Open Directory Project: www.dmoz.org/add.html.

Start an affiliate programme. Affiliates earn a commission when a visitor to their site clicks the link to your sales page and then makes a purchase. Concentrate on sites with related content.

Get links to and from similar high-traffic, quality sites. Look for sites that serve the same audience as your site but are not competitive. Also contact sites that link to your competition. For more information, see www.directhit.com/ and www.about.com.

Get a listing in relevant databases in the Search Engine Guide: www.search engineguide.com/searchengines.html.

Write articles! Become known as an expert in your field by writing articles that you post to your site. Submit these to other websites and *e-zines*. Include *hyperlinks* back to your own site.

In late 2003, a graphic and amusing illustration of the power of link popularity engineering could be seen by entering '*weapons of mass destruction*' into the Google search engine (www.google.com). The top link went to what looked like a standard 'This link cannot be displayed' message, but, on reading, was actually 'These weapons of mass destruction cannot be displayed', followed by witty and satirical text at the expense of government(s) apparently unable at the time to find weapons of mass destruction. At the bottom of the page there was a link to 'Get the WMD 404 tee shirt'. This linked to www.coxar.pwp.blueyonder. co.uk/about.htm, where you could indeed buy the T-shirt and also WMD mug, mouse mat and boxer shorts. There was also a link directly to books from Amazon such as *The Battle for Iraq*.

So how did the WMD site achieve its top Google rating? The answer is a combination of viral marketing and link popularity engineering. The author e-mailed friends and asked them to link their sites to the WMD site, and to pass on the message to their own friends. The network quickly grew to carry enough links to gain top rating on the search term. The WMD story thus illustrates the importance of link popularity engineering, even when based only on links (which may be on reciprocal deals) with virtually no financial investment needed.

CHAPTER SUMMARY

- e-Shoppers are avid users of the Web and use Web search engines and directories to guide their search
- e-Retailers can set up the web pages on their sites to make them more attractive to e-shoppers – to focus their search
- It can be arranged that the web page addresses appear in relevant directories
- It can also be arranged that the web page addresses are picked up by the search engines used by the majority of e-shoppers
- Use Web logs and other systems to determine how often your web pages get accessed

In the following chapter we consider what happens when potential e-shoppers find the e-retail site – the design and interactivity issues.

Case study 5.1: AUBUCHON

When searching Google for 'Christmas light sets', the second-ranked link to appear was Aubuchon Hardware, a family-run New England chain of 140 New England hardware stores. As a result, Aubuchon now sells more light sets in California than in Massachusetts, its home state. 'Search engines are great because we have so many different products', said William E. Aubuchon IV, who runs the website. Aubuchon uses two strategies to have its name appear for any of the 40,000 products. With the help of iProspect, a firm that helps companies improve visibility in search engines, it has tweaked the wording on its web pages to make them closer to the top of search engine results. It also buys text advertisements, typically called sponsored listings, which appear above and to the side of the actual search engine results. Now over 50 per cent of Aubuchon's online business comes from search engines.

'We're not a destination site, like Home Depot [the US leading hardware company], but search engines help people find us when they are looking for a specific product such as Christmas light sets', said Mr Aubuchon. 'Instead of us chasing customers around, on search engines the customers chase us around.' According to Aubuchon, search engine marketing will help the company double its online sales this year.

Source: Summarized and adapted from the *New York Times*, 4 December 2003

Case study 5.2: L L BEAN (www.llbean.com)

In the US, L L Bean has been a pioneer of mail order, selling goods to rural farmers since way back in the mid-1800s. Today, the company has put a reputation for customer responsiveness, helpfulness, cheerfulness and reliability to use in becoming world leader in e-retailing outdoor equipment and clothing, with an efficient, award-winning site. But the L L Bean site is not just about selling – it is packed with useful information about the outdoors. For example, when someone searches for a campground (or campsite in UK parlance), say in British Columbia (Canada), L L Bean comes high up the listings. The link will go immediately to a huge, easily accessible amount of information not just on camping, but also on trails (walks) and activities in national parks all over the world. For instance, the 'Park search' link is ideal to 'Plan your next adventure with . . . 2200 worldwide park listings'.

The home page links easily to clothing, maps, books, camping and outdoor equipment, and outdoor information is always high on the agenda, with, for example, 'Preserving Acadia: L L Bean helps protect Maine's National Park'.

The moral seems to be that a good site does not necessarily do 'hard' selling, and that useful related information can lead surfers to shop from an e-retail site.

QUESTIONS

Brief feedback to these questions is included at the back of the book.

Question 5.1

What is the *one* thing I can do to get my website noticed?

Question 5.2

I put up a good web page some months ago, but nobody is accessing it much nowadays.

FURTHER READING

Chaffey, D., Mayer, R., Johnston, K. and Ellis-Chadwick, F. (2003) *Internet Marketing: Strategy, Implementation and Practice*, Harlow: Pearson Education.

Ray, E. and Ray, D. (1998) *The AltaVista Search Revolution*, Berkeley, CA: Osborne McGraw-Hill.

REFERENCES

Childers, T.L., Carr, P.L. Peck, J. and Carson, S. (2001) 'Hedonic and utilitarian motivations for online retail shopping behaviour', *Journal of Retailing*, 77 (4): 511–535.

Dennis, C. and Papamatthaiou, E.-K. (2003) 'Shoppers' motivations for e-shopping', *Recent Advances in Retailing and Services Science, Sixth International Conference*, The European Institute of Retailing and Services Studies, Portland, Oregon, 7–10 August.

Dennis, C.E. and Richardson, O. (2004) 'e-Retail: paradoxes for suppliers and consumers', in L. Budd and L. Harris (eds), *e-Economy: Rhetoric or Business Reality?*, London: Routledge.

eMarketer (2003) *Portal Plays: Strategies and Developments of the 'Big Three'*, New York: eMarketer.

Fink, D. and Laupase, R. (2000) 'Perceptions of website design characteristics: a Malaysian/Australian comparison', *Internet Research: Electronic Networking Applications and Theory*, 10 (1): 44–55.

Gehan, M. (2003) *Search Engine Marketing: The Essential Best Practice Guide*, www.search-engine-book.co.uk.

NAMNEWS (2003) 'US: eBay tells analysts growth can be sustained', *NAMNEWS: The Original Newsletter for Key Account Managers*, EMR-NAMNEWS, London, www.kamcity.com/namnews.

Nielsen, J. (2000) *Web Usability: The Practice of Simplicity*, Indianapolis: New Riders.

Nielsen NetRatings (2003) www.nielsen-netratings.com.

Price Waterhouse Coopers (2003) www.e-port.ru/corporate/pressa/strategic_perspective.html.

Rodgers, S. and Sheldon, K.M. (2002) 'An improved way to characterise Internet users', *Journal of Advertising Research*, 42 (5): 85–94.

Rohm, A.J. and Swaminathan, V. (2004) 'A typology of online shoppers based on shopping motivations', *Journal of Business Research*, 57 (7): 748–757.

Shehan, K.B. (2002) 'A typology of Internet users' online sessions', *Journal of Advertising Research*, 42 (5): 62–71.

Shim, S., Eastlick, M.A., Lotz, S.L. and Warrington, P. (2001) 'An online prepurchase intentions model: the role of intention to search', *Journal of Retailing*, (77): 397–416.

Wolinsky, A. (1999) *The History of the Internet and the World Wide Web*, Berkeley Heights, NJ: Enslow.

WEB LINKS

www.communicationsteam.com/mb/archive/march2003/main2.htm
David Murphy looks at the fine art of making sure that your website is search engine friendly (see Bibliography).

www.pandia.com
For a European perspective on search engines, lots of information and a helpful free search engine tutorial.

www.search-engine-book.co.uk
Download a free report, rankings test, e-marketing newsletter and more.

www.searchenginewatch.com
Offers a free daily newsletter, *SearchDay*, to keep you up-to-date with developments.

Recommended by Sunday Times *(UK) Doors, 15 June 2003:*

metacrawlers
www.dogpile.co.uk, www.vivisimo.com

engines
www.google.co.uk, www.alltheweb.com

directories
www.search.yahoo.com, www.excite.co.uk

Chapter 6

e-Store design: navigability, interactivity and web atmospherics

LINKS TO OTHER CHAPTERS

- Chapter 1 – The world of e-retailing
- Chapter 7 – e-Service

KEY LEARNING POINTS

After completing this chapter you will have an understanding of:

- The overall nature, purpose and scope of e-store design
- Navigability as a fundamental design issue
- Interactivity as a higher-level e-store design issue
- Design enhancement through web atmospherics
- An integrated approach to e-store design
- The importance of clarifying the objectives and strategy of the e-retailer *before starting* to create or redevelop an e-store design

ORDERED LIST OF SUB-TOPICS

- What is e-store design?
- The purpose and scope of e-store design
- Why is store design more important for e-retailers?
- Start e-store design with navigability
- Progress to interactivity
- Building e-relationships through interactivity

- Enhancements through web atmospherics
- All together for an integrated approach to e-store design
- The role of objectives and strategy in guiding e-store design
- Conclusions
- Chapter summary
- ❖ Case study
- ❖ Questions
- ❖ References and further reading
- ❖ Web links

WHAT IS E-STORE DESIGN?

The purposeful design of the e-retailer's site is usually referred to as *e-store design*. This includes listing products or services for sale, providing product information including a product description and price for each item, enabling users to move about the site, providing a method of ordering and paying for merchandise, and generally listing broader company policies, such as security, privacy and guarantees if given. Apart from providing information, it is also necessary to design in other features, such as graphics and, in some cases, audio.

THE PURPOSE AND SCOPE OF E-STORE DESIGN

Simply put, e-store design is part of the retail mix that helps the e-retailer market their business generally, and more specifically, to sell merchandise. All elements of the retail mix have a role to play, but clearly having a place to buy the merchandise is a fundamental part of the process.

There are some similarities to traditional (offline) retailing in which the shop and the way it is designed (including infrastructure, layout and visual presentation) is a necessary part of the shopping (buying) process. Another similarity to offline retailing is that store design has a *broader* purpose than just being a place to buy. Store design plays a bigger marketing role in that different designs create different images. The store design might convey an image that really reinforces the merchandise in a particular store, which makes it more likely that customers seeking that type of merchandise will purchase something from that particular store.

So it pays both offline and online stores to invest in choosing the right store design that fits the image they want as well as making it easy for customers to buy what they want. The e-retailer and the traditional retailer have to think carefully about basic functional activities like layout movement and checkout, as well as more symbolic issues like creating the right look and feel of the store.

Scope of e-store design includes layout, visuals, interactivity, information search engines, checkout facilities and the posting of policies. Each of these elements needs to be specified, coded and made operational.

Mini case study 6.1: CLOTHING ONLINE SEARCHES (www.gap.com/home_gap)

This is a typical e-retail site that offers catalogue products for consumers to buy. The home page has a menu selection for gender and age for a range of clothing covering uses and seasons. The catalogue items include scanned photographs of garments with a description and price. The site includes a basket for collecting items and functions for purchasing and delivery details.

These direct purchase sites are less popular for consumers than was first thought. It would seem that people prefer to touch and examine certain products before making a decision.

WHY IS STORE DESIGN MORE IMPORTANT FOR E-RETAILERS?

We have already established that store design is important to both traditional retailers and online retailers. The reader may have already guessed that e-store design is relatively more important for online retailers and might even be considered the most important part of their retail mix. Why?

The main reason is that store design has bigger scope with e-retailers. Store design in traditional offline retailing is generally confined to the physical aspects of the store, such as the infrastructure and layout. The online scope of store design is greater because it also includes what used to be covered by interaction with the salesperson. Almost everything has to be covered by what is on the computer screen, so the e-store design is clearly a very important domain. Additionally, areas like customer service and after-sales service that were separate departments in offline retailing, now have to be incorporated into the e-store design. This further increases the scope and importance of e-store design.

Mini case study 6.2: ONLINE CAR SEARCHES (autos.msn.com/home/new_research.aspx)

This site provides information on new cars and includes data on make, model, dealership, specification, quotes, prices and insurance, as well as a photogallery. It is a typical site in this retail category, but additionally offers a link to multimedia presentations that provide 360-degree views of the exterior and interior of the motor vehicle. The function can be controlled for both speed and vertical views directly by the user.

The site is similar to others such as those selling boats, motorcycles, caravans, etc. and includes new and second-hand cars. This is useful for searching for unique or hard-to-find items such as collectables and is convenient for consumers and sellers alike and provides a greater market reach.

START E-STORE DESIGN WITH NAVIGABILITY

Navigability is the most fundamental building block of e-store site design. By navigability we mean the ability of the user to move around the site easily and efficiently, that is, without getting lost. If users have to travel through several topics or layers to find information, they will get frustrated or lost, possibly causing them to exit the site prematurely. Thus a key objective of good navigation design is to minimize travel, depth and redundancy when moving around within a site.

Another way of thinking about navigation design is to ask three basic questions in terms of a user at a point in time on an e-site:

1. Where am I at the moment?
2. Can I get back to where I have been?
3. How can I go forward to a particular location?

For well-designed sites, these three questions are readily answered for most users. If a user struggles, then the site is badly designed.

Exercise 6.1: Go to an e-retailer site and make a couple of moves around the site. Now answer the three basic questions above. Write down on a piece of paper how well this particular site answers these three basic questions. If the answers are not good, what could the e-retailer do to improve its e-store design? Can you find a site that is really good at this function?

Another study has developed a checklist to assist with evaluating the navigability of a site. Merrilees and Fry (2002) have come up with the following points:

1. Is navigation easy?
2. Is navigation efficient?
3. Is navigation fast?
4. Does layout of the site make it easy to use?
5. Does the site have a good menu system?
6. Overall, is the design simple and user-friendly?

Exercise 6.2: Briefly go back to the site that you used for Exercise 6.1. Now answer the six new questions about site design. Do you get more or less the same answers as to how well the site performs? Would you agree that you need both lists to get the right answer?

Although navigation design might be seen as a technical function, it nonetheless needs to address fundamental requirements that create a user-friendly experience. Two checklists have been presented here to help the reader evaluate existing sites or, alternatively, to guide the development of a new site or a new e-store design for an existing site.

Different devices can be used to facilitate this process, including links that can take the user back to the home page from any page, or have clear menu signposts of how to proceed. The reader can learn from experience of which sites do a good job on this fundamental process. As an example, one site (an online second hand bookstore used several times by one of the authors) has a good recovery system if a user accidentally double-clicks on the 'order' button. The instructions enable an e-mail to be sent or offer suggestions of another way of proceeding without re-keying in everything again. However, while these suggestions for recovery are good, would it not be better to re-design the site so that it does not collapse if someone does inadvertently double click instead of single click?

PROGRESS TO INTERACTIVITY

Interactivity is another fundamental aspect of e-store design. In simple terms, it refers to the interaction between the user of an e-site and the site itself. Thus this refers to a *person–machine interaction*. However, this relationship has more depth than say the relationship that you have with an ATM or even your home computer doing desktop work. The extra depth comes about because the *machine* in the e-retailer context is an ongoing *entity*, with a capacity to provide service, sell goods, transact money, be cheerful or grumpy, be there tomorrow for you and so on. Such extra depth makes this particular person–machine interaction *virtually* (but not quite fully) that of a person-to-person interaction.

Another way of illustrating this is to compare the *user–e-retailer interaction* in the e-world to that of the *consumer–salesperson interaction* in the bricks and mortar world. With a traditional offline retailer, if as a customer you have a question about a product, it is common to ask a salesperson. Salespeople are also important if you want to pay for merchandise or, alternatively, if you want to return goods. Instead of a salesperson, these functions are handled by a computer interface. Usually the answers are built into the program, such as a description of the product or a mechanism to order and pay for the merchandise. Discrete questions can be asked, but are usually handled as part of a *frequently asked question (FAQ)* routine. If this does not provide an answer then a separate e-mail might be called for, though most e-retailers do not encourage this option because it is deemed too time-consuming.

Thus the user–e-retailer interaction has to anticipate the sorts of questions that might be normally asked of a salesperson and, where possible, to automate these procedures into the design of the e-store. Obviously it is important to convey the right tone and mood. It is better to have a friendly and helpful 'sales assistant' and this also applies to the user–e-retailer interface.

The difference between the online e-retailer and the offline bricks and mortar retailer can be exaggerated. Traditional offline retailers have increasingly become more self-service in their orientation with less personal service from sales assistants. To some extent this trend is even true with normal department stores which used to be very labour-intensive. The move to more reliance on self-service has been achieved through more effective layout of the store and visual merchandising, such as more helpful product tags. In other words, it has become necessary for offline retailers to improve their skills in selling merchandise with less or no help from salespeople. This is exactly what an e-retailer does, so in a sense it is really an extension of existing offline trends rather than a radically different way of selling.

We can take a closer look at interactivity in the e-retail sense by examining how the academic literature views it. Most of the interpretations of interactivity have a strong communication element, which builds on the analogy with the salesperson interaction in the offline world. Five major impressions or dimensions of online interactivity can be highlighted. The most common impression of interactivity from the literature is that it is primarily *communication*-based. Infrequently, other activities, such as downloading software or making a purchase, are noted as forms of interactivity that seem to have something else other than communication as the driving force. In such cases, we would wish to highlight the communication or information aspects of those activities. Second, interactivity is about *two-way communication*. This spans communication from the viewer to the firm and from the firm to the viewer, as well as simultaneous interaction between the two parties. All three aspects of two-way communication need to be addressed in better understanding the meaning of interactivity. Third, a special feature of Internet interactivity is the ability to *personalize* and possibly customize the situation for an individual. Fourth, a number of writers have emphasized the ability of the individual to *control* the communication and *learn* as a noteworthy feature of the interactive process. Fifth and finally, a broader more holistic role of interactivity has been noted as an important contributor to building up the total *shopping experience* on the Internet.

Based on a wide body of Internet-related literature, Merrilees (2002) developed the following checklist of aspects of interactivity:

- site helps the viewer participate, learn and act;
- good two-way communication;
- site facilitates feedback from the viewer to the retailer (directly via the Web and/or e-mail);
- the overall shopping experience is very pleasant and enjoyable;
- the site develops a close, personalized relationship with the viewer;
- any query or question that you have can be answered quickly and efficiently;
- site has good interactivity (capstone item).

The reader interested in following through with more reading on interactivity can see the references in Merrilees (2002), with some of the key ones given at the end of this chapter (p. 148).

BUILDING E-RELATIONSHIPS THROUGH INTERACTIVITY

Given the importance of communication in developing *offline* quality relationships, it seems likely that the same may be true in the e-commerce context. Kolesar and Galbraith (2000) suggest that establishing a relationship with customers is harder to achieve in an e-retail context because alienation makes it harder to create the kind of bond that is often enjoyed between other service providers and their customers. They argue that, because the Internet as a medium is less personal than other retail channels, surrogates for direct personal interaction must be provided in an e-retail transaction.

The issue of managing customer relations in e-commerce begs the question as to what the strategic drivers of effective e-relationships are. Some writers (Lindstrom and Anderson 1999; Carpenter 2000) argue that e-relationships are critical for developing strong e-retail sites. One of the few empirical papers demonstrating the importance of interactivity in developing quality e-relationships is by Merrilees (2002), who studied www.amazon.com for books and an Australian online grocer, www.coles.com.au.

The relationship between interactivity and higher-quality relationships between users and the e-retailer (as perceived by the user) was very strong.

Box 6.1:
PIONEERING MAJOR ARTICLE ON WEB ATMOSPHERICS

One of the first major journal academic studies of web atmospherics was that of Eroglu *et al.* (2001). The paper supports the idea that various online cues could influence outcomes like satisfaction, amount purchased and time spent online. Their emphasis is on the process by which these cues work and they begin by adopting two types of atmospheric qualities, namely high task-relevant environment and low task-relevant environment. The high-task cues include product description, price, terms of sale, delivery, product reviews, return policies, product pictures and navigation aids. Low-task cues include unrelated special offers, colours, borders and background patterns, icons, image maps and affiliations. Sites are likely to have a different mix of high-task and low-task cues, so there is a need to get the balance right. The authors argue that there is a greater need for high-task cues for segments of customers who are either high-involvement or very sensitive to their environment's atmosphere.

ENHANCEMENTS THROUGH WEB ATMOSPHERICS

Web atmospherics have an analogy to traditional offline retailing. Retailers in the latter environment have long added to the atmosphere of the store, in the belief that the feel and look of the store would encourage shoppers to spend more time there and to buy something or something extra. To a certain extent, atmosphere is strongly influenced by visual merchandizing, that is, the way the merchandise is presented to the customer. The patterns of the displays and the use of colour and textures are sometimes offered in a real-life setting, such as a bedroom to sell beds. Such displays can take on various tones, such as sophistication, stylish or economic, depending on the target market of the retailer. Music and other audio can reinforce the mood that the retailer is attempting to create.

The same principles apply to e-store design. The visual look of the e-store can change the perception that viewers have of the store. If controlled properly and if they are aligned to the profile of the target market, then web atmospherics can stimulate an increase in sales.

Although it makes sense that the use of visuals might help, caution is needed in the extent to which they are used by the e-retailer. Some visuals are a good thing, but there are two major caveats if they are overused. Overuse of visuals applies when it results in slow downloading time. So, even if all users really liked visuals, they would get frustrated if there were long delays until each visual fully

Mini case study 6.3: BELLS AND WHISTLES ADDED FOR SPECIAL EFFECTS (www.denbighfarm.com)

This is a site for Denbigh Farm Bed and Breakfast in the Lockier Valley, Australia. It illustrates a site that has 'bells and whistles' with an interesting presentation. The home page has contemporary music, while the menu bars make a typewriter tap and school bell ring when selected. The site includes the normal array of menus with links to other tourist sites, bookings, queries and e-mails.

The gallery displays a number of smaller photographs that are magnified onto a centre screen when the cursor is passed over them. Bordering the pages are merging pictures superimposed by the menus. The site is interesting with the original design, colours, sounds and displays.

appeared. This is a clear case in which the e-store design should be pilot tested before being fully launched. Second, not all e-retail users want a lot of visuals. There is a big segment of users who primarily want product and price information, and want it quickly and efficiently, in order to buy well-specified products like dry groceries, books or CDs. This segment may be bigger than for offline shopping, where there is a segment of shoppers who want to get into a supermarket quickly and get out quickly. Notwithstanding such a large segment, there might be an opportunity to show a realistic colouring of, say, fruit in the store, as an aid to online fruit purchases as part of an online grocery store. Most online grocery stores have a very limited fresh food department.

Using music and visuals, such as 3-D displays and downloadable video clips, e-retailers can create web atmosphere. One way of tackling the problem is to provide a 'click here for broadband' (for a more sophisticated, high memory requirement version).

A number of detailed studies by Vrechopoulos and colleagues, including Vrechopoulos (2001), Vrechopoulos *et al.* (2001, 2004) and Pramataris *et al.* (2000), have provided considerable insight into e-store layout design. His approach essentially combines layout (which we discuss under the heading of navigation) and web atmospherics, in that some forms of layout have enhanced atmospherics. Much of the work by Vrechopolous is based on experimental study with online grocery shopping, but it has wider implications. Vrechopoulos (2001) gave his subjects a choice of three types of layout, holding everything else constant. The three layouts were the grid approach (rows and columns of shelves – a very hierarchical way of selecting goods, dominating brick supermarkets), the free-flow approach (more chaotic but exciting and common in fashion stores) and the racecourse approach (circular route to selecting goods). It is argued that the grid approach dominates conventional supermarket design, which it does, though in Australia there is a big swing towards combining a large grid section for dry grocery products with a large free-flow section for fresh fruit and vegetables, so it is a qualified agreement that the grid dominates conventional supermarket layout design.

The results of Vrechopoulos' study quickly eliminated the racecourse design, making it a two-horse race as to which layout design was best for online grocery shopping. Although not unanimous, it was nonetheless found that the free-flow approach was superior to the grid method in terms of satisfaction with users. The grid and free-flow e-retail layouts are illustrated in Figures 6.1 and 6.2 respectively. Vrechopoulos states that there is a good argument for being cautious about simply adopting the conventional retailing principles and applying them to an e-retailing context. One might challenge, at least slightly, the conclusion that free flow is a better layout design than grid for online grocery shopping. This might depend on whether it involved regular users of online grocery sites or non-users, because the latter might have liked the 'variety' and interesting aspects of free-flow design compared to a possible greater need for a grid design by regular users. In any case, the study does highlight the need for e-retail sites that service frequent, routine, regular purchases to recognize the need to go beyond simple linear models of layout design and as well incorporate more interesting

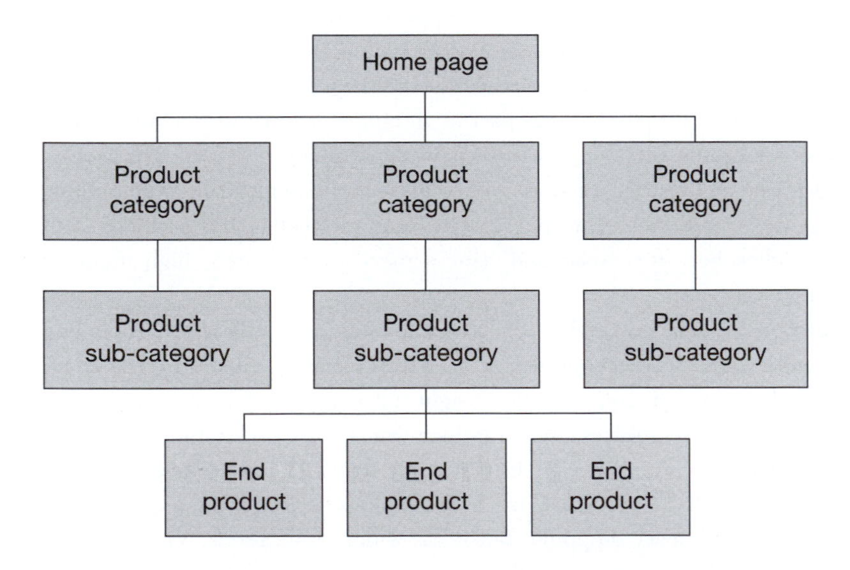

Figure 6.1 *Simplified representation of a grid layout e-retail store*

Source: The authors, based on Vrechopoulos (2001)

atmospherics in layout via the free flow. Perhaps the best solution of all comes when Vrechopoulos proposes a new layout design that he calls the 'freegrid', which is a hybrid of the grid and free-flow designs. See Figure 6.3 for a schematic representation of the freegrid e-retail layout.

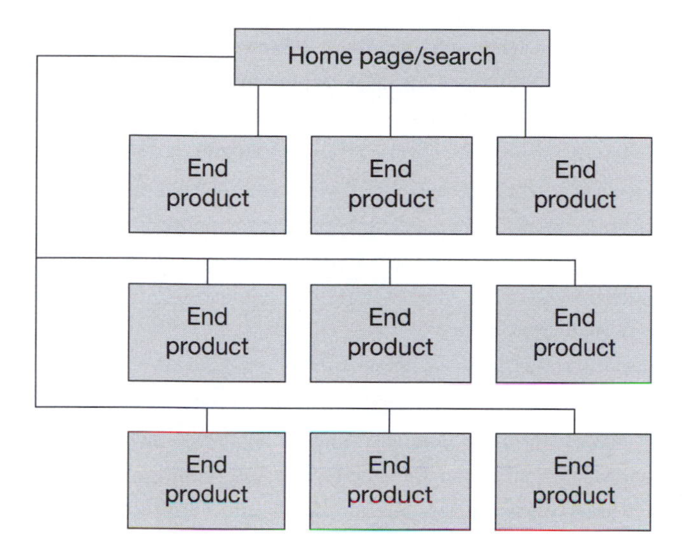

Figure 6.2 *Simplified representation of a free-flow layout e-retail store*

Source: The authors, based on Vrechopoulos (2001)

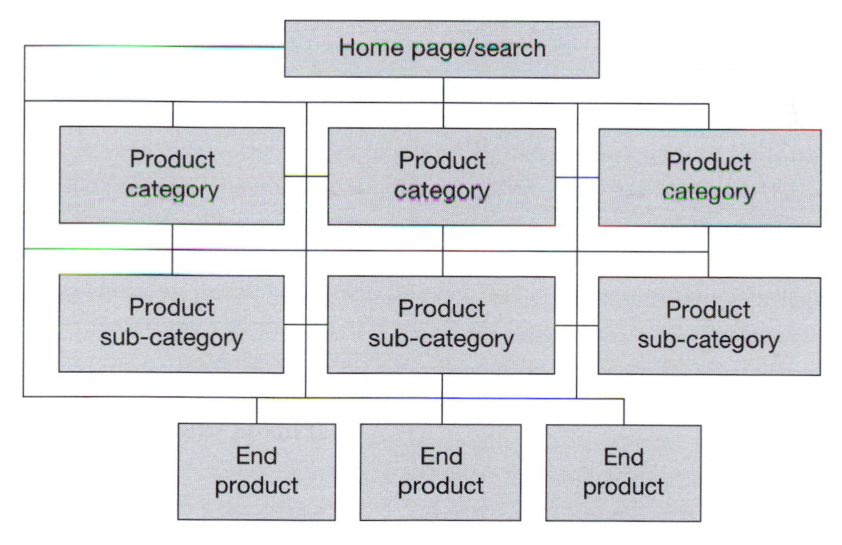

Figure 6.3 *Simplified representation of a freegrid layout e-retail store*

Source: The authors, based on Vrechopoulos (2001)

Box 6.2:
WEBSITE DESIGN FEATURES TO SELL 'LOOK AND FEEL' GOODS ONLINE

Chicksand and Knowles (2002) present a paper counter to much common opinion and argue instead that 'look and feel' sites, such as clothing, beauty products and furniture, do have a potentially important role to play in e-retailing. In a study of 45 such e-retailers they found a clear majority did have a good design in terms of the basics: layout, navigation, information and image. In contrast, only a small minority seemed to make strong use of web atmospherics, such as customization, colour management, technology and chat communication lines. Thus they argue that part of the reason why these types of sites have not spread at the same rate as other e-retail sites may be due to the underutilization of web atmospheric cues in these sites.

Chicksand and Knowles (2002) refer to a number of 'good practices' that might be relevant for 'look and feel' (and potentially any) e-retailers to go further with their web atmospherics. Examples using technological advances include the 'My Virtual Model' option on the Lands End site, allowing shoppers to create virtual models of themselves online. Thomasville Furniture uses zoom view technology, allowing shoppers to view home furnishings in minute detail, down to wood grain and moulding detail.

Personalization and customization examples include Eddie Bauer's virtual closet, whereby a customer can choose items of clothing and see how they match by viewing them on a 'Style Builder' program. Beauty product e-retailer www.EZFace.com allows consumers to download a photo of themselves and preview make-up products that will be added to the photo. Online apparel firm www.Fanbuzz.com customizes styles, colours, graphics and sizes, though charges a 10 to 20 per cent premium for doing so.

Smell can be enhanced through peripheral devices that can be plugged into a computer. DigiScent has designed a product called the iSmell Personal Scent Synthesizer, which receives code from the website and emits the relevant smell.

Online colour can be improved through technology that, for example, downloads a cookie, which then reads the monitor's colour output. This issue is important because colours can be difficult to gauge when looking at a computer screen, with each monitor displaying colours differently. Retail support companies, such as E-Color, Imation, Pantone and WayTech, are targeting e-retailers selling goods such as clothing that rely on colour presentation.

Exercise 6.3: As a follow up to the Vrechopoulos study just discussed, look up two or three online grocery e-retailers and compare and evaluate the layout design in them. Does this reinforce your thinking or change your thinking about this issue? Sites might include: www.coles.com.au; www.woolworth.com.au; and www. greengrocery.com.au. Or you can click on to any of the UK e-grocery sites.

ALL TOGETHER FOR AN INTEGRATED APPROACH TO E-STORE DESIGN

This chapter has focused on three important concepts that influence e-store design, namely navigability, interactivity and web atmospherics. Designers of e-stores should pay a lot of attention to each of these concepts if they are to really satisfy users of e-retailing. Checklists have been given in each section to guide students, designers and e-retailers themselves on ways of achieving higher standards of performance with navigability, interactivity and web atmospherics considered separately.

In this section we show how the three key concepts fit together in the total design of the e-store. That is, rather than treating navigability, interactivity and web atmospherics as three separate pieces of an e-store design, we want to show how they interface with each other. The interrelationships between the three concepts provide greater insight into e-store design, enabling the designer to incorporate synergies across the components.

Figure 6.4 shows graphically how the concepts interface with each other. Navigability is really the base of the system because it (twice) influences other things but is not in turn influenced by them. Thus it should be seen as the base building block in an e-store design.

The first influence that navigability has is on web atmospherics. If you think about what this says it makes sense. The more freely, easily and efficiently that a user can move around an e-store site, then the more readily can the user enjoy the web atmospherics, be it nice visuals, special deal offers, book reviews, audio or whatever. Alternatively, if the site is slow and frustrating, then the viewer is less likely to appreciate the web atmospherics and, indeed, the atmospheric effects could even be counter-productive.

The second influence that navigability has is on interactivity. Again this makes sense for broadly similar reasons. The more freely, easily and efficiently that a user can move around an e-store site, then the more readily and willingly can the user interact with the e-retailer. Alternatively, if the site is slow and frustrating, then the viewer is less likely to stay longer on the site, even less likely to engage in a more deep and meaningful way, and will probably not want to revisit in the future.

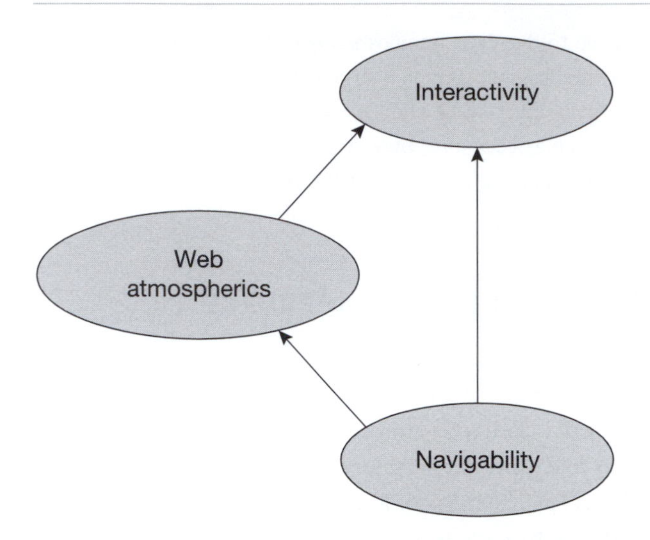

Figure 6.4 *An integrated framework for e-store design*

Figure 6.4 also depicts another interrelationship, that is, from web atmospherics to interactivity. This is likely to be a very strong relationship. What it says is as follows: users who enjoy the web atmospherics are more likely to seek interactivity with the e-retailer. So if the nice visuals, the book reviews, the audio, the special deals or whatever the particular web atmospherics are positively perceived, then more interactivity will be sought in the future. In such a case, the user will engage more with the e-retailer and a stronger, communication-based relationship will be formed.

In summary, this section augments the insight that the separate key concepts of navigability, interactivity and web atmospherics provide for e-store design. Figure 6.4, a *model of e-store design*, helps us see how the three key design concepts fit together, providing a more powerful and holistic way of seeing the big picture.

THE ROLE OF OBJECTIVES AND STRATEGY IN GUIDING E-STORE DESIGN

The integrated model presented in the previous section is a good way to pull your thoughts together in terms of designing the components and linkages across the components of an e-store site. Helpful information has been given to assist in this design, or redesign, task. However, although we have mentioned it in passing, there is one missing piece of critical information, namely the objectives and strategy of the e-retailer.

Most likely, a common objective of e-retailers is to sell as much as possible online, or at least enough (critical mass) to make the online operation viable. If this is the case then it is necessary to make the e-store experience a positive one, with easy and efficient navigation, relevant interactivity to solve any problems and sufficient web atmospherics to make it interesting and enjoyable. If navigability and interactivity are deficient, then online users will get frustrated and abandon their trolleys. It is therefore important to have a good understanding of online consumer behaviour in designing the ideal e-store site.

Another objective, but not a generic one, is to create the appropriate image for the e-store. An e-retailer might wish to convey an image of high quality, another that of a discounter, while others might wish to build a unique image. Each of these objectives would require an entirely different e-store design, so clearly it is necessary to be sure about the specific e-retail objectives *before* designing the e-store.

CONCLUSIONS

We have seen how e-store design is about creating desirable features on the e-store website, particularly the technical components of navigability and interactivity. Although such features can be considered to be technical in the first instance, in the final analysis they are more about the human–machine interface. That is, what sort of e-store design is going to appeal to the type of customer that the e-retailer is targeting? Thus it is important to have a good profile of the typical customer and to be clear about the strategic objectives of the e-retailer.

The question of optimal e-store design is a challenge for all e-retailers and all students or designers inputting into this process. Part of our approach in this chapter has been to provide conceptual tools (such as concepts like navigability and interactivity, checklists and maps like Figure 6.4) to help answer the question. It is up to the reader to follow through with this challenge, partly by evaluating existing sites and partly by leveraging this learning into a blueprint for success.

CHAPTER SUMMARY

The concept of e-store design is about creating desirable features on the e-store website, particularly the technical components of navigability and interactivity.

The main components of e-store design that we have focused on include:

- navigability
- interactivity
- impact on e-relationships
- web atmospherics.

We have also provided an overall framework (Figure 6.4) that graphically integrates these various components and shows the interrelationships between them. Another integrating device is the need to underpin the e-store design with explicit objectives that need to be achieved by the e-retailer and which closely reflect the strategy of the e-retailer.

In the next chapter we will consider the emphasis that e-retailers need to place on providing service to customers.

Case study 6.1: NIKE (www.nike.com)

Introduction

Nike, named after the Greek winged goddess of victory, was formed in 1972 by Bill Bowerman, the legendary University of Oregon track coach, along with student Phil Knight, who was a middle distance runner for Bowerman. Currently Nike employs over 22,000 people worldwide in every continent in the world. Nike owns facilities in Oregon, Tennessee, North Carolina and The Netherlands, and operates leased facilities for 15 Nike Towns, over 70 Nike Factory Stores, 2 Nike Goddess boutiques and over 100 sales and administrative offices worldwide.

Personalization/customization

Nike opened its e-retail store in 2001. A key feature is the Nike ID initiative scheme, which allows consumers to customize shoes not only with colours and styles but also with a name or message. Nike also allows customers to personalize the performance technology of its shoes for new models such as the Rival, a shoe that can alternate between a track shoe and a road shoe.

However, allowing customers to customize their shoes does not overcome the problem of personalization, such as not actually being able to physically try on the products. Thus, Nike concluded that consumers want to try on trainers similar to the ones they are purchasing. To overcome this, Nike devised a project that would incorporate Web-based technology via the use of Web kiosks in all 'Nike Town' stores. These kiosks encourage shoppers to become designers and try on products, thereby increasing satisfaction regardless of where they bought their trainers.

Interactivity

Nike allows customers to customize their own marketing campaigns! In the UK this takes the form of an interactive game based on Europe's largest sport: football (soccer).

Leading players in the European league, such as Luis Figo, Roberto Carlos and Edgar Davids, play in a tournament game. Individual customers play as one of these characters and join the elite force.

Usability

Web usability looks at the design of the interface and navigation of the site. Usability is often the most neglected aspect of websites, yet in many respects it is the most important. If visitors can't use the site, they leave and may never become customers. Moreover, the average user is impatient and has approximately a five-second attention span on the Web.

Nike uses clear, consistent icons, graphic identity schemes, and graphic or text-based overview and summary screens. These give users confidence, and allow them to find what they are looking for without wasting time. Creating a website with creative flair helps depict a flamboyant and expensive brand design, but importantly it also helps portray an innovative organization and allows consumers to relate back to the offline store. Furthermore, creativity and ease of use helps keep the site in the memories of the user. This is known as making the site 'sticky'.

A good online customer experience can also lead to higher offline sales, depending on the firm's strategy. For example, Gray Nicholls, a sporting equipment manufacturer and supplier to other businesses like Nike, has created on its retail site a 'Store locator' that gives information on the local bricks and mortar store nearest to a customer's location. Even if customers do not want to purchase online, they are able to visit one of the stores where they can enjoy the physical atmospherics that might induce them into purchasing products.

Navigation aids

Many Web gurus list web navigation to be a key driver of online purchases. The majority of Web users are mainly concerned with accomplishing their goal of locating the correct product efficiently, and purchasing the product quickly. In a physical retail store context, consumers navigate for desired products by identifying representations of the store layout and by understanding the logic used to organize, categorize and merchandize goods. Most user interactions with web pages involve navigating *hypertext* links between documents. The main problem in websites is that 'you don't know where you are' within the organization of information, thus it is essential that clear navigational aids are provided to inform consumers of where they are and where they have to go. Such a procedure is facilitated by 'progress icons'. Progress icons tell you where you are in the process, and where you still have to go. Nike uses progress pages to inform users of progress in the customization process of their trainers. This allows the customers to actually see how long the process will take. It also encourages repeat online sales.

Navigation schemes

The navigation scheme uses a broad and shallow approach, requiring fewer clicks to reach the same pieces of information than would a narrower, deeper one. The disadvantage can be that the design of the screen potentially becomes cluttered. The Nike site allows users to switch from differing regions with just one click, e.g. from the UK to the US site.

Visuals

Visual elements in web atmospherics study the colour, text style and design attributes of the site. A major goal is to look at the quality of images used, text fonts and whether the site downloads quickly, say within ten seconds. Nike has developed the site using Macromedia Flash, which is a dynamic Web application tool that allows cross-platform implementation and interactive development that normal standalone HTML cannot create. However, a major issue with Flash is that not all users have macromedia flash or flash plug-ins installed on their machines and, thus, would not be able to view the site to its full potential. This would not adhere to usability heuristics, as it would rule out users with less computational power. A method around this would be to provide an alternative HTML site with reduced graphics and images. Though it would not deliver the same graphical impact, it would enable transactions for users with less computing power.

Images

The Nike site uses quality images and graphics, essential in portraying a quality brand image online. Furthermore, high-quality images have been used to show the product in as much detail as possible. However, as stated earlier, this may cause problems with downloading, as consumers are not patient enough to wait while graphics download.

Text

The product information provided is in-depth, but uses short concise sentences that should be clear to any reader. The font is Verdana, which is the industry standard for web pages. This font is useful as the characters are spaced and have good readability.

Conclusion

Nike has produced a dynamic website which uses high-quality images along with good font structure so that the website is user-friendly and can be read easily. Furthermore, Nike has allowed customization of the products and made the site interactive in the form of a game. Navigation aids inform the user of where they are in the design process of customized trainers, again increasing user-friendliness.

However, it is a major problem that full e-commerce transactions cannot take place on all the sites. This may be due to cultural differences in the take-up of e-commerce, but there may also be legal problems facing Nike in some countries. Another major problem is that it does not offer all the products online, except to US e-shoppers.

The Nike site might be improved by:

- Allowing full e-commerce transactions on all sites
- Allowing shoppers to purchase all Nike goods and services
- Personalization techniques online through 3-D modelling
- Increasing interactivity by offering chat rooms and forums.

Source: This case study was kindly contributed by Vijay Sisoda

QUESTIONS

Brief feedback on these questions is included at the back of the book.

Question 6.1

Why do you think design issues are more important for e-retailers than for offline (brick) retailers?

Question 6.2

Two checklists have been presented in this chapter (a three-point list and a six-point list – see pp. 132 and 133)) to assist in the evaluation of the navigability of an e-retail site. How would you develop these two lists into a 'metric' that quantifies these points?

Question 6.3

How could an e-retailer use the metrics developed in Question 6.2 to help improve its navigability performance?

Question 6.4

What is e-interactivity and how would you measure it?

Question 6.5

How does interactivity help an e-retailer build a stronger relationship with its customers?

Question 6.6

Consider two different types of e-retailers. Name them. What sort of web atmospherics would be best for each of them (not necessarily what they are currently using)?

REFERENCES AND FURTHER READING

Navigability

Merrilees, B. and Fry, M.-L. (2002) 'Corporate branding: a framework for e-retailers', *Corporate Reputation Review*, 5 (2/3): 213–225.

Interactivity

Carpenter, P. (2000) *E-Brands: Building an Internet Business at Bottleneck Speeds*, Boston, MA: Harvard Business School.

Kolesar, M.B. and Galbraith, R.W. (2000) 'A services-marketing perspective on e-retailing: implications for e-retailers and directions for further research', *Internet Research: Electronic Networking Applications and Policy*, 10 (5): 424–438.

Lindstrom, M. and Anderson, T. (1999) *Brand Building on the Internet*, Melbourne: Hardie Grant.

Merrilees, B. (2002) 'Interactivity design as the key to managing customer relations in e-commerce', *Journal of Relationship Marketing*, 1 (3/4): 111–125.

Web atmospherics

Chicksand, L. and Knowles, R. (2002) 'Overcoming the difficulties of selling "look and feel" goods online: implications for website design', *IBM e-Business Conference*, Birmingham University, UK.

Eroglu, S., Macleit, K. and Davis, L. (2001) 'Atmospheric qualities of online retailing: a conceptual model and implication', *Journal of Business Research*, 54 (2): 177–184.

Pramataris, K., Vrechopoulos, A. and Doukidis, G. (2000) 'The transformation of the promotion mix in the virtual retail environment: an initial framework and comparative study', *International Journal of New Product Development and Innovation Management*, 2 (2): 163–178.

Vrechopoulos, A. (2001) 'Virtual store atmosphere in Internet retailing: measuring virtual retail store layout effects on consumer buying behaviour', unpublished Ph.D. thesis, Brunel University, London.

Vrechopoulos, A., Papamichail, G. and Doukidis, G. (2001) 'Identifying patterns in Internet retail store layouts', in P. Pardalos and V. Tsitiringos (eds) *Financial Engineering, e-Commerce and Supply Chain*, Dordrecht, The Netherlands: Kluwer Academic Publishers.

Vrechopoulos, A., O'Keefe, M., Doukidis, G. and Siomkos, G. (2004) 'Virtual store layout: an experimental comparison in the context of grocery retail', *Journal of Retailing*, 80 (1): 13–22.

WEB LINKS

www.creativegood.com
White paper on creativity.

www.macromedia.com
Usability white paper.

Chapter 7

e-Service

LINKS TO OTHER CHAPTERS

- This chapter builds on Chapter 6 – e-Store design: navigability, interactivity and web atmospherics, in particular.

KEY LEARNING POINTS

After completing this chapter you will have an understanding of:

- The overall nature, purpose and scope of online service
- The many facets of e-service
- Different classifications of e-service
- The importance of measuring e-service performance
- Two different ways of developing metrics for evaluating e-service
- The concept of e-retail service quality

ORDERED LIST OF SUB-TOPICS

- e-Service as the fourth stage of e-commerce development
- Three approaches to e-services
- A second taxonomy of e-service
- The self-service myth
- e-Service performance
- A critical incident approach to e-service performance

E-SERVICE AS THE FOURTH STAGE OF E-COMMERCE DEVELOPMENT

The literature on *e-service* has by and large followed the commercial thrust of Internet marketing development. Initially, the most common application by firms and use by users was through the website itself, often a basic overview of the company and more in keeping with having a public relations 'presence' in the e-commerce world. The next most common application was to post more detailed information about products, and conversely this was the second most common use by users. The third wave of application is the now dominant interest in e-selling, that is, the use of the Web to sell or buy goods. This takes us to the fourth and emerging wave, one that is still greatly underutilized, namely e-service.

Essentially, e-service offers the potential for some of the more advanced applications of Internet technology. For example, firms could use intelligent agents to provide extraordinary service, by tracking and datamining previous histories through Internet sites and developing known patterns of users' requirements. Customer relationships can be developed, based on prior 'modelled' understanding of which offers a consumer is likely to respond to (see Cravens *et al.*, 2000). This is a special case of market segmentation to a market of one. As another application of work by Brookes *et al.* referred to in Cravens *et al.* (2000, p. 4), a manufacturer of washing machines could include in its warranty agreement the electronic capability of monitoring the ongoing usage of the machine. Suppose that, after the machine has been bought, the household has a new baby. If detergent dosage or load patterns place strain on the motor, the machine could have the built-in communication capability to automatically page the manufacturer's service depot. The depot receives a message for a service representative to visit the household and adjust the washing machine before it becomes a problem. In this way, while both the information technologies and the servicing component are largely unobtrusive to the household, they are nonetheless essential to maintaining customer satisfaction and potential loyalty.

The literature has started to discuss e-service, but it is somewhat unstructured. For this reason, a review of the literature plays a particularly important front-end role in this chapter and we provide a simple classification of the literature to assist. We have included a separate section debating whether self-service is a myth for e-service. Our own position on this matter is made clear. We follow the literature review with a proposed, more systematic, typology of e-service, which could be useful to readers beyond this chapter.

> **THINK POINT**
>
> Try and anticipate what the difference is between service that is offline on the one hand and service that is online on the other hand. Are they different? Are they the same? Are there just a few slight differences or nuances between them?

THREE APPROACHES TO E-SERVICE

We have identified three types of e-service literature. The first is what we call the *macro* or *very broad view* of e-service, namely that e-service is effectively synonymous with e-commerce. An *intermediate view* of e-service is that we can study the provision of *specialist services* made available by *specialist service providers* that help service Internet users (both individuals and companies). The third perspective on e-service is what we term a *micro perspective*, namely the provision of particular and varied detailed customer services within a site as *part* of the website – user interface.

At the broadest level is the view that e-commerce per se is an electronic service to customers – one that provides greater convenience. This view places e-commerce as an option available to customers, providing another channel of distribution or information. For example, instead of spending, say, an hour to physically access and purchase from a bookstore, the customer has the option to purchase the same electronically. As a further example, a company may use the Web to provide information about the company's offering to assist consumers in their product search, without necessarily enabling the consumer to purchase through the Web.

A related macro view of e-service is the *services marketing* perspective on e-retailing (Kolesar and Galbraith, 2000). They argue that e-retail offerings are service offerings and exhibit many of the same characteristics as other non-Internet-based services. They further argue that Internet services can be evaluated by similar criteria, such as responsiveness, empathy and the establishment of trust through courtesy and competency. The principal service provided by e-retailers is a search and evaluation facility that potentially saves time and effort for the consumer. The task of the e-retailer is to provide a website design that caters to different shopping styles, provides evidence to reduce risk and also educates the user in a shopping mode that may differ to what they are used to in conventional retail shopping.

There is now a considerable number of papers that have applied the macro perspective of e-service to a specific industry. For example, Muir and Douglas (2001) have studied how service delivery has changed in legal services with the rise of e-commerce. They argue that the quality of service is potentially improved with the Web. A Web presence allows legal practices to be more transparent and to offer greater access to information for customers by way of improving their services. It is suggested that this improved communication may lead to a reduction in complaints against solicitors.

An *intermediate perspective* of e-service is the provision of *electronic services* from *specialist providers* to users of the Internet and intranets. Thus we have a market (external or internal) in which key electronic services are similar to products and sold or exchanged in a market to general users of the Web. There is a huge variety of specialist firms that offer their services (products) to Web users. Web designers form a stereotypical group in this category, but also included are all types of suppliers of a wide range of Internet services, such as portal providers or providers of any specific link in the Internet network. For example, consider the commercial services offered by Compuserve, Prodigy, America Online and e-world. The pages of the national financial newspapers are filled with the advertisements of companies offering such Web-enabling services, some claiming to offer an integrated service.

Electronic trust services are specialist e-services that provide reassurance and trust to the financial and privacy security of Internet information flow. There is a number of third-party commercial service providers who guarantee protection of either the financial security or the personal confidentiality of information flows. A special case of this situation is the role of the electronic signature, an issue discussed by Travers (2001), who is particularly concerned with the status, planning and implementation of electronic signatures, in the context of the UK Electronic Communications Act 2000. He argues that electronic signatures can be considered within a knowledge management framework and proposes a six-part system that incorporates people, clients, knowledge matters, business development and training. Travers notes that the Electronic Communications Act provides:

- an approvals scheme for businesses providing cryptography services such as electronic signature services and confidentiality services;
- for the legal recognition of electronic signatures and the process under which they are verified; and
- for the removal of obstacles in other legislation to the use of electronic communications and storage in place of paper.

A somewhat unusual example of a specialist e-service is the provision of electronic money (Buck, 1997), which could be redefined as a trust-service, but Buck did not do so in his paper. He notes that there is a range of online payment systems, including credit systems (e.g. Payflow Pro), debit systems (e.g. BankNet), token-based mechanisms (e.g. Digicash) and electronic cash schemes (e.g. Mondex). Such mechanisms vary considerably in terms of safety, privacy protection and trustworthiness.

An example of a specialist e-service within an internal market is that of an e-mail-mediated help service (Hahn 1998). Hahn analysed 265 help-service responses from service logs and found, among other things, that users and help-service staff held different internal models for ideal e-mail communication. Users desired a fairly simple exchange of communication, that is, a clear question followed by a quick, simple response. Staff, on the other hand, envisaged the need for a more complex interrelationship, over several messages.

This takes us to the third perspective of e-service, namely the *micro* approach. Perhaps the dominant element in this field is the role of information. Some authors see information-based marketing as a potential competitive advantage (Weiber and Kollmann, 1998). Other scholars see the Web as important for tracking and gathering customer feedback (Sampson, 1998; Sen *et al.*, 1998). Still other writers focus on the role of e-information as an aid to facilitating consumer search (Ward and Lee, 2000; Ratchford *et al.*, 2001).

A second significant micro area of e-service is that of interactivity. Despite the importance of interactivity for websites, there is still no consensus as to what should be included by this phenomenon. For example, Schloerb (1995), Shih (1998), Steuer (1992) and Welch *et al.* (1996) interpret interactivity very narrowly, as relating to speed of feedback and control. See also the related studies by Ghose and Dou (1998), Ha and James (1998) and Wu (1999). It is particularly in Merrilees (2002) that a broader perspective is given to interactivity. He embraces a more multi-dimensional approach to the concept of interactivity. Included factors are two-way communication between the e-retailer and the user; the ability of each party to communicate with the other including through e-mail; the ability to personalize the situation for the individual user; and the ability of the individual to control the communication and learn from it. The broader approach to interactivity is the approach taken in the current chapter (see also Chapter 6).

Finally, there are numerous other Internet studies that emphasize particular aspects of e-service besides information or interactivity. For example Mols (2000), in his study of Danish retail banking, examined the role of more individualized services for consumers and their need for a close relationship with the bank. As a final example of a difficult-to-classify study of providing services on the Internet see Mathur (1998) who takes a financial accounting approach to the topic.

In summary, we have used our three-part classification of macro, intermediate and micro as an initial way of structuring the literature, as it exists. This is not to say that we endorse all perspectives of the literature. In particular we have reservations about the macro perspective. In a sense, the use of the World Wide Web by a retailer to market its organization as an online e-retailer is no more a services marketing exercise than the use of catalogues makes Lands End a services marketer. The *service component for an e-retailer* is the sum total of the ancillary support mechanisms provided by the retailer and the channel intermediaries to aid the Web prospective buyer to select, pay for and receive the merchandise. The e-retailer may provide services for the consumption of the prospective buyer through the Web channel, but this still does not make the channel a service unto itself. Thus we prefer the intermediate and micro perspectives of initial classification and our empirical research design is more in keeping with the micro perspective. A more refined taxonomy of e-services is developed below.

Mini case study 7.1:
BRITISH LIBRARY (www.bl.uk)

This is a free service provided by the British Library in London that includes a 'turn the page' function. This technology is new to websites and is only available for three articles at the time of going to press. The home page offers a range of services provided by the library and is easy to use with simple menu selection and navigation.

Of interest is the 'turn the pages' of Leonardo da Vinci's notebook. This technology displays a scanned image of the original notebook and allows the user to turn pages using the cursor in a way similar to a real book. To enter this site, select 'turn the pages' on the home page and follow the instruction. To use this facility a Shockwave driver is required and can be downloaded free in two minutes from the same site. This is an interesting site for those who are interested in history.

A SECOND TAXONOMY OF E-SERVICE

We initially used a three-way classification of the e-service literature, namely macro, intermediate and micro, as a way of sorting the literature in this fragmented domain.

Our thinking on this topic has progressed to another proposed taxonomy of e-service, as given in Figure 7.1. Not all of the aspects covered in this taxonomy are addressed in the empirical part of our chapter that follows in the next section.

However, the Figure 7.1 taxonomy is put forward as an initial framework that can be debated by interested academics or practitioners.

THE SELF-SERVICE MYTH

Before leaving the literature, it is useful to discuss a crucial issue in the e-service area referred to by Moon and Frei (2000). They give the example of customers visiting a typical airline website and being confronted by a self-service search engine. If they know exactly when and where they want to travel, the website will generate a list of feasible flights. However, the search process becomes complex

Consumer awareness of site existence

- Search engines i.e. www.google.com
- Portals, i.e. www.yahoo.com
- Print media stories
- Broadcast media stories
- Website banner advertising
- Web links from channel partners

Consumer awareness of faults and risks in using certain websites

- Print media stories
- Broadcast media stories
- Website banner advertising
- Web links from channel partners
- Alerts issued by consumer groups and government agencies, e.g. www.bbb.org

Consumer confidence in products and/or the website

- Written and tabled comparisons provided by portal sites or journals, e.g. www.pcmag.com
- Comparisons and recommendations from consumer groups, e.g. www.choice.com.au
- Third-party rankings of sites and products, e.g. *Top 100 (undiscovered) Web Sites* from www.pcmag.com

Payment options

- Credit card provider indemnities, e.g. Citibank iCard (www.citigroup.com.au)
- Online credit systems, e.g. Payflow Pro (www.verisign.com)

Confidence in privacy and security

- Third-party verification of a site's policies, e.g. www.verisign.com
- Use of secured document systems, e.g. www.microsoft.com/Windows/ie/using/howto/digitalcert/using.asp
- Site is part of a well-known online group or cybermall, e.g. www.jumbomall.com

Figure 7.1 *Web ancillary services that influence e-retail trust*

if they wish to find the cheapest airfare and are flexible on the dates and destinations. Moon and Frei are sceptical of the usefulness of the self-service approach to e-service and suggest that the customer is likely to have a much more satisfying experience if they call the airline's call centre for handling more complex situations.

Co-production is proposed by Moon and Frei (2000: 26) as a better model than self-service for e-commerce. In the co-production model the company undertakes many of the tasks in shopping and buying, relieving the burden on the customer. The new model recognizes that, although customers like having choices, they do not want too many and appreciate pre-screened alternatives geared to their needs. Co-production also understands that customers want to state their preferences only once. Moon and Frei conclude that e-commerce firms should focus on customer service *not* self-service, and give illustrative examples of companies like Dell Computer Corporation. Dell performs a host of back-end transactions that are invisible to customers, such as grouping products by customer segments and displaying only in-stock items.

The current authors tend to endorse the sentiment of Moon and Frei in that we agree that it would be foolish for owners of e-sites to provide a minimalist infrastructure and simply to let users do their own thing. Our only objection is what to call the 'co-production model'. We are content to keep calling it a *self-service model*, but one that is designed appropriately and optimally. Indeed, we believe that the challenge is for e-commerce firms to strive for an optimal self-service design capability. The current chapter will shed light on this question, but much more research is needed on this topic. For a very interesting and relevant study, see Dabholkar (2000). His review of research into what consumers want from technologically-based self-service options suggests that speed, control and privacy are generally required. However, two additional attributes that positively influence the attitude of consumers towards computer technology are ease of use and fun or enjoyment. Web designers searching for the most effective design are advised to consult Dabholkar (2000).

We should point out that the same issue has been debated with conventional retailing. Some *weak* retailers have taken the view that *self-service* equals *no service* and have provided very little help to consumers, using the opportunity to reduce their costs (in particular fewer sales staff). This approach will only leave consumers frustrated and unable to find what they want and so they are likely to leave the store very unhappy. In contrast, as Merrilees and Miller (1996) note, for better-performing stores 'self-service' does not mean 'no service'. The best self-service stores, like IKEA, Wal-Mart and many superstores, appreciate that self-service needs to be designed in such a way that it delivers good service, albeit of a kind other than personalized service. Thus *good self-service design* in *conventional retailing* includes a well-organized store, with good layout, good signage, helpful visual displays and ready access to product information. Merrilees and Miller (2001) have argued that the approach taken by superstores represents a new self-service paradigm of retail service. Broadly speaking, the same good self-service design principles readily transfer from conventional retailing to e-retailing.

E-SERVICE PERFORMANCE

Knowing what is meant by e-service is an important first step in managing an e-retail business. However, it is necessary to take another step, namely the measurement of how well an organization is performing in each e-service activity. At this point it is clear that we only have a limited understanding of which e-service functions are important to consumers and how well e-retailers deliver these services. For this reason, the next section in this chapter introduces some much-needed new research, namely a study of critical incidents in e-service delivery. Our critical incident analysis is followed by an examination of the role of e-service metrics as a management tool. In turn we discuss an alternative measure of e-service performance, namely e-retail service quality.

A CRITICAL INCIDENT APPROACH TO E-SERVICE PERFORMANCE

This section outlines the results of new research initiated especially for this book. A content analysis of 138 e-retail sites was undertaken by four judges in order to assess the nature and effectiveness of e-service across those sites. It was suggested that a good way of getting started might be with book, music, gift and department store sites, because these represent a high share of the e-selling transaction activity. The final discretion as to sites chosen was left to the individual judges. The main criterion for selection as a judge was expertise in analysing e-retailer websites. Notwithstanding each judge's expertise, further controls were built into the evaluation process through careful briefing and training of the judges. This briefing included careful instruction to make sure that all items were fully understood by each judge and that all judges had the same meaning for each. Another instruction was that each judge was to spend about 10 to 15 minutes moving through the site to understand its features and its content before answering the various set questions. Each site was analysed in the same way.

A survey instrument (protocol) was designed for each judge to use with each site. A wide number of site attributes were assessed on a Likert scale of 1 to 7, depending on whether the judge agreed or not that the site performed well on a particular attribute. There was also an open-ended section of the survey instrument where the focus was on the overall level of e-service for the site, based on a 1 to 7 Likert scale. On the same page the judge was asked to describe up to three important critical incidents/areas (if any) that positively contributed to their assessment of the overall level of e-service. Additionally, up to three important critical incidents (if any) could be listed that detracted from the level of e-service.

Results

POSITIVE CRITICAL INCIDENTS

Initially we present the incidents that positively contributed to e-service. We do this in two ways. First we can note those positive facilitators to e-service across the *total* sample of 138 sites. We also break the results into *high-service sites* and *low-service sites*. High-service sites are those sites that were rated highly on the basis of the perceived overall level of e-service, that is, those sites that scored a 5, 6 or 7 out of 7. Those sites that scored 1 to 4 were called low-service sites.

As Table 7.1 shows, across the total 138 sites, the three most positive incidents that contributed to e-service were:

- interactivity and communication (56 per cent of all sites);
- special offers (33 per cent);
- information (20 per cent).

The next most important batch included:

- variety of items for sale (14 per cent);
- frequently asked questions (FAQs) (a separate type of interactivity) (12 per cent);
- ease of use (12 per cent).

Table 7.1 Positive critical incidents affecting e-service (percentage)

e-Service element	*Overall sites (n=138)*	*High-service sites (n=89)*	*Low-service sites (n=49)*
Interactivity	56	72	27
Special offers	33	39	20
Information	20	26	10
Variety of items for sale	14	16	12
FAQ	12	17	2
Ease of use of site	12	13	10
Security/privacy	8	11	2
Delivery	7	9	4
Returns	4	4	0

Note: Figures may add to more than 100 per cent because of multiple incidents

Other less important facilitators of e-service included security/privacy references (8 per cent), goods delivery (7 per cent) and returns policy (4 per cent).

If we compare high-service and low-service sites, we more or less get a similar picture of what is important. One key difference shown in Table 7.1 is that the number of positive incidents of good e-service is a lot lower in low-service sites. Thus interactivity and special offers remain the highest two facilitators of good e-service, but the rate of incidence is about twice as much in high-service sites. For example, in low-service sites there is a 27 per cent incidence of interactivity (compared to 72 per cent in high-service sites) and a 20 per cent incidence of special offers (compared to 39 per cent in high-service sites). A number of key determinants of e-service in high-service sites are downgraded in low-service sites. These include information, FAQ, security/privacy and returns.

NEGATIVE CRITICAL INCIDENTS

Apart from coding those elements of e-service that contribute to the overall level of e-service of a site, we have also analysed those elements that have reduced the overall level of e-service. We have retained the same classification of elements, but now we refer to negative critical incidents. That is, interactivity now refers to a lack of interactivity or a low level of service from this element. The same applies to the other eight elements of e-service.

Table 7.2 now shows the pecking order of negative critical incidents that affect overall e-service. The two most important negative incidents are a narrow variety

Table 7.2 Negative critical incidents affecting e-service (percentage)

e-Service element	*Overall sites (n=138)*	*High-service sites (n=89)*	*Low-service sites (n=49)*
Variety of items for sale	15	8	29
Delivery	14	8	27
Interactivity	11	6	20
Information	10	4	20
Ease of use	8	1	20
Returns	8	4	14
FAQ	4	2	8
Security/privacy	4	3	6
Special offers	3	3	4

Note: Figures may add to more than 100 per cent because of multiple incidents of goods for sale (15 per cent of sites had this problem) and poor delivery service (14 per cent of sites). Other problem areas of e-service included interactivity (11 per cent), information (10 per cent), ease of use (8 per cent) and returns policy (8 per cent). The other three elements, FAQ, security/privacy and special offers, were rarely mentioned as a negative incident.

We have extended this analysis to a comparison of high-service and low-service sites. As we would expect, the number of negative incidents is almost thrice as great in the low-service sites. Variety and delivery were the top biggest problem areas for both types of sites, but had an incidence rate of less than 10 per cent in the high-service sites (compared to more than a quarter of the low-service sites). For the rest of the e-service elements, the most notable difference in the rankings is that of ease of use. It was the equal third highest problem area among low-service sites, but the lowest (and almost non-existent with a 1 per cent incidence) among the high-service sites.

LOGISTIC REGRESSION OF HIGH–LOW SERVICE SITES

We can extend our analysis from an enumeration of the critical incident elements (as a form of Pareto analysis), to a binary logistic regression analysis in which we can predict which sites fall into the high-service or low-service categories. The dependent variable is binary (either one type of site or the other). The independent variables are the nine dummy variables denoting positive critical incidents and the nine dummy variables denoting negative critical incidents.

Table 7.3 Logit regression differentiating high-service and low-service sites

*Dependent variable**	*Beta coefficient (standardized)*	*t-value (absolute)*
Positive interactivity incidents	0.37	5.69
Negative information incidents	–0.27	4.36
Negative delivery incidents	–0.23	3.76
Negative interactivity incidents	–0.23	3.74
Negative ease of use incidents	–0.22	3.50
Positive FAQ incidents	0.21	3.40
Positive information incidents	0.17	2.80
Positive special deals	0.17	2.72
Negative variety of items	–0.15	2.35

Note: *Binary variable: 0=low-service site; 1=high-service site

The results are shown in Table 7.3. Overall the degree of explanation is high, with an adjusted coefficient of determination of 0.53. Nine of the dummy variables were significant at the 5 per cent level. The model predicts very well, with an 88 per cent hit rate.

The six major e-service elements that shunt a firm into either a high-service or low-service category were:

- positive interactivity incidents
- negative information incidents
- negative delivery incidents
- negative interactivity incidents
- negative ease of use incidents
- positive FAQ incidents.

In addition, less important influences were positive information incidents, positive special deals and negative variety of items for sale incidents.

Multiple regression analysis of overall service rating

Given that we have recorded the actual overall service rating of the site, on a 1 to 7 scale, we can also analyse the data with conventional multiple regression analysis, with the overall service rating as the dependent variable and the same independent variables as before. This is another way of testing the robustness of our results, although the logistic regression and the multiple Ordinary Least Squares (OLS) are testing slightly different models and therefore we would not expect exactly the same results to be produced.

Table 7.4 summarizes the results. The adjusted coefficient of determination is good, at 0.56. Eight variables were significant. The six most important e-service elements explaining the overall service rating were:

- positive interactivity incidents
- negative delivery incidents
- negative ease of use incidents
- negative information incidents
- positive information incidents
- negative interactivity incidents.

Additionally, positive variety of the offerings had a marginal influence on overall service rating, while positive deals and negative variety of items were not quite significant.

If we compare Tables 7.3 and 7.4, we see that essentially the same elements are at work. However there are slight differences, with some elements appearing

Table 7.4 OLS regression determining overall site e-service rating

Dependent variable (overall e-service rating)	*Beta coefficient (standardized)*	*t-value (absolute)*
Positive interactivity incidents	0.39	6.19
Negative delivery incidents	–0.28	4.76
Negative ease of use incidents	–0.26	4.38
Negative information incidents	–0.25	4.27
Positive information incidents	0.24	4.03
Negative interactivity incidents	–0.22	3.76
Positive variety of items incidents	0.13	2.16
Positive special deals	0.11	1.85 (n.s.)
Negative variety of items	–0.11	1.76 (n.s.)

Note: n.s. denotes not significant at the 0.05 level

in one table only, and the pecking order changing marginally. For example, a positive FAQ service might elevate an e-retailer into the high-service category (Table 7.3), but did not have any discernible influence on the overall rating regression (Table 7.4).

E-SERVICE METRICS: A MANAGEMENT TOOL

Our research in the previous section revealed that interactivity was overwhelmingly important for achieving a perception of high e-service. This finding is even stronger when we add frequently asked questions (FAQs) to its role because this is a form of interactivity. In a sense the emphasis on interactivity is akin to the importance of personal service in the conventional literature. Interestingly, personal service was found to be the most important type of customer service in conventional retailing (see Merrilees and Miller, 1996: Chapter 14). Interactivity in the e-context includes two-way communication, the ability of the e-retailer to communicate to the user and the ability of the user to communicate with the e-retailer, responsiveness in answering questions (including the special case of FAQ) and personalization of the process (see also Merrilees 2002; Chapter 6 in this book).

Even without measurement, interactivity is clearly a good candidate as a capstone element in a powerful e-service program. Chapter 6 provides guidance on how an e-retailer could effectively do this. Similarly, we recommend that an e-retailer should audit its interactivity every year or so, along the lines suggested in the previous section (using, say, a critical incident analysis). If interactivity is found to be too low or not as high as desired, then steps can be undertaken to increase it, through, for example, increased customization or other means.

A second key finding of our research study is that interactivity needs to be supported by special offers, information, variety of items for sale and ease of use, as part of an integrated approach to e-service. An e-service audit of an e-retail site should incorporate all components of e-service.

A third key finding of our research is also very important for the practice of good e-service. We have shown that it is not sufficient to create and manage *positive e-service experiences*. Equally, the firm's e-commerce strategy needs to be able to handle *negative critical incidents*. The first point is that *even high-service sites* experience periodic problems in e-service. For example, Tables 7.1 and 7.2 show that high-service sites, while generally having a very high (72 per cent) positive incidence of interactivity, nonetheless had a 6 per cent (that is, non-zero) incidence of negative interactivity. The same pattern occurs in the areas of product variety and delivery. Firms need to take steps to continuously improve (that is, lower) the rate of negative incidents. Ideally, more interactivity may need to be built in if all other aspects of interactivity fail – this is the ultimate approach to service-failure recovery. Perhaps it is a toll-free phone service that is needed as a service in the last resort?

A fourth key finding of our research that needs to be carefully considered by websites is that the solution for sites attempting to increase their e-service capability is not simply to *add* more information, an FAQ service or similar facility. Such actions are a necessary, though insufficient condition to becoming a high-service site. Take information, for example. Information incidents, both positive and negative, were important in determining membership of the e-retailer in a high-service or low-service category and the overall level of e-service of the site. Yet there was only a slight difference (and one that was *not* statistically significant) in the quantity of information across high-service and low-service sites. This suggests that the problem for some sites is not the *quantity* of information, but rather the *quality* and *relevance* of information. Thus the high rate (20 per cent) of negative incidents about information on the low-service sites (see Table 7.2) may be due to overemphasis on the wrong information, that is, the wrong details, rather than the lack of information in general.

In summary, we suggest that e-retailers should regularly monitor or audit all of their e-service, at least as frequently as annually. The critical incident approach is a simple way of doing this and the method is robust because it captures both positive and negative incidents in e-service. Notwithstanding the merit of this approach, there are alternative ways of evaluating e-service and we turn to one of those in the next section.

E-RETAIL SERVICE QUALITY: AN ALTERNATIVE PERFORMANCE METRIC

Retail service quality entails the application of service quality as both a concept and measure to retailing. The landmark study in this respect is Dabholkar *et al.* (1996). One advantage of using a measure of (retail) service quality is that it represents a composite measure, pulling together a number of components of service, such as personal service, store design and problem-solving. So, instead of having to say that six or seven or whatever components of service are performing at the individual service level, we can combine our assessment into a composite service quality measure.

More recently, researchers have extended their scope of retail service quality from conventional retailing to also include Internet or e-retailing. These studies include Zeithaml *et al.* (2000), Francis and White (2002a; 2002b), Janda *et al.* (2002) and Wolfinbarger and Gilly (2002). Each study uses slightly different dimensions (or items under each heading) of e-retail service quality, but generally the dimensions include:

- website design
- security
- ordering system
- delivery system
- communication.

The five dimensions of e-retail service quality provide an umbrella approach for e-retailers wishing to use an alternative measure of e-service performance. We offer no view as to whether this approach or the critical incident approach is better. Indeed, e-retailers could quite easily use both sets of metrics to evaluate their e-service, as they complement each other.

At the time of going to press a major new article on e-retail quality has appeared, namely Wolfinbarger and Gilly (2003). This article seems to be the most comprehensive and methodical of all of the articles in this field and so we should highlight its findings. Four components of e-retail quality were identified, namely:

- website design (navigation, order processing, personalization);
- fulfilment/reliability (receipt of correct goods, delivery on time);
- privacy/security (security of credit card payments and privacy of shared information);
- customer service (responsive to customer inquiries).

In terms of the predictive power of these four components, two of them (website design and fulfilment) were found to be the most important in contributing to overall quality, satisfaction and return purchases.

ADDITIONAL GUIDANCE ON PRACTICAL E-SERVICE PROVISION

The chapter already provides a number of practical tools that could help the improved delivery of e-service for e-retailers. First, key concepts, such as interactivity and delivery, have been highlighted as having special importance. Second, the idea of e-service metrics is another practical tool ready for actual use by e-retailers. In addition to these ideas and tools, the reader might wish to consult a number of 'how to' books, including Sterne (1996), Cusack (1998) and Zemke and Connellan (2001).

CONCLUSIONS

This chapter has provided two taxonomies of e-service as a contribution to an otherwise indistinct field, and has also made a statement about the self-service myth in e-service, suggesting a semantic resolution of the debate. Indeed, the challenge to Web designers and Web marketers is to find the *optimal self-service* design for interactive marketing. In part, the fieldwork conducted in this study helps to make a contribution to this pursuit.

The research part of the chapter has evaluated critical incidents in a sample of 138 e-retailer sites. We have analysed the total number of websites in the sample as well as sub-samples of *high-service* and *low-service* websites. We have also contrasted *positive* critical incidents from *negative* critical incidents. Perhaps an unexpected result, we found that the main e-service elements that drive positive e-service are *not* the same as the elements that cause negative critical incidents in e-service. Interactivity in particular, strongly supported by special offers and information about the product and firm, was the key component of positive e-service. In contrast, negative e-service experiences were most often associated with a lack of variety of items for sale and poor delivery arrangements.

We have suggested that interactivity could be the key capstone element for e-retailers trying to build a powerful e-service program, with support from information, ease of use, variety and special offers. There is also a need to manage *service failure recovery*, that is, the myriad of negative critical incidents. This may lead to the ultimate form of interactivity – namely an interactive service that handles the collective failure in all the other interactive mechanisms.

CHAPTER SUMMARY

The service component for an e-retailer is the sum total of the ancillary support mechanisms provided by the e-retailer and the channel intermediaries to aid the Web prospective buyers to select, pay for and receive the merchandise. Two different taxonomies or classifications were used to explore the nature of e-services. We also argued that self-service is not a myth for e-services and should not be taken for granted. It needs to be properly designed to genuinely help the e-customer.

Further, evaluating e-service performance is important for e-retailers, if they are to fully understand what attributes are needed by customers. Two different ways of measuring e-service performance were given, namely a critical incident approach and an e-retail service quality approach.

In the following chapter, we draw together the issues of site design, products and e-service with a consideration of branding for the e-retailer.

Case study 7.1: LEGAL SERVICES: BELL LEGAL GROUP (www.belllegal.com.au)

This is a legal services site of the Bell Legal Group on the Gold Coast, Australia, that offers a full range of legal services from corporate to individual issues. The site is typical of a service provider with a professional appearance and an abundance of information on the services that they provide. This site differs from many others due to the music and voice commentary on the home page.

The menu offers: our people, a group that lists employees' qualifications and experience with portrait photographs. It has the usual menu selection for contacts and queries with linked pages to a large range of predominantly Government websites related to legal matters ranging from privacy codes to taxation issues. The notion of providing an extra service through linkages to established sites is a fairly easy and cost-effective way of adding value to customers. Essentially it is a public service that is an option available to any e-commerce firm.

Case study 7.2: MOTORING ORGANIZATION: RAC (www.rac.co.uk)

This is a UK motoring organization that offers a range of services from breakdown to insurance coverage. The site is representative of a large organization that offers a multitude of services and requires careful navigation to locate particular information. This is made even more difficult with the amount of linked advertising and special deals scattered over the pages. If followed carefully the menu items on each page are self-explanatory and will lead to the desired location. The site is typical of similar motoring organizations worldwide that offer online services and information on their core and related products. While some of the site is intended to gain customers, there are some parts could be seen as public service, such as traffic conditions.

The home page includes connection to localities, insurance for vehicles, property and holidays, motoring information for breakdown, technical reports and car care, holiday information, accommodation deals, vehicle hire, ship/airline bookings and tours. It also covers a range of finance options for loans and insurances as well as legal matters. The site is interesting enough, with standout colours, and is complemented with related photographs, coupled with an abundance of graphic deals.

QUESTIONS

Brief feedback on these questions is included at the back of the book.

Question 7.1

What is the difference between the macro and the micro view of e-service?

Question 7.2

Why do Moon and Frei (2000) prefer the co-production model of e-service rather than the self-service model?

Question 7.3

Do you agree that the factors that contribute to *good* e-service are different from the factors that contribute to *bad* e-service? Why?

Question 7.4

Explain how e-service metrics can help an e-retailer better manage their business.

REFERENCES AND FURTHER READING

Buck, S. (1997), 'From electronic money to electronic cash: payment on the net', *Logistics Information Management*, 10 (6): 289–299.

Cravens, D., Merrilees, B. and Walker, R. (2000) *Strategic Marketing Management for the Pacific Region*, Sydney: McGraw-Hill.

Cusack, M. (1998) *Online Customer Care: Applying Today's Technology to Achieve World-Class Customer Interaction*, Milwaukee, WI: ASQ Quality Press.

Dabholkar, P. (2000) 'Technology in service delivery: implications for self-service and service support', in T. Swartz and D. Iacobucci (eds) *Handbook of Services Marketing & Management*, Thousand Oaks, CA: Sage.

Dabholkar, P., Thorpe, D. and Rentz, J. (1996) 'A measure of service quality for retail stores: scale development and validation', *Journal of the Academy of Marketing Science*, 24 (1): 3–16.

Francis, J. and White, L. (2002a) 'A model of quality determinants in Internet retailing', *Proceedings of 2001 ServSIG Services Research Conference: New Horizons in Services Marketing*, AMA, pp. 59–67.

Francis, J. and White, L. (2002b) 'Exploratory and confirmatory factor analysis of the Perceived Internet Retailing Quality (PIRQ) Model', *Proceedings of ANZMAC*, Melbourne, Victoria.

Ghose, S. and Dou, W. (1998) 'Interactive functions and their impacts on the appeal of Internet presence sites', *Journal of Advertising Research*, 38 (2): 29–43.

Ha, L. and James, E. (1998) 'Interactivity reexamined: a baseline analysis of early business websites', *Journal of Broadcasting & Electronic Media*, 42 (4): 457–470.

Hahn, K. (1998) 'Qualitative investigation of an e-mail mediated help service', *Internet Research: Electronic Applications and Policy*, 8 (2): 123–135.

Janda, S., Trocchia, P. and Gwinner, K. (2002) 'Consumer perceptions of Internet retail service quality', *International Journal of Service Industry Management*, 13 (5): 412–431.

Kolesar, M. and Galbraith, R. (2000) 'A services-marketing perspective on e-retailing: implications for e-retailers and directions for further research', *Internet Research: Electronic Networking Application and Policy*, 10 (5): 428–438.

Mathur, L. (1998) 'Services advertising and providing services on the Internet', *The Journal of Services Marketing*, 12 (5): 334–345.

Merrilees, B. (2002) 'Interactivity design as the key to developing Internet relationships', *Journal of Relationship Marketing*, 1 (3/4): 111–125.

Merrilees, B. and Miller, D. (1996) *Retailing Management: A Best Practice Approach*, Melbourne: RMIT Press.

Merrilees, B. and Miller, D. (2001) 'Superstore interactivity: a new self-service paradigm of retail service', *International Journal of Retail & Distribution Management*, 29 (8): 379–389.

Mols, N. (2000) 'The Internet and services marketing: the case of Danish retail banking', *Internet Research: Electronic Networking Applications and Policy*, 10 (1): 7–18.

Moon, Y. and Frei, F. (2000) 'Exploding the self-service myth', *Harvard Business Review*, 78 (3) (May–June): 26–27.

Muir, L. and Douglas, A. (2001) 'Advent of e-business concepts in legal services and its impact on the quality of service', *Managing Service Quality*, 11 (3): 175–181.

Ratchford, B., Talukdar, D. and Lee, M. (2001) 'A model of consumer choice of the Internet as an information source', *International Journal of Electronic Commerce*, 5 (3): 7–21.

Sampson, S. (1998) 'Gathering customer feedback via the Internet: instruments and prospects', *Industrial Management & Data Systems*, 98 (2): 71–82.

Schloerb, D. (1995) 'A quantitative measure of telepresence', *Presence: Teleoperators and Virtual Environments*, 4 (1): 64–80.

Sen, S., Padmanabhan, B., Tuzhilin, A., White, N. and Stein, R. (1998) 'The identification and satisfaction of consumer analysis-driven information needs of marketers on the WWW', *European Journal of Marketing*, 32 (7/8): 688–702.

Shih, C. (1998) 'Conceptualizing consumer experiences in cyberspace', *European Journal of Marketing*, 32 (7/8): 655–663.

Sterne, J. (1996) *Customer Service on the Internet: Building Relationships, Increasing Loyalty and Staying Competitive*, New York: John Wiley & Sons.

Steuer, J. (1992) 'Defining virtual reality: dimensions determining telepresence', *Journal of Communication*, 42 (4): 73–93.

Travers, T. (2001) 'Electronic trust services will inspire the next chapter of e-commerce in 2002', *Business Information Review*, 18 (4): 24–33.

Ward, M. and Lee, M. (2000) 'Internet shopping, consumer search and product branding', *Journal of Product & Brand Management*, 9 (1): 6–20.

Weiber, R. and Kollmann, T. (1998) 'Competitive advantages in virtual markets: perspectives of "information-based marketing" in cyberspace', *European Journal of Marketing*, 32 (7/8): 603–615.

Welch, R., Blackman, T., Liu, A., Mellers, B. and Stark, L. (1996) 'The effects of pictorial realism, delay and visual feedback, and observer interactivity on the subjective sense of presence', *Presence: Teleoperators and Virtual Environments*, 5 (3): 263–273.

Wolfinbarger, M. and Gilly, M. (2002) '.comQ: dimensionalising, measuring and predicting quality of the e-tail experience', *Marketing Science Institute Working Paper Series*, Number 02.100.

Wolfinbarger, M. and Gilly, M. (2003) 'eTailQ: dimensionalising, measuring and predicting etail quality', *Journal of Retailing*, 79 (3): 183–198.

Wu, G. (1999) 'Perceived interactivity and attitude toward website', *Annual Conference of American Academy of Advertising*, Albuquerque, New Mexico.

Zeithaml, V., Parasuraman, A. and Malhotra, A. (2000) 'A conceptual framework for understanding e-service quality: implications for future research and managerial practice', *Marketing Science Institute Working Paper Series*, Number 00.115.

Zemke, R. and Connellan, T. (2001) *e-Service: 24 ways to keep your customers – when the competition is just a click away*, New York: AMACOM.

Chapter 8

Branding on the Web

LINKS TO OTHER CHAPTERS

- Chapter 1 – The world of e-retailing
- Chapter 6 – e-Store design: navigability, interactivity and web atmospherics
- Chapter 7 – e-Service

KEY LEARNING POINTS

After completing this chapter you will have an understanding of:

- The nature of branding on the Web
- The role of interactivity and trust in building strong e-brands
- The nature of the e-retail mix in branding
- The notion of the overall e-retail offer
- How to choose an appropriate e-retail offer for an e-retailer
- e-Branding and how to use this concept to strengthen the overall e-retail offer

ORDERED LIST OF SUB-TOPICS

- Branding in conventional retailing
- Different approaches to branding on the Web
- Branding as hype: the narrow meaning
- e-Brand development I: start with the brand concept

- e-Brand development II: build the brand platform
- e-Brand development III: implement through the brand elements
- e-Brand development IV: the special role of interactivity and trust in building strong e-brands
- The role of the e-retail mix in branding
- What is the overall e-retail offer?
- A framework for choosing an optimal e-retail offer
- Conclusions
- Chapter summary
- ❖ Case study
- ❖ Questions
- ❖ References and further reading

BRANDING IN CONVENTIONAL RETAILING

Branding has become one of the most striking developments of conventional (bricks) retailing over the past decade. This has become a worldwide trend, led to some extent by well-known American retailers like The Gap, Home Depot, Toys R Us and Wal-Mart. The same is true in the UK, led by The Body Shop, Tesco, Sainsbury's and Marks & Spencer. In Australia brand leaders include Woolworths, Coles, Big W, Flight Centre and David Jones. In the Australian case, retailers occupy six of the 20 largest and most valuable brands. So branding has become a big business in its own right and good retailers can add value to the organization through clever brand management. We thus have a good reason to see how we can apply branding principles to the e-retailing context.

Before leaving this section we need to clarify that by the term *retailer brand* we are referring to the overall brand of the retailer across all of their business. The Body Shop is a brand that increases in value whenever that retailer improves their overall retailing performance. In a sense a retailer brand is a *corporate brand* or an *organizational brand*. In contrast, there is also something called a *store brand* or *own brand* or *private brand*, which is one that attaches to certain *products* within the store. In the UK the use of own or private brands is very high – up to 30 per cent of all products in some retail categories. For the purposes of this chapter we mainly refer to branding in the corporate/organizational sense rather than in terms of particular products.

DIFFERENT APPROACHES TO BRANDING ON THE WEB

Branding is a major consideration in developing an e-retail business. However, what we mean by branding and how should it be implemented vary according to different perspectives. Some people see branding in a fairly narrow sense – essentially part of the product decision. In this sense it is basically a logo, symbol or slogan. So an e-retailer might add the slogan 'serving you better' to its home page website. Of course, in the example given, there could be a presumption that the e-retailer really does serve you better, but the reality might be otherwise. In other words, a consultant or someone has advised the e-retailer to add a slogan and may even have supplied the words, without necessarily establishing that the policies and design of the e-retail site really do make a difference in the service. If this were the case, then consumers using such a site would get cynical and possibly angry and may eventually deliberately boycott such a site as soon as service gets bad or even ordinary. Branding yourself as something that you are not is worse than no branding at all, because you raise consumer *expectations* about the quality of what they will get.

An alternative, almost opposite, approach to branding is not to diminish it to a *small part* (the symbolism) of the product offer, but to suggest that it represents *everything* about the e-retailer. For this meaning the

> *e-brand* is a summary of the unique package of benefits offered by and distinctively associated with the e-retailer.

This definition of a brand for an e-retailer is a very powerful way of looking at branding. It also means that to understand branding you have to look at what lies behind the brand name. The brand name is just the tip of the iceberg. One has to look deeper and ascertain what is the *substance* and *essence* of the brand: Nike is not just a name or a swish; additionally there is meaning associated with the quality and performance of the products and the associated uses of those products.

We begin by reviewing the notion of branding as hype, that is, the narrow meaning of branding as simply a symbol, logo or slogan. Although we have already argued that this is too superficial, it nonetheless is an approach taken by many marketers and e-retailers. Indeed, the narrow definition of branding is similar to that (incorrectly) used by the American Marketing Association over the past decades. We then move to the definition of an e-brand used by this book, namely one that takes a broad approach to branding. Next we ask how we can build a *specific e-brand* to suit a particular e-retailer and market. We focus on the special role of interactivity, that is, relationships, in building a strong e-brand. This takes us into related issues about the nature of the e-retail mix and how to develop a market position in cyberspace.

BRANDING AS HYPE: THE NARROW MEANING

We have referred to the narrow meaning of branding as a sign, symbol or slogan. Another way of expressing this is to view branding as part of web atmospherics.

One can inject slogans, visuals, pop-ups and colours to create a particular 'branding' impact. A good example is Sanity, the Australian CD store. The physical store is relatively cool and hip, with lots of metal, ducting and exposed ceilings creating a very industrial look. The online site is very similar, with an extreme use of black colour to convey the same cool and hip image.

There are many e-retailer sites that have a high image/personality impact as soon as you click on. Good examples would include the sites *Yahoo!* and *Priceline.com*, where it is quickly obvious what the mood of each site is. Personality plays a big part in these sites. Not so much for these particular examples, but for some e-retailers, the high impact, strong personality is the main approach to branding. The reader might try to identify examples of e-retailers who have a *primarily* narrow-hype approach to branding.

There is nothing absolutely negative with this approach, *but it misses opportunities* to use branding in a more powerful way. For example, in the case of Sanity online, the cool and hip web atmospherics can be reinforced through careful selection of the product range of CDs offered. The other danger with the narrow, hype approach to branding is that in some cases it could be misleading, for example when 'serving you better' is not fulfilled in the experience of the customer, as discussed in the last section.

E-BRAND DEVELOPMENT I: START WITH THE BRAND CONCEPT

Our broader approach to *e-branding* is one that taps into all of the basic principles of branding used in the offline world. We begin with our new definition of branding that puts an emphasis on the distinctive package of benefits offered to customers (see p. 172).

So a useful way of starting the process of *brand development* is to appreciate that the brand name is only a part of the story and the *essence* of the brand has to be built. The central aspect of a brand is something called *brand identity*. What exactly is the meaning of the brand? What does the brand stand for? What sort of things or attributes do you (as a consumer) associate with the brand? Fundamentally this is the first step in building a brand. It is not enough to say that 'we are an e-retailer selling CDs', because that is too general and does not uniquely identify a particular e-retailer. Brands require a degree of focus and selectivity. For example, you could aim to be *the* CD e-retailer with the fastest delivery in a particular region (as far as logistics will allow) or a specialist in 1960s' music or heavy-metal music or whatever. This process needs to be continued until a unique package of benefits is created. As can be seen already though, uniqueness is not necessarily based purely on product differentiation; it could equally be based on service or image differentiation.

Although an image can be based on a variety of attributes, the end result has to be a simple, clear brand image that is very quickly comprehended by the consumer. If this is not the case, then there is need to further clarify and simplify. The authors propose the one-second test. Mention the word 'McDonald's' and within one second most consumers have a very good impression of what is conveyed by that brand. Within a second most people can conjure up the image of fast food, quick service, clean floors and Ronnie McDonald. This is not to say that everyone has the same positive image of McDonald's – far from it; even if there is a majority with a positive image there could also be a large minority with a negative image. The same is true for most brands. In summary, the first step in brand development is to develop a clear and strong brand identity (*brand concept*) – one that gives the company a competitive advantage in the market.

In the context of e-retailing, Lindstrom and Anderson (1999) devote a chapter to the development of a Web concept briefing. They suggest two sections for the Web concept, first outlining the market position of the brand and, second, developing the brand platform. The first of these sections concentrates on being clear about how your brand is perceived in the market, including such things as budget or premier brand, degree of quality, degree of service, etc. The second section covers the core values of the brand, its personality, the target audience profile and their experience with the Internet.

E-BRAND DEVELOPMENT II: BUILD THE BRAND PLATFORM

After the brand identity or brand concept is decided, the next step is to elaborate on this concept in terms of developing a solid brand platform foundation. The four key aspects of a brand platform (see Lindstrom and Anderson, 1999: 146) include role, personality, achievement and brand back-up.

The e-retailer needs to ascertain the purpose of the brand, how it can help people's lifestyle and the functional and emotional benefits being offered. This view links into the very nature of the brand, that is, what is the brand concept? What are the core values of the brand? For example, the predominant values of the Libra site (associated with the feminine hygiene product, Libra pads) are feminine, cool and confident. The personality of the brand includes the look and feel of the brand. Helpful ways for the e-retailer to approach this issue include associating the brand with an animal; for example, a cheetah is fast. Another approach is for the e-retailer to think in terms of the personality of the typical user and to build that into the e-retail site.

Achievement, the third aspect of the brand platform, refers to the realized differentiation of the e-retailer brand compared to competitors.

Brand back-up, the fourth aspect of the brand platform, asks whether the site is authentic. Can the claims or promises be backed up? Is the brand trustworthy?

Before leaving this section, we return to the suggestion made above that the e-retailer could establish what the personality of the typical user is and then use that to guide the development of a personality for the e-retail site. Notwithstanding, e-retailers need to be careful not to stereotype personalities. For example, it has been shown that there is not a single 'teenage personality', though there are some common needs, such as high expectations, speed and a need to be entertained and constantly diverted (Lindstrom, 2001: 258). There is also a fascinating question about whether people adopt a 'mask' when interacting with a computer, so that the screen social self is different from the real social self (Wallace, 1999). Research has only just begun on these sorts of issues, but they are important in terms of what ideal personality benchmark is needed when designing an e-brand and e-store in general.

E-BRAND DEVELOPMENT III: IMPLEMENT THROUGH THE BRAND ELEMENTS

Brand elements are the points of contact between the brand and the consumer. Banner advertisements are an example. Other examples include the myriad of signals sent from the e-retailer site to the consumer. The price of a product and the quality of the service are examples. Web atmospherics are another brand element that needs to be designed to reflect the desired look and feel of the brand and its personality. Communication and interactivity could also be considered branding elements.

In broad terms, the brand elements are all of the elements of the e-retail mix or the marketing mix. These brand elements need to be controlled and adjusted correctly if the design of the brand concept and the brand platform are to be successfully applied. Designing the right brand is really important and needs to be carefully thought out. But this will not come to much unless the brand elements are properly aligned to the brand platform. In other words, formulating a good brand is very important, but equally important is the execution or implementation of the brand through the brand elements.

E-BRAND DEVELOPMENT IV: THE SPECIAL ROLE OF INTERACTIVITY AND TRUST IN BUILDING STRONG E-BRANDS

The previous three sections represent the essential features of a three-stage framework, comprising brand concept, brand platform and brand elements, on how to develop an e-brand.

More detailed information on how to progress the three-stage e-brand development process can be found from either conventional books on brand-building (see Aaker, 1991, 1996; Kapferer, 1997; Keller, 2003) or from the increasing number of new books that are explicitly devoted to branding on the Web. Some of the better books include Lindstrom and Anderson (1999), Moon and Millison (2000), Carpenter (2000), Lindstrom (2001) and Braunstein and Levine (2000); see also Accenture (2001).

In one way or other we have already covered the potential role of trust and interactivity. Trust was referred to as 'back-up' – the fourth aspect of the brand platform (the need for credibility), while interactivity was mentioned as one of several brand elements to be used to help implement the brand platform. Notwithstanding the fact that we have already mentioned these two factors, we now wish to highlight the extraordinary role that they might contribute to the power of an e-brand.

We have referred to the increasing number of books explicitly devoted to e-branding. Interactivity and trust are two of the more common themes running through all of these books. Lindstrom and Anderson (1999), Carpenter (2000) and Braunstein and Levine (2000) particularly emphasize interactivity. Moon and Millison (2000) emphasize trust, while Lindstrom (2001) emphasizes both trust and interactivity. In a related way, Accenture (2001) highlights the role of the online experience as a brand builder. The predominance of the interactivity and trust themes in all of the major published works on e-branding is unlikely to be coincidental. At face value it makes sense – e-retailers are experiential brands. That is, consumers' perceptions of e-brands are driven by their total experience on the website, with interactivity being a central aspect of the experience.

Although the views that interactivity and trust are the key to e-branding come across very strongly from the authors of these e-branding books, we need to remind ourselves that the views are based on the *opinions* of the authors. It is true that these opinions are very informed because the authors tend to be experts, often with a lot of e-brand consulting experience. One of the few empirical academic studies to explicitly test the proposition that interactivity and trust are the key determinants of successful e-branding is found in Merrilees and Fry (2002). They showed that brand attitudes to the online CD e-retailer CDNOW.com were shaped by interactivity, trust and navigability, while trust in turn was primarily driven by interactivity. Another study to support this last relationship is in Merrilees and Fry (2003).

To see these connections more clearly we can further develop the model presented in Figure 6.1 (p. 138). This figure represented a schematic way to guide e-store design, namely by developing interactivity through web atmospherics and navigability. The three components of navigability, web atmospherics and interactivity can now be extended to three more components, namely trust, brand attitudes and brand loyalty. Figure 8.1 is a six-component *model of e-branding*.

Figure 6.1 shows an e-retailer how to develop interactivity, namely through a combination of navigability and web atmospherics. Having developed interactivity, this can be used by the e-retailer to build trust with the consumer.

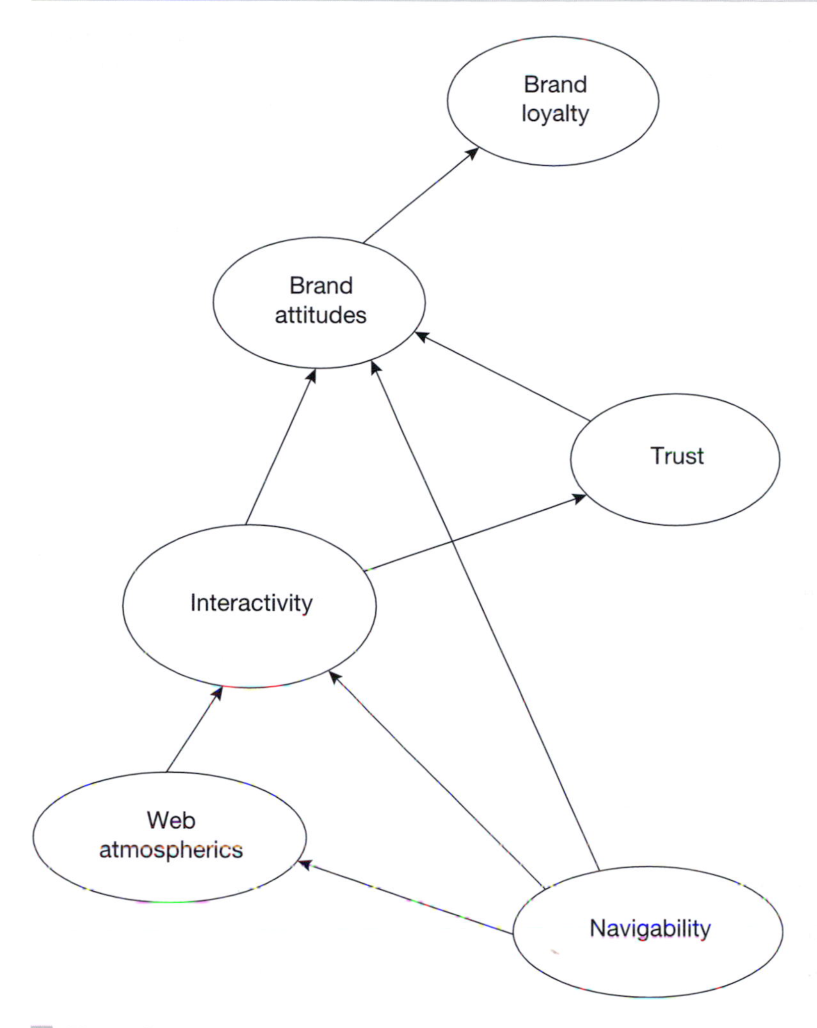

Figure 8.1 *An integrated framework for e-branding*

Source: Adapted from Merrilees and Fry (2002: 216)

In other words, the more contact/communication between the two players and the more willing the e-retailer is to answer questions and solve problems, then the greater the trust. Trust is built on a solid relationship between the e-retailer and the consumer.

The next stage in the process is critical for brand-building. Figure 8.1 shows that strong brands are driven by three elements that (in order of importance in the CDNOW site) are interactivity, trust and navigability. Importantly, the stronger the dialogue between the two parties (interactivity), the more highly regarded is the e-retailer (brand attitude). Trust reinforces this relationship and can be enhanced through appropriate cues, including privacy and security policies.

The final step in the Figure 8.1 framework is the link from brand attitudes to brand loyalty. Users with a more positive brand attitude to the e-retailer are more likely to return to the site and to repeat purchase. Such a final link is the clincher that it is worthwhile for the e-retailer to nurture a strong brand, with a fundamental requirement to pay close attention to interactivity and trust.

We conclude by saying that, from the point of view of both e-brand experts (the likes of Lindstrom, Anderson, Braunstein, Levine, Carpenter and Moon) and academic research, e-retailers wishing to build strong e-brands need to invest in both interactivity and trust.

So far in this chapter we have used a traditional brand-building framework, starting with the brand concept, moving to brand platform and then to brand elements, with a special look at interactivity and trust. An even more traditional way of approaching these issues is through the notion of the e-retail mix and market positioning. We now turn to this approach, which should reinforce some of the ideas already presented and further help the e-retailer to focus their marketing activities.

Mini case study 8.1: TWO OF THE GREATEST E-BRANDS: AMAZON.CO.UK AND EBAY.CO.UK

(See the case studies on pp. 46–51 and 104–105 respectively for more on these e-retailers.)

There is little debate that Amazon and eBay are two of the greatest e-brands since e-retailing began. Neither company was the absolute pioneer in the book or auction categories respectively. However, they were pioneering in the way they did e-business.

Amazon was the first online company to *explicitly* walk the customer through each step of the five-step purchasing process and essentially became the benchmark for most e-retailers. Indeed the entire site was developed keeping the customer foremost in mind, to ensure a satisfactory customer online experience. The five-step approach was later upgraded to the '1-click ordering technology' and the company was actually awarded a patent on this. Later, Amazon sued Barnes and Noble for infringement, causing critics to argue that the patent office was too liberal in awarding e-commerce rights. Amazon's strong customer service begins with a very personalized greeting each time a customer clicks back on, using a first name basis coupled with memory of the categories of interest to the user. Amazon is also very strong in terms of security and fast delivery. In the Australian book e-retailing case on pp. 183–184, Amazon generally outgunned the two local e-retailers in practically every aspect of the e-retail mix (see the Figure 8.2 *snake diagram* on p. 184), demonstrating just how good the Amazon brand is in a competitive situation. Amazon generally appears as a case study in many best practice e-commerce books (see for example Seybold, 1998: 123–138). For a more in-depth story about the Amazon business model approach and how this has evolved over time see Spector (2000).

With its current name, eBay is slightly more recent than Amazon (ignoring its previous life as Auction Web), with the auction category closely following books and CDs as early popular areas. It is particularly well known for its feedback ratings and the way in which categories are laid out. The ratings method seems to be a major contributor to building trust that is really critical for an auction trader attempting to bring buyers and sellers together.

To give a brief snapshot of just some of the eBay happenings throughout just one year (namely 1997) we can draw on Cohen (2002). Up to mid-1997, eBay still had fewer than 40 employees. The new staff being added had to fit in with the culture of eBay, which was itself changing. Marketing and business development was becoming more formalized. For example, rather than relying on organic growth, a pact was made with Netscape for ads that would drive traffic to eBay's site. It also launched a major public relations offensive. Further, CKS Interactive, a leading Silicon Valley branding expert, was called in to reposition the eBay brand and redesign its website. Customer surveys indicated some positive news; that the brand conveyed a crisp, clear message about what the company was trying to be – an online trading platform. The eBay website today still proclaims that its mission is '*to provide a global trading platform where practically anyone can trade practically anything*'. Later in 1997, eBay had to do battle with some tough competitors: Auction Universe and Onsale Exchange. For further instalments on the history of eBay see Cohen (2002).

One of the real strengths of eBay is that it provides a sense of community, which is a higher-level form of interactivity. Revisit our discussion of interactivity in Chapter 6 (pp. 133–135). The intention is to create a network that is more than just buying and selling. Additionally, users can have fun, shop around, discuss topics of interest, share information, get to know one another and pitch in.

Auction sites require trust, safety and privacy if they are to succeed. Davis and Benamati (2003) argue that eBay has performed very highly in this respect, in terms of privacy and protecting users against fraud. Additionally, as discussed by Joines *et al.*, (2003), one of the main reasons for using a site like eBay is to save time and money.

THE ROLE OF THE E-RETAIL MIX IN BRANDING

Chapter 1 introduced the concept of the (e-)retail mix. Just as there are the 4Ps in the conventional marketing mix, there are various components of the (e-)retail mix. In Chapter 1, we used the memory aid 'Sale the 7Cs' to simplify the components of the (e-)retail mix.

The retail mix is an important concept in conventional retailing. As we explained in Chapter 1, these components include personal service, advertising and in-store promotions, pricing, visual merchandising and other parts of store design and location, among others. The retail mix is a bit like the marketing mix in that the components represent the various marketing function activities that can be controlled by the retailer in order to influence the consumer. For example, if a retailer wants to sell more merchandise so as to reduce surplus inventory, they can have a 'sale' using a combination of the price and promotion components of the retail mix. As another example, a retailer may improve their image by upgrading the tone and materials of the visual merchandise displays. In each example, a different combination and direction of the retail mix is used, depending on the objectives of the retailer.

The same principles apply to the e-retail mix. In other words, the e-retail mix is an aid to the e-retailer to assist in the achievement of desired marketing objectives. Different e-retailing objectives require a different e-retail mix. As outlined in Chapter 1, price levels, price specials and advertising remain in the e-retail mix as per the marketing mix and the conventional retail mix. Sometimes there might be subtle differences in execution, such as banner ads, pop-up ads or pop-up special offers, but the essence of the component remains the same. In contrast, for some components of the retail mix, the e-retail mix counterpart takes on a radically different form. For example, the very important personal service in conventional retailing becomes 'interactivity' in the e-retail mix (see Chapter 6, pp. 133–135). Other types of customer service in conventional retailing become part of e-service in the e-retail mix (see Chapter 7). As another example, store design in conventional retailing becomes site design in the e-retail mix (see Chapter 6). A special part of store design, namely visual merchandising, becomes web atmospherics in the e-retail mix (see Chapter 6, pp. 136–139). Another important part of store design, in conventional retailing – layout – becomes layout and navigability in the e-retail mix (see Chapter 6, pp. 137–139). Further, location in conventional retailing becomes global with universal access in the e-retail mix, instead of a fixed physical site, though supplemented by portal and e-mall alliances (see Chapter 9). Finally, although convenience was always indirectly represented in conventional retailing through the location component, it is now worth *explicit* consideration in the e-retail mix context because of the special significance of convenience for e-retailing consumers. Taken together, the elements of the e-retail mix can be seen as representing the package of benefits offered by the e-retail brand.

WHAT IS THE OVERALL E-RETAIL OFFER?

The overall e-retail offer is the particular package of offerings made by the e-retailer to the consumer. For example, an e-retailer might specialize in second-hand books and offer a wide search capacity combined with a good deal on the books offered. The restriction to second-hand books is a speciality in the product area, while emphasis is primarily given to wide choice and fair prices. The overall e-retail offer therefore focuses on three elements of the e-retail mix, namely product specialization, wide search and low prices, with less attention to other elements of the e-retail mix, such as e-service (transaction processing and delivery) and web atmospherics.

The reader might now see the connection between the previous section (describing the e-retail mix) and this one (understanding the e-retail offer). The e-retail offer represents the value proposition made by the e-retailer to the consumer. It represents a particular package or combination of the e-retail elements. The e-retailer has an infinite number of combinations of the e-retail mix to choose from. The next section addresses how the e-retailer chooses the best package of offerings.

A FRAMEWORK FOR CHOOSING AN OPTIMAL E-RETAIL OFFER

There is a number of issues that the e-retailer must work through before choosing what seems to be the best package of benefits to the consumer. First, the notion of *trade-offs* must be addressed. It is not possible for an e-retailer to offer the best of everything because sometimes attributes are opposites. It would not be possible or desirable for a company to offer the highest quality and the lowest price. Similarly, a high-service, high-convenience e-retailer would require a lot of finances and resources to make that happen, so it would be very difficult to also present as the cheapest site. Thus there is a trade-off between convenience (service) and low price. An e-retailer needs to be clear upfront and decide which of convenience or low price they want to emphasize.

Second, the issue of trade-offs raises a related point about exactly what are the strengths of an organization? In other words, the optimal e-retail offer (mix) should highlight those areas in which the e-retailer has a particular strength. For example, an e-retailer might decide that they are particularly effective in logistics and therefore might emphasize speedy and reliable delivery service as a key part of their value package to consumers. The same outcome might arise from an e-retailer who jointly has a large bricks network of stores that might be used for e-retailer consumers to more easily return goods that are not satisfactory. As a different example, another organization might have strong Web design skills, helping it build user-friendly navigation links or clever forms of interactivity.

Third, the issue of trade-offs is not confined to extreme cases like high convenience vs. low price. In fact it applies to all pairs of e-retail mix elements. Even if it had a lot of resources it would be too difficult for a company to try to move in all directions at the same time; it gets too confusing for all concerned. Ultimately it becomes necessary to focus scarce resources in a particular direction.

Michael Porter developed a model some time ago suggesting that companies needed to choose between differentiation and low cost (with niche business a third choice). A more modern approach to strategy formulation comes from Cravens *et al*. (2000) who develop four alternative generic strategies for firms to choose from, namely *branding*, *innovation*, *channel management* and *price leadership*.

CONCLUSIONS

Branding on the Web is about selecting a unique or distinctive package of benefits to be offered to the consumer in a way that gives a competitive advantage to the e-retailer. From the outset we make it clear that branding is more than the name of the e-retailer (URL). It is about the essence and substance of the e-retailer and might relate to the products, services or image of the particular e-retailer.

Branding does not come naturally to many retailers or e-retailers, but rather presents quite a challenge as to how to do this well. To assist with this process the book presents a three-stage brand development framework for e-retailers. Critically, it is clear that branding needs to start with a clear understanding of exactly what is the brand, in terms of its meaning and identity. The brand platform is the next stage and develops the detailed components of the brand concept, including core brand values, personality, point of difference and credibility. Finally, the third stage focuses on implementation, which requires alignment between the brand platform and the brand elements that are at the sharp (consumer) edge.

Special attention has been given to interactivity and trust as the key to building a strong e-brand. This position is supported by the literature, essentially that of e-brand consultants. However, one particular academic study is also used to support the notion that interactivity and trust are the key drivers of strong e-brands. A diagram (Figure 8.1, p. 177) is used to help reinforce how these components fit together to drive brand attitudes and brand loyalty.

CHAPTER SUMMARY

There are different approaches to branding on the Web, ranging from the very narrow approach focusing on web atmospherics to a more strategic approach. The strategic approach is akin to the methods used by branders in traditional settings and follows a three-stage process. Brand development goes through the following three stages:

- start with the brand concept (brand identity);
- then build the brand platform;
- then implement through the brand elements (including interactivity and web atmospherics).

A related, though different, approach to Web strategy is through manipulation of the e-retail mix. The e-retail offer represents a particular package or combination of the e-retail elements. This chapter provides guidance for the e-retailer in selecting the best package of benefits to offer to the consumer.

In the next chapter we consider the potential for expanding the audience for an e-retail offer by being represented with other e-retailers on an e-mall.

Case study 8.1: THREE AUSTRALIAN BOOK E-RETAILERS (www.dymocks.com.au; www.bookworld.com.au; www.amazon.com)

Merrilees (2001) applies this new four-type generic strategy framework to three Australian book e-retailers. He concludes that *Amazon* is currently using the dual strategies of branding and channel management; *Dymocks* is using mainly a channel management strategy; and *Angus & Robertson* is using a low price strategy. For example, the Dymocks channel management strategy is built around responsiveness to customer needs, a convenient returns policy and a book club program to nurture their own loyal base of customers.

The generic strategy framework provides a guide to the selection of an optimal e-retail offer. Simply put, an e-retailer should choose from the four generic strategies, with the possibility (as in the Amazon case) that dual strategies could be chosen. Once the generic or dual generic strategies are chosen, it is still necessary for the e-retailer to shape the generic strategy in a distinctive way to reflect that particular e-retailer. Thus both Amazon and Dymocks use a channel management strategy, but each formulates this in a slightly different and unique way.

An alternative way of moving towards an optimal e-retail offer is to pinpoint a unique *market position* on a map, relative to other competitors. One limitation of most textbook maps is that they are two-dimensional, so we would be limited to two attributes, when in practice there are many elements in the e-retail mix as discussed earlier. A somewhat novel way to compare different e-retailers on a map when there are four or five or more key attributes (e-retail mix elements) entails the researcher using a *snake diagram*. An example of this is Figure 8.2, which shows the three Australian book e-retailers assessed against seven e-retail mix elements, including low price, latest books, wide selection, fast delivery, fair and easy returns policy and close personal relationship (see Merrilees 2001). Based on a survey of users, readers can apply this technique to any e-retail category.

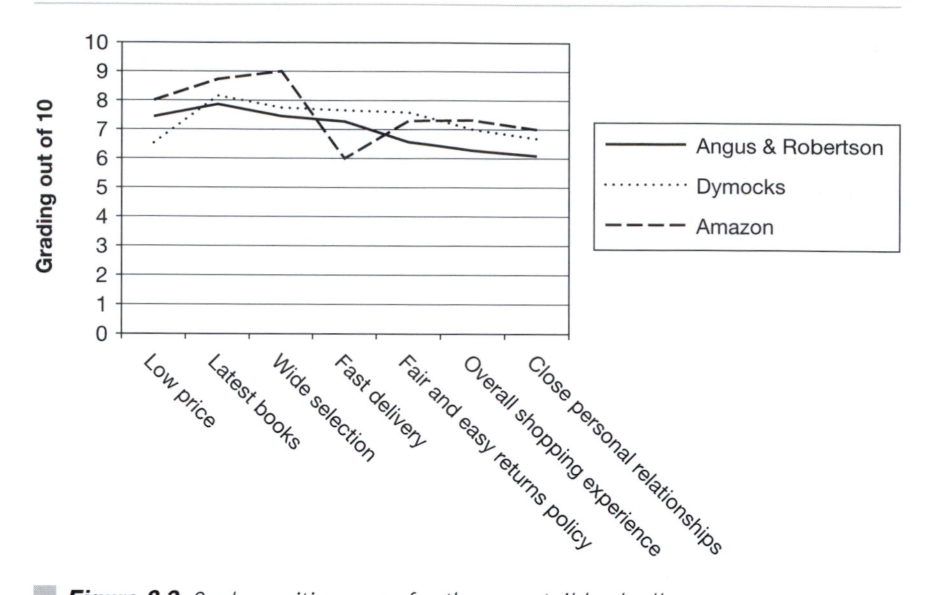

Figure 8.2 *Snake position maps for three e-retail booksellers*
Source: Adapted from Merrilees (2001), p. 179

QUESTIONS

Brief feedback to these questions is included at the back of the book.

Question 8.1

A common mistake in branding or the understanding of branding is to treat it very narrowly as a sign, symbol or slogan. What is wrong or limiting with this approach?

Question 8.2

Briefly summarize the three-stage approach for e-brand development outlined in Chapter 8 (pp. 173–175).

Question 8.3

The brand platform stage of e-brand development includes the need to develop the personality of the e-brand. Select a particular e-retailer and show how you would use web atmospherics to develop the brand of this particular e-retailer.

Question 8.4

Chapter 8 has really highlighted the importance of interactivity and trust as necessary for building strong e-brands. Why have these two aspects been highlighted in this role?

Question 8.5

Why are Amazon and eBay regarded as such strong e-brands?

REFERENCES AND FURTHER READING

Aaker, D. (1991) *Managing Brand Equity*, New York: Free Press.

Aaker, D. (1996) *Building Strong Brands*, New York: Free Press.

Accenture (2001) 'Beyond the blur: correcting the vision of Internet brands', www.cio.com/research/ec/cc_market.html.

Braunstein, M. and Levine, E. (2000) *Deep Branding on the Internet*, Roseville, CA: Prima Venture.

Carpenter, P. (2000) *E-Brands: Building an Internet Business at Bottleneck Speeds*, Boston, MA: Harvard Business School.

Cohen, A. (2002) *The Perfect Store: Inside E-Bay*, Boston, MA: Little, Brown and Company.

Cravens, D., Merrilees, B. and Walker, R. (2000) *Strategic Marketing Management For The Pacific Region*, Sydney: McGraw-Hill.

Davis, W. and Benamati, J. (2003) *E-Commerce Basics: Technology, Foundations & E-Business Applications*, New York: Addison Wesley.

Joines, J., Scherer, C. and Scheufele, D. (2003) 'Exploring motivations for consumer Web use and their implications for e-commerce', *Journal of Consumer Marketing*, 20: 90–108.

Kapferer, J. (1997), *Strategic Brand Management* (2nd ed.), London: Kogan Page.

Keller, K. (2003) *Building, Measuring and Managing Brand Equity*, Upper Saddle Valley, NJ.: Prentice Hall.

Lindstrom, M. (2001) *Clicks, Bricks & Brands*, Melbourne: Hardie Grant.

Lindstrom, M. and Anderson, T. (1999) *Brand Building on the Internet*, Melbourne: Hardie Grant.

Merrilees, B. (2001) 'Do traditional strategic concepts apply in the e-marketing context?' *Journal of Business Strategies*, 18 (2): 177–190.

Merrilees, B. and Fry, M. (2002) 'Corporate branding: a framework for e-retailers', *Corporate Reputation Review*, 5 (2/3): 213–225.

Merrilees, B. and Fry, M. (2003) 'E-trust: the influence of perceived interactivity on e-retailing users', *Market Intelligence & Planning*, 21 (2): 123–128.

Moon, M. and Millison, D. (2000) *Firebrands: Building Brand Loyalty in the Internet Age*, Berkeley, CA: Osborne McGraw-Hill.

Seybold, P. (1998) *Customers.com*, New York: Random House.

Spector, R. (2000) *Amazon.com*, New York: Harper Business.

Wallace, P. (1999) *The Psychology of the Internet*, Cambridge: Cambridge University Press.

Chapter 9

e-Malls

LINKS TO OTHER CHAPTERS

This chapter builds on the following chapters in particular:

- Chapter 1 – The world of e-retailing
- Chapter 6 – e-Store design: navigability, interactivity and web atmospherics
- Chapter 7 – e-Service
- Chapter 8 – Branding on the Web

KEY LEARNING POINTS

After completing this chapter you will have an understanding of:

- The nature of online malls
- How to transfer lessons from conventional malls to online malls
- The need to explore mall look-alikes, including ancillary malls
- The value of using case studies to get more insight
- The role of interactivity and trust in building strong e-brands
- The importance of interactivity in building e-mall trust
- The importance of mall design (navigability) and tenant mix (quality) in building interactivity

ORDERED LIST OF SUB-TOPICS

- Conventional (bricks) malls
- Lessons from conventional malls for online malls
- Multiple category e-retailers
- Shopping bots: intelligent shopper assistants or virtual mall?
- Portals and other quasi e-malls
- Examples of e-malls
- Case study
- Lessons from Australian case studies of e-malls
- e-Malls as ports of entry for newly started businesses: the tenant perspective
- Conclusions
- Chapter summary
- ❖ Questions
- ❖ References and further reading

CONVENTIONAL (BRICKS) MALLS

In most Western countries malls have gradually become the dominant shopping location for much of what we buy. At the same time malls have become more competitive with each other and now use a variety of extra methods including promotions and entertainment to capture the highest market share (see Sit *et al.*, 2003). As with other chapters, we continue to draw upon an understanding of conventional retailing in order to guide e-retailing businesses. So initially we need to identify the key principles that are important in conventional mall marketing and management. From this benchmark we can then draw lessons for e-malls.

THINK POINT

Before outlining the conventional mall principles it is interesting to reflect on a puzzle. How many e-malls does the reader know about, let alone use? One suspects that the typical reader does not know very many and perhaps a large number of you may not know any! Of itself your lack of information does not really matter, because by the end of the chapter you will know some and have visited them.

Conventional malls are not all the same, though some have been criticized for being too similar in terms of the retailer tenants in them. Each mall is different in some respect. Sometimes it is simply a size matter, with contrasts across jumbo malls, medium to large conventional malls, down to small neighbourhood malls. In other cases they differ as to special or unusual features, with extreme examples of the wave pool or submarine ride at West Edmonton Mall in Canada or the Lego store and many rides at Mall of America. Malls differ as well in terms of their specialization, with differences in the format. Many malls adopt the conventional format of having fashion, home and food components. But some are more specialized, such as *power centres* (a small number of large superstores, catering to bulky purchases like furniture, bedding, carpets or electrical goods) or *factory outlet centres* (giving the opportunity to buy well-known brands like Wedgwood or Nike at discount prices). Another point of difference between malls is the different emphasis given to entertainment, with some malls putting on fashion and other shows or having electronic games parlours. Careful selection of tenants could also differentiate one mall from the others, for example by grouping a lot of trendy, independent fashion designers.

A recent Australian study (Sit *et al.*, 2003) has pulled together the literature on conventional malls. The study has identified four main areas which shape the image of a mall, including:

- merchandise (types of tenants, quality, assortment, pricing);
- accessibility (ease of access to the centre and within the centre);
- services (including signs, escalators, restrooms);
- atmospherics (including ambience, music, decor).

These four broad areas tend to appear repeatedly in the growing number of studies of shopping malls. The four areas thus represent a starting point for any mall owner to define what sort of brand they want to be. Notwithstanding, Sit *et al.* (2003) note that the academic studies have neglected some factors that could be important in differentiating shopping centres, namely entertainment, food and security. These authors note that entertainment and food in particular seem to be increasingly used as a method of shopping mall differentiation.

A recent British study (Dennis *et al.*, 2002), based on a study of six British malls, has provided more detailed insight into the branding of conventional malls. An interesting finding by Dennis *et al.* was that consumers were able to associate a personality with a particular shopping centre. One shopping centre studied was described as 'dull and boring and old-fashioned – lower working class or elderly'. As an animal it was like a cat or dog – not exciting, just OK. In contrast, another centre was described as like a tiger, lion or peacock – strong, vibrant, big and colourful. Dennis *et al.* conclude with some advice about active brand-management of malls. The first step is to focus on key attributes like quality, service, atmosphere and infrastructure. Second, choice of the right market positioning is important in creating a point of difference. Third, internal marketing has the potential to help. Finally, well-blended communication can develop credibility.

There is also a broad literature that focuses on how to build a good relationship between the shopping centre landlord and the retail tenant (see Howard, 1997; Roberts and Merrilees, 2003). Howard suggests that in the past too much attention has been placed by landlords on property as a financial investment, rather than investing in the relationship between the landlord and the tenant. Roberts and Merrilees empirically show that stronger cooperation between the landlord and the tenants (such as joint promotions or joint planning of tasks) can improve the performance of the mall. The same authors also show that trust is a precondition for tenants to be willing to cooperate.

THINK POINT

If we include small neighbourhood shopping centres, then the majority of Australian, British, American and other Western country shoppers would visit a mall or centre at least once every two weeks. For a sizeable minority, much of the shopping and even a lot of the social lifestyle are mall-based. *Why is there such a contrast between the role of the conventional mall and that of the e-mall?* Why is the e-mall not utilized to the same extent? Think about this issue yourself and work out what *you* regard as the main answer. We will return to the issue at the end of the chapter.

LESSONS FROM CONVENTIONAL MALLS FOR ONLINE MALLS

One of the key lessons from conventional mall management that applies to online mall management is the need to manage the *business-to-business* (B2B) relationship between the online mall landlord and the e-retailer tenants. There is a need for the online mall landlord to build a trusting relationship with its online tenants. Most likely, interactivity or cross-communication may be the best way to do this, which is consistent with the Australian case study evidence (pp. 193–196) (although this evidence only relates to communication between the online mall and customer/users of the mall, and not tenants per se). Additional mall management issues include things like leasing arrangements and policies. The terms of the lease need to balance the needs of both the landlord and the tenant and to provide financial incentives to expand the online tenant business as much as possible.

Another lesson from conventional mall management is the need for the online mall landlord to provide appropriate and reliable services to the e-retailer tenants.

In an online context, appropriate services might include a well-designed mall, referring to the architecture, including access entrances and layout. Deck (1997) highlights the importance of navigation and other architectural design issues for successful e-malls. Second, services might also include 'decor', which in this context might mean ensuring that each e-retailer has neat and clean premises, rather than a shabby, disorganized appearance. Decor might also include the appropriate 'atmosphere', an issue that most conventional mall studies highlight. Third, traditional mall management includes 'security', which in the online context might entail a third-party guarantee (from the online mall manager, who in turn might outsource this service to a regular third-party vetting firm) that each e-retailer tenant in the online mall has secure facilities for financial transactions online.

Yet another lesson from conventional mall practices is the need to market the online mall in various ways. One way this could be done is through advertising, possibly online. There could also be a coordinated mall-wide promotion for a limited time, say a 10 per cent off deal. A further marketing tool relates to the selection of the tenant mix. Usually the tenant mix is not accidental, but rather is planned and designed to project a particular image (brand) of the mall. Malls can be upmarket, no frills, entertainment-based and so on. Some malls are very specialized, such as factory-outlet or power centres. An online mall owner can deliberately create a particular mall brand image and might be judged on how consistently they could execute this image. This is a fundamental aspect of mall marketing. Atmospherics can also be interpreted as a marketing tool, supporting the overall e-mall brand image.

Finally, Chapter 8 provides a useful input into online branding, drawing on practical book references as well as recent academic research. The main finding from e-retailer branding is that interactivity and trust are very important influences in terms of creating online brands.

MULTIPLE CATEGORY E-RETAILERS

Although not strictly an e-mall, it is interesting to consider multiple category e-retailers. Amazon is probably the best-known example in this situation, where a single-site owner sells goods across multiple retail categories, including books and CDs. In fact Amazon resembles an online department store in this respect. Perhaps surprisingly there are not many explicit online department stores. An Australian example was d-store, which had about 20 departments, though this has now ceased operating as an online department store.

Although multiple category e-retailers provide an interesting source of ideas and inspiration that may be useful for e-malls, to date there is very little academic research investigating such a format. Merrilees (2001), among other authors, has studied Amazon, but purely in terms of a single category (books) and not in terms of multiple categories. No doubt a lot of the well-known good properties of Amazon flow over to the multiple category situation, but there is still a need to ascertain how convenient and useful the site is for searching and buying multiple categories of goods on a *single* shopping trip. Further, how many users actually buy more than one category of goods from Amazon in a single trip?

THINK POINT

The lack of academic studies on Amazon in terms of its potential usefulness to buy more than one category of goods in the one shopping trip does not stop you, the reader, from simulating such a trip. Click on to Amazon and see how easy or not it would be to buy from say two categories of goods. Can you suggest any improvements in the design of the site to improve on the user-friendliness of Amazon for consumers who might wish to use it as an online department store (that is, multiple rather than a single category of goods)?

SHOPPING BOTS: INTELLIGENT SHOPPER ASSISTANTS OR VIRTUAL MALL?

Shopping bots are tools that help e-shoppers identify, locate and compare products available from e-retailers (Rowley, 2000: 298). There can be a consumer/shopper perspective or an e-retailer one. In the former sense shopping bots are another tool for searching the Internet and are not very different from an online directory or a search engine.

Alternatively, we can conceptualize a shopping bot from the perspective of the *e-retailer*, who forms a contractual relation (like a tenant) with the *provider* of the shopping bot (like a landlord). It is in this sense that the shopping bot can be considered as a virtual mall, which helps e-retailers present and project their merchandise to the public (Rowley, 2000).

Bots tend to be either comprehensive or specialized (say books, music, CDs, gifts) in terms of product categories carried. Rowley (2000: 300) lists about 20 shopping bots and suggests the following overall site for a general listing of the shopping bots: www.smartbots.com.

Category search is a common approach to moving through a bot. As an example, storesearch.com invites shoppers to select a department; the next screen displays a series of product categories in that department; then, choosing one of these categories will display a number of merchants.

Rowley (2000) does address the difficulty of how the consumer might choose across shopping bots. Some shopping bots seem more suitable for certain products, but it is difficult to generalize. There is also a number of traps to watch out for, with a need for the correct level of specificity and specification. For example, a searcher might specify both the author and title of a book, but there might not be an exact match because of the way the shopping bot database is set up. Ironically, in this hypothetical case, a lower level of specification, such as only the author's name, might be more successful in locating the book. In another case, 'running shoes' might be more successful than 'shoes' or 'sports shoes'. It is hard to see how anything other than one's own experience, or praise or complaints from friends, can guide the selection of shopping bots. More academic research might help us on this matter.

PORTALS AND OTHER QUASI-E-MALLS

We have just seen that shopping bots can be considered to be a type of virtual mall. We should also acknowledge that there are many additional Internet listing and search tools or intermediaries and other third-party sites that also contribute to the world of e-commerce. Yahoo! is probably the most famous site, but there are hundreds of sites that also contribute a similar or related linking of parties through the network. We simply acknowledge this component of the e-retail sector, leaving it to other researchers to elaborate on their role (see for example Dong and Su, 1997).

EXAMPLES OF E-MALLS

An e-mall is sometimes referred to as a cyber-mall or a virtual mall or an e-shopping centre. It brings together a number of separately owned e-retail sites to a single virtual location, with the individual e-retailers paying rent to the centre management, as in an offline mall. A British example of such an e-mall is www.indigosquare.com.

An interesting example of an American (fashion) niche mall is www.fashion-world.com. This mall has about 100 fashion retailers in it, categorized by floor, which include Main Street and an outlet clearance floor (Hill, 2000).

In the Australian case there were recently two e-malls of prominence, namely www.ozeshopping.com.au and www.sofcom.com.au.

The e-mall should *not* be confused with a related system in which consumers can be guided to a particular offline (bricks) shopping centre, where they can use special deal coupons downloaded from the central system. For an American version of this latter system, see www.myshoppingcenter.com.

The same sites are provided by Australian bricks malls, with similar announcements of book signings, promotions and general information about the tenants in each of the malls in the multi-mall portfolio of the mall owner. See, for example, www.westfield.com.au and www.harbourtown.com.au. A slightly different approach has been taken by the South Australian Government, which has developed its own online mega-mall, with a category-based listing of a wide range of online vendors: www.sacentral.sa.gov.au/shopping/online.

We are restricted to giving just a few examples of online malls. However, the reader is invited to discover other e-malls, either in their own country or in other countries.

Case study 9.1: AUSTRALIAN RESEARCH INTO E-MALLS (www.ozeshopping.com.au; and www.sofcom.com.au)

This chapter is a little different from other chapters in that, instead of several smaller case studies, we have one mega case study of two Australian malls. The details of the case study follow in the next section.

AN AUSTRALIAN RESEARCH STUDY OF TWO e-MALLS

The authors have developed a questionnaire based on the literature, deriving issues important to Internet users/shoppers relevant to their attitudes towards purchasing from e-malls. Respondents were asked to familiarize themselves with two predetermined Australian sites, namely www.ozeshopping.com.au and www.sofcom.com.au, and explore the two sites' features before answering a set of Likert scale-based questions.

By way of broad description, there was a difference in the overall image of the two sites. Ozeshopping was fairly close to what you might term or imagine a regular (online) shopping mall. It had an anchor store, which was an online department store (dstore), and more than 30 tenants, including many well-known Australian bricks and clicks e-retailers (such as Sanity or Strathfield). The site was fairly organized and looked like a solid upper-middle market mall. In contrast, sofcom had an entirely different image. It came across as much more variable in the types of tenants, from sophisticated to somewhat 'seedy'. Most of the tenants could be said to have a strong tourist-Australiana image, making it more of a niche mall. It had an anchor store (e-store; an electrical goods store) and had a higher proportion of pure clicks retailers.

In constructing the survey items specific to this study, prior studies were reviewed to extrapolate items examining Web usage and branding theory research. Then a survey was designed with items intended to capture the underlying multi-item constructs of e-brand attitudes, e-interactivity, e-trust, navigability and retailer-quality. Each survey item was measured on a seven-point scale of (1) disagree very strongly to (7) agree very strongly.

The current study focuses particularly on the potential roles of interactivity and e-trust *inter alia* in influencing brand attitudes with respect to e-malls. Both *interactivity* and *e-trust* have previously been shown to be powerful and central determinants of brand attitudes with respect to a particular e-retail site (Merrilees and Fry, 2002) and the same might be expected with respect to e-malls.

The study consisted of 116 Australian undergraduate marketing students from a large regional area. Given the nature of the study, only those who had indicated that they had used the Internet were selected to participate in the study. The student sample *met the minimum conditions* needed for this study in that they (1) were familiar and experienced with the Internet for information search and (2) were of an age (mostly 18–25) that comprises a major segment in the Internet buying market. Importantly, as the study focuses on purchase intention rather than actual purchase, it was not critical that respondents had previously purchased via the Internet. All respondents had access to the Internet, either privately or through university facilities. The sample consisted of an equal number of males and females with a median age of 21 years.

Modelling the determinants of e-mall brand attitudes

This entailed estimating the various paths of the model, with the emphasis on a multiple regression of the determinants of e-mall brand attitude, for each e-mall separately. Table 9.1 summarizes the regression analysis that explains e-mall brand attitude. It should be noted that the statistical fit is good, with adjusted R-squares of 0.66 and 0.57.

Table 9.1 *Determinants of brand attitudes in two Australian e-malls*

Variable	*Ozeshopping e-mall*	*Sofcom e-mall*
Constant	–0.37	–0.20
	(1.1)	(0.6)
e-Trust	0.54	0.54
	(6.06)**	(6.69)**
Interactivity	0.32	0.29
	(3.62)**	(3.62)**
Adjusted R-square	0.66	0.57
F-ratio	106.3**	71.8**

Notes: * denotes significant t or F value at 5 per cent level;
** denotes significant t or F value at 1 per cent level

The main finding in Table 9.1 is that both e-trust and interactivity were key determinants of brand attitude for the sample of users of the two Australian e-malls. The standardized beta coefficient on the e-trust variable was 0.5, meaning that for every additional *two* points of e-trust (measured on a seven-point scale), there will be a *one*-point increase in positive brand attitude towards that e-mall. Similarly, the beta coefficient on the interactivity variable was approximately 0.33, which means that, for every *three* points of interactivity (measured on a seven-point scale), there will be a *one*-point increase in positive brand attitude towards that e-mall. Both of these two variables were significant at the 1 per cent level, with high t-values. No other variables had a statistically significant effect on brand attitude.

Modelling the determinants of e-mall trust

The results of ascertaining the determinants of e-mall trust produced only one statistically significant variable, namely interactivity (see Table 9.2). There was a high beta coefficient of interactivity on e-trust for both of the e-mall sites. That is, the greater the level of interactivity, the greater the level of e-trust that was significant at the 1 per cent level.

Table 9.2 *Determinants of e-trust in two Australian e-malls*

Variable	*Ozeshopping e-mall*	*Sofcom e-mall*
Constant	1.30	1.81
	(4.31)**	(5.30)**
Interactivity	0.78	0.62
	(12.98)**	(8.26)**
Adjusted R-square	0.60	0.38
F-ratio	168.4**	68.3**

Notes: * denotes significant t or F value at 5 per cent level;
** denotes significant t or F value at 1 per cent level

Modelling the determinants of e-interactivity

The regression results are shown in Table 9.3. The perceived interactivity of each e-mall can be largely explained by a combination of both the site navigability and the quality of the retail mix in the mall.

Table 9.3 *Determinants of interactivity in two Australian e-malls*

Variable	*Ozeshopping e-mall*	*Sofcom e-mall*
Constant	1.25	1.28
	(3.02)**	(4.57)**
Navigability	0.49	0.55
	(5.15)**	(6.88)**
Retail mix quality	0.21	0.26
	(2.21)*	(3.23)**
Adjusted R-square	0.42	0.50
F-ratio	40.5**	55.8**

Notes: * denotes significant t or F value at 5 per cent level;
** denotes significant t or F value at 1 per cent level

LESSONS FROM AUSTRALIAN CASE STUDIES OF E-MALLS

The main finding of our empirical work is that both e-trust and interactivity were crucial in forming brand attitudes towards each of the two Australian e-mall sites studied. In broad terms this finding is similar to earlier research that had found the same two variables were also crucial in forming brand attitudes at the site of an individual e-retailer, CDNOW (Merrilees and Fry, 2002). Thus these two variables seem fundamental in explaining brand attitudes of sites that use a variety of *business-to-consumer* (B2C) business models.

However, there are some subtle differences in comparing brand attitudes across e-retailers and e-malls. With the *e-retailer site*, interactivity was the most important determinant of brand attitudes, while with the two *e-mall sites* e-trust was relatively more important. This suggests that, with the more complex and multi-retailer site, trust seems to be a bigger issue. This makes sense in that trust is more difficult to assess if there are multiple retailers and doubts can arise if trustworthy retailers are juxtaposed with less trustworthy retailers.

Trust is most likely a key factor in *any* company's reputation, whether in e-commerce or not. This seems likely because trust is akin to being reassured that the specific company will look after the interests of the user or consumer and protect them in all respects. It is a form of meta-guarantee – one that goes beyond just a product guarantee. Trust is likely to be even more important in the context of e-retailers and extremely important for e-mall owners. This is because major consumer concerns over the adequacy of credit card security or the way that privacy matters are handled could deter the completion of transactions, especially if different firms have different security and privacy policies.

The issue of e-trust can also be explored by comparing the Table 9.2 results across the two e-malls. The sofcom.com.au site is different from the ozeshopping.com.au site in that it has less of the large, well-known branded bricks retailers and more smaller retailers and pure e-retailers. These characteristics make it harder for the sofcom e-mall to gain the trust of users. This may be why the constant term in the sofcom mall is larger and more significant than that for the ozeshopping mall; that is, 1.81 vs. 1.30.

The study breaks new ground in explaining brand attitudes in the e-mall context. The two most important drivers of e-mall brand attitudes were *e-trust* and *e-interactivity*. These relationships were both large (that is, large regression beta coefficients) and highly statistically significant (at the 1 per cent level). Thus the model suggests that e-trust and e-interactivity are two key elements in successful Web branding of e-mall sites.

The results suggest that trust is relatively more important for e-malls compared to individual e-retailer sites in terms of developing Internet brand attitudes. This may be due to the diversity of retailers in the mall context and the inclusion of smaller retailers and pure e-retailers. Owners and prospective developers of future e-mall sites need to be cognizant of the need to develop an overall strategy of trust building. This includes the need to put in place various explicit policies and implement other mechanisms that help project confidence and trust to the consumer and other stakeholders. It also requires careful selection of online tenants, that is, those who will instil trust among e-mall consumers. Finally, and perhaps most importantly, e-mall sites need to develop interactivity, because this is fundamental to e-trust specifically and ongoing relationships more generally.

E-MALLS AS PORTS OF ENTRY FOR NEWLY STARTED BUSINESSES: THE TENANT PERSPECTIVE

It has been obvious that the main perspective that we have taken so far has been that of the e-mall owner. From this perspective we have questions like how should the e-mall be designed so as to be attractive to e-retailer tenants and to potential users or consumers of the e-mall? Although it has been implicit, another perspective is that of the tenant. This leads to a different set of questions. Do I need a presence in an e-mall for my business? If so, what would a suitable e-mall look like? Which one(s) should I become a tenant in?

An appropriate answer to some of these questions is almost certainly connected to the consumer evaluation of an e-mall. The two Australian case studies of e-malls were on the basis of users or consumers assessing an e-mall. If consumers or users rate an e-mall highly then that would be a positive cue to an e-retailer who is considering becoming a prospective tenant. However, it is not a simple matter of a prospective tenant choosing the most popular e-mall site for consumers. The reason is that the best or most popular e-malls will also have the highest rents. A prospective tenant may like to have a high-traffic, high-selling e-mall presence, but may not be able to afford it. This lesson is derived from conventional retailing. McDonald's likes to have high-traffic sites; but it has to pay a lot for them. Within a conventional mall, rents differ for different stalls (micro sites) depending on the traffic flows. The same principles apply in cyber-space.

Additional issues in how tenants might choose or use an e-mall are discussed in Hill (2000) and O'Hara (2001).

Moving on from the rent issue, the e-mall presents a great means for an upstart online organization to get a presence (Hof, 2000). Sometimes the upstarts become the main players. Hof (2000) describes the case of Indianapolis-based National Wine & Spirits Inc. wanting an online presence. Rather than potentially getting upstaged, the company formed its own e-mall (eSkye.com Inc.) that was a national marketplace for beverage makers, distributors and retailers to buy and sell online. Hall (1998) and Strom (1998) also elaborate on the idea that e-malls are a useful means not only to help launch or expand e-retailers, but in some cases to totally create the e-retailer! So one of the services provided by some e-malls is to help create the e-retailer from scratch.

CONCLUSIONS

The e-mall presents a challenge to e-retailers' aspirations to have full coverage on the Web. Shopping in the conventional bricks world is greatly facilitated by the presence of malls and in fact they tend to dominate the way we shop. Yet the two *think points* at the beginning of this chapter suggest that a completely different situation applies in the e-world, with a minimal role to date for the e-mall. Why is this the case? Perhaps one answer is that there is in fact a range of close substitute sites that resemble online malls. Such sites include portals, search engines and shopping bots. Similarly there are major category e-retailers that resemble a virtual department store, like Amazon or eBay, and these are also substitutes for an e-mall.

An alternative answer is that it is not entirely clear that there is a major need for a multi-category, multi-owner e-mall. Although there is a real and established need for a bricks mall in which we can pick up the bread, milk, newspaper and a video from, say, three different vendors at a local mall, is there an equivalent situation where we need to go to an e-mall for the same type of experience? For the majority of consumers the answer is probably no, with a few exceptions.

On the other hand, there might be a high demand for a mega e-retailer in a particular category (e.g. Amazon or CDNOW) or one offering multiple categories (e.g. Amazon or eBay). There could also be a reasonably large demand for a specialized or single-category e-mall, such as fashion.com (see Hill, 2000) or defence.com (see O'Hara, 2001). With this view we speculate that the dominant current and probable future use of cyberspace is primarily a single or limited use shopping expedition, with a constrained view as to the type of e-malls needed. Our viewpoint is consistent with the immediate and instant gratification nature of e-retailing shopping, focused on *immediate needs* though not *immediate consumption*. We envisage a norm of limited online shopping expeditions, focused on gift buying, fashion buying or e-grocery purchasing for example, but rarely a combination of all these tasks in the one 'trip'.

Having established that the most desirable type of e-mall is a highly focused and specialized one, what is the best way to design such an e-mall? This chapter has argued that there are lots of lessons to be drawn from conventional bricks malls, in terms of choosing the right array of tenants, merchandise, quality, services and support. Relationship marketing and management is also likely to be a big issue. Specifically, and drawing on the two Australian case studies, interactivity and trust were seen as the most crucial means of building the e-mall brand. Such a finding is consistent with what we found in Chapter 8 in terms of individual e-retailers wishing to build their brands.

The case study was able to provide further understanding in terms of advice about how to develop trust in an e-mall site. This can be a big challenge for any e-mall, as it is necessary to convey not just the overall trustworthiness of the mall, but also each e-retailer tenant in it. Such a challenge is especially great for an e-mall with a large proportion of pure clicks retailers in it, such as the sofcom e-mall. The finding in Table 9.2 (p. 195) was that interactivity was the main way of building trust in an e-mall. However, this was somewhat less effective in the sofcom e-mall, meaning that e-malls with a high proportion of pure clicks tenants have to work harder in building trust and ultimately a strong brand.

Finally, we can ask the question of how e-mall owners should develop interactivity, that is, a closer relationship between consumers and the overall e-mall site. The answer here is a combination of more effective navigability (site design) and retail mix quality (mix of tenants).

There still remain some unanswered questions, particularly for more developed e-malls, such as fashion.com. What is the role of web atmospherics for the value of such sites? What is the best way of handling the security and privacy guarantees? What is the best way of handling returned goods? What is the scope to internationalize such e-malls? Future research is needed to resolve these issues, though the reader might provisionally come up with their own solutions or approach.

CHAPTER SUMMARY

As in other chapters, we started by examining conventional (mall) retailing practices and principles as a basis for designing the appropriate e-retail (e-mall) system. The main finding from conventional mall marketing is the need to control the brand image through the tenant mix, merchandise quality, services and atmospherics, as well as building a good landlord–tenant relationship.

More or less the same principles, suitably adapted, apply in the case of e-malls. Careful selection of the tenants and the quality of merchandise was important, with a suggestion not to have too many pure clicks e-retailers as tenants. A healthy proportion of bricks and clicks e-retailers relative to clicks e-retailers helps to build familiarity with the consumer and contributes to greater trust of the e-mall overall.

As noted, e-malls are not radically different from single-ownership e-retailers covered in other chapters, but there is a greater threshold in terms of 'acceptance' (trust towards) an e-mall. Part of the problem with trust in an e-mall relates to the general lack of familiarity with e-malls and a lack of a norm or experience in how to use e-malls. Just as Amazon invented a simple five-step model for how e-shoppers could use an e-retailer, there is a need to do something similar for e-mall shopping. Not surprisingly, trust and interactivity were found to be the main influences on the strength of an e-mall brand.

In the following chapter we will investigate how business models may be useful to e-retailers.

QUESTIONS

Brief feedback to these questions is included at the back of the book.

Question 9.1
What is important in managing conventional malls?

Question 9.2
How do you *translate* the principles in managing conventional malls to e-malls?

Question 9.3
Do you regard a shopping bot as an intelligent agent or a virtual mall? Why?

Question 9.4
Why are e-malls less dominant in cyberspace than bricks malls are in physical space?

REFERENCES AND FURTHER READING

Deck, S. (1997) 'Ease of navigation key to successful e-malls', *Computerworld*, 14 July: 4.

Dennis, C., Murphy, J., Marsland, D., Cockett, W. and Patel, T. (2002) 'Measuring image: shopping centre case studies', *International Review of Retail, Distribution and Consumer Research*, 12 (4): 353–373.

Dong, X. and Su, L. (1997) 'Search engines on the World Wide Web and information retrieval from the Internet: a review and evaluation', *Online and CD-ROM Review*, 21 (2): 67–81.

Hall, E. (1998) 'Viaweb store 4.0 makes i-commerce setup simple', *InfoWorld*, 2 February: 47.

Hill, S. (2000) 'To de-mall or e-mall? Shaping Web shopping', *Apparel Industry Magazine*, February: 36–37.

Hof, R. (2000) 'e-Malls for business: the new web rush is from companies forming electronic marketplaces', *Business Week*, 13 March: 32–34.

Howard, E. (1997) 'The management of shopping centres: conflict or cooperation?' *The International Review of Retail, Distribution and Consumer Research*, 7 (3): 249–261.

Merrilees, B. (2001) 'Do traditional strategic concepts apply in the e-marketing context?' *Journal of Business Strategies*, 18 (2): 177–190.

Merrilees, B. and Fry, M. (2002) 'Corporate branding: a framework for e-retailers', *Corporate Reputation Review*, 5 (2/3): 213–225.

O'Hara, C. (2001) 'Defense e-mall changes hands', *Federal Computer Week*, 19 February, 15 (4): 1.

Roberts, J. and Merrilees, B. (2003) 'Managing the mall relationship: does trust lead to cooperation?', *ANZMAC Conference Proceedings*, Adelaide.

Rowley, J. (2000) 'Shopping bots: intelligent shopper or virtual department store?' *International Journal of Retail & Distribution Management*, 28 (7): 297–306.

Sit, J., Merrilees, B. and Birch, D. (2003) 'Entertainment-seeking shopping centre patrons: the missing segments', *International Journal of Retail & Distribution Management*, 32 (2): 80–94.

Strom, D. (1998) 'Building your online storefront', *InfoWorld*, 2 February: 45, 47.

Chapter 10

e-Retailing models

LINKS TO OTHER CHAPTERS

- Chapter 4 – Understanding and communicating with the e-consumer
- Chapter 6 – e-Store design: navigability, interactivity and web atmospherics
- Chapter 7 – e-Service
- Chapter 9 – e-Malls

KEY LEARNING POINTS

After completing this chapter you will have an understanding of:

- The categorization of e-retailing business models
- The electronic shopping test to assess a product's suitability for e-retailing
- Assessing the fit between an organization's objectives and the available business models

ORDERED LIST OF SUB-TOPICS

- What is a business model?
- The retail participant groups in a retailer's environment
- Distribution channels
- Revenue streams
- Assessment of the fit between organizational objectives and the business models

- Assessment of product suitability for e-retailing using the de Kare-Silver electronic shopping 'ES' test
- Chapter summary
- ❖ Case study
- ❖ Questions
- ❖ Further reading
- ❖ References
- ❖ Web links

WHAT IS A BUSINESS MODEL?

Though often quoted in Internet and e-commerce literature, the term business model has no uniform definition. In this text, we will define an Internet business model as follows:

> An Internet business model is an organization's strategic business system for producing a customer-oriented value proposition. The business system is composed of one or more targeted customer segments; hardware and software architecture, the organization's product offering; the organization's business partners; and associated resources required to achieve the organizational objectives.

As suggested by Eduard (2001), many retailers carry out their business through the 'influence of the five retail participant groups within the business environment' as displayed in Figure 10.1.

Figure 10.1 *The influence of the five retail participant groups within the business environment*

Source: Adapted from Eduard (2001)

THE RETAIL PARTICIPANT GROUPS IN A RETAILER'S ENVIRONMENT

Customers

Central to the retailer's marketing concept is the customer. To satisfy customer needs and wants an organization must comprehend the nature of their relevant customer base. Useful for this purpose is the segmentation of the customers into logical groups, for example geographic regions or purchase frequency.

Staff

The majority of interactions between staff and customers have until recently required at least one physical exchange of communication in the presence of both parties. Improvements and the increased availability of telecommunications technologies has enabled more of these communication exchanges without the need for either party to see, or hear speech from, the other party. Such a change in communications operational procedures often provides reduced transaction costs for the retailer, though it does require a revision of staff operations and training to successfully support the customer transactions.

Shareholders

Persons owning shares in a retailer require information on the operation and strategy of the organization to be able to monitor the investments. In the pre-online era, the shareholder was restricted to information from printed annual reports, the annual general meeting, direct mail and telephone enquiries made to the retailer. Now, with the Web, the shareholder may interact with the retailer by monitoring the retailer's website for breaking news, by exchanging e-mail correspondence with retailing staff, and by exchanging comments with other shareholders through online newsgroups.

Suppliers, partners and dealers

Operation of retail activities is not done in isolation. Retailers require business suppliers and stakeholders to provide merchandise supplies, financial systems, logistics, legal advice and ancillary services. Online architecture made up of the Internet and electronic data interchange systems enable the business suppliers and partners to keep the stakeholders informed of activities with a minimum of delay and thereby permit quicker responses and feedback.

Community

The community is composed not only of current and prospective shoppers but also individuals and groups that will exert influence upon others who will in turn determine the operating environment of the retailer. Growth in community awareness of environmental, ethical and social welfare issues leads to greater attention being paid to business operations. Members of the community seek to acquire information on the activities of retailers and any potential negative effects on the environment, such as the use and disposal of packaging waste. Organizations can use Internet information facilities (i.e. web pages or newsgroups) to provide public relations communications to emphasize positive corporate environmental issues and counter negative impressions held by the community.

From interactions with these five retail participant groups, the retail organization may anticipate positive or negative outcomes that will be quantitative or qualitative. Quantitative outcomes in the business environment are most readily revealed as the number of units sold, the revenue figures generated, returns on investment and company share price. Not as easy to measure, though still essential to the successful operation of a business, are qualitative outcomes. Examples of qualitative outcomes include customer loyalty, client satisfaction, employee loyalty, corporate image and supplier confidence.

THINK POINT

With so many academic articles written on the significance of qualitative outcomes, e.g. customer loyalty, why aren't these issues as prominent in published summaries of retailing activities as sales revenues and inventory costs?

Categorizing e-retailing business models

For the e-retailer to integrate the needs of the five retail participant groups, adapt to the merchandise mix offered and still meet the business objectives, the e-retailer may select from a variety of business models. Initially, the e-retail business models are categorized by 'distribution channel', that is, how the customers will access the retailer's merchandise mix. Following this, the business models may be categorized by the 'revenue stream' used to maintain the sales activity for the retailer.

DISTRIBUTION CHANNELS

The logistics for the retailer and prospective customer to establish contact and achieve an exchange of merchandise for payments have not always required a physical store. Apart from the physical bricks and mortar store, the retailing channel is also achievable through 'direct retailing' and online through a 'virtual retailer'.

Virtual retailer

The introduction of commerce on the World Wide Web gave rise to the development of a new retailing form, the pure Web-based retailer, also known as a 'virtual retailer' or 'pureplay e-retailer'. Perhaps the best-known virtual retailer is Amazon, which started selling books over the Web in 1995. The virtual retailer enables Internet users to participate in retailing activities previously restricted to store-based retailers, i.e. product and price comparisons and payment systems, but in a speedier and more convenient manner.

Bricks and mortar retailers

With the establishment of the virtual retailer came a renaming of the traditional retailer to accommodate the e-commerce environment. Retailers retaining a physical store presence are now termed bricks and mortar retailers. A significant difference between the virtual retailer and the bricks and mortar retailer is the ability of the prospective bricks and mortar retail customer to physically inspect store merchandise before making a purchase and exiting the store.

Direct retailers

'Direct retailers' have utilized a variety of distribution methods to provide a retail space for the customer. Examples of direct retailers have included catalogue marketing since the 1800s, e.g. the Sears catalogue; door-to-door selling, e.g. Avon since the 1960s; telephone shopping since the 1970s, e.g. Lands End (www.landsend.com); and 24-hour television shopping since the 1980s, e.g. QVC (www.qvc.com).

Categorizing hybrid retailers

Marketers today are not restricted to just bricks and mortar, direct and virtual categories of retailing. In between these categories are the three hybrid forms of retailing: the 'clicks and bricks retailer', the 'catalogue retailer' and the 'digital retailer'.

Clicks and bricks retailer

The clicks and bricks retailer has a physical store for consumer shopping and also conducts Web-based retail operations through the Internet. In the majority of cases, such a retailer originally transacted business as a bricks and mortar retailer, e.g. Harrods, then adopted the Web for additional sales coverage. In other cases, an established direct retailer or virtual retailer, e.g. Dell computers, will establish a store-based retail outlet to provide potential customers with the opportunity to physically examine merchandise. As such, the retailer counters one of the leading objections to online purchases – the inability to personally view and inspect items before making a purchase.

Catalogue retailer

Portal-based catalogue-marketing companies have been very successful in meeting their marketing and sales objectives. By developing websites that are online representations of printed brochures and catalogues, the catalogue companies are able to widen their distribution network without replacing or alienating their postal clients. The positive outcomes in this channel are reduced distribution costs; the expansion of the potential customer base; and speedier, more convenient, feedback to prospective clients.

Digital retailer

Consumer access to the Internet has provided a logical environment for the distribution and exchange of items that are deliverable in a digital form. Currently, popular digital items sold by retailers over the Internet include recorded music and computer software. While visiting a digital retailer's website, the Internet user may sample such items, e.g. hear the music or trial software, before making a purchase decision. Once happy with the sampled digital product, the Internet customer may download the complete digital product and arrange for payment.

REVENUE STREAMS

Customer-centred e-retailing business models are often categorized by the revenue stream achieved by the online retailer. The four revenue business models are based on advertising, merchandise sales, transaction fee and subscriptions.

Advertising-based e-retailing

The retailer generates revenues by selling advertising space on their website. As one of the original revenue models of the Internet, portals such as Yahoo! have charged third parties a flat fee for placing an advertisement on their web page or charge for each visitor who clicks on the advertisement. This is known as the 'click-through' rate to a third party's website. Organizations such as Double Click (www.doubleclick.com) can monitor the traffic coming to a website by way of cookie files and provide this site traffic data to the e-retailer for marketing decisions. A few years ago this service caused complaints from Web users about invasion of privacy, to which Double Click responded with a revised Privacy Policy that has placated much of this criticism and maintained the organization's competitive advantage.

Merchandise sales e-retailing

As with the traditional bricks and mortar retailer, this revenue business model produces revenue from the sale of the retailer's merchandise over the Web, e.g. Sanity (www.sanity.com.au) selling recorded music.

Transaction fee e-retailing

Similar to the concept of brokerage, retailers may charge a third party for the marketing of merchandise to the retailer's customers. The most successful Internet example of transaction fee e-retailing is eBay (www.ebay.com), where the auction facilitator receives a fee once the successful bidder has finalised an online auction using eBay's online technology.

Subscription e-retailing

An adaptation of direct marketing, the subscription-based e-retailing revenue model allows consumers to access merchandise facilities, usually in a digital form, and through a subscription, e.g. the *New York Times* (nytimes.com) for Web-based archival news stories.

> **THINK POINT**
>
> Many sites provide free content or content at reduced cost through subsidies provided by advertising revenues. This revenue requires the site to monitor and record website traffic with such devices as cookie files. If site visitors get the advantages of such free or subsidised content, why are many people so against their Web usage being monitored?

ASSESSMENT OF THE FIT BETWEEN ORGANIZATIONAL OBJECTIVES AND THE BUSINESS MODELS

In selecting the business model suited to a retail operation, the retailer will initially assess their marketing and sales objectives for the three principal retail channels: bricks and mortar, direct retailers and virtual retailers. Samples of these objectives are given in Table 10.1 for the five retail participant groups using a

Table 10.1 Assessment of retail channels in meeting a retailer's objectives for customers

Retailer's objectives for customers	*Retail channel*		
	Bricks and mortar	*Direct*	*Virtual*
Inform prospects of product details/features	5	3	4
Demonstrate product features	5	1	2
Stimulate prospect interest and customer demand by communicating details about the retailer's available and pending merchandise lines	5	3	4
Advise prospects and customers of retailer's achievements (e.g. sales levels, awards)	3	5	3
Provide merchandise access to potential customers in multiple geographic locations (domestic *and* international)	2	4	5
Total score for the retail channel	20	16	18

five-point scale: one point is given for low and five points for high, representing the level of potential in each retail channel. Note that objectives are *samples* and not an exhaustive list. A retailer's unique environment may require the retailer to add or remove objectives from the samples in this table.

Scoring the retailer's objectives for customers

The potential for a retail channel to meet the individual objectives for customers is assessed on a scale of 1 to 5. A retail channel with little potential to meet an objective scores 1 increasing to 5 for a retail channel with a high potential to meet the customer objectives. Using the series of objectives in Table 10.1 and totalling the scores for each retail channel, the maximum potential score is 25.

The structure of each retail channel and the method of accessing the channel's target audience provide advantages for communicating certain information and appealing to certain human senses. For communicating information that appeals to the customers' senses of sight, sound, touch, taste and smell, there is currently no better medium than the face-to-face interaction possible in a physical retail store. This conclusion is reinforced by the 20/25 score for the bricks and mortar retailers in Table 10.1.

Restricted to audio and static visual images, direct retailers cannot provide moving images of new products or a tactile experience for a customer and this resulted in a score of 16/25. Encouragingly, research into direct retailing shows that such customers often retain the retailer's marketing correspondence to be reread in the future. Such correspondence may include details (e.g. retailer achievements) often overlooked while browsing in a retail store or un-clicked on the retailer's website.

Though computer software and hardware facilities for the Web are improving to encompass audio, video and tactile reproductions of the real world, the experience is still not a replacement for the communication facilities and immediate feedback of the store environment. As an advantage over the direct retailers, the virtual retailer's ability to include moving video and online search facilities enables improved demonstration ability for merchandise offered, giving the virtual retailer a score of 18/25.

Globalization created by the Internet means that many retail names formerly restricted to domestic markets have become internationally recognized brands. While some retailers have attempted to establish a physical bricks and mortar presence in overseas markets, the logistical costs and unique requirements of the overseas locations has for some retailers resulted in major losses and eventual withdrawal from the overseas market.

Direct retailers have utilized the well-established international postal and courier systems for decades. With little more than a sales orientation, many direct retailers have accepted orders from overseas customers, packaged the orders and passed the distribution responsibility to transport groups such as DHL (www.dhl.com) or FedEx (www.fedex.com). The transport groups arrange pick-up of the packaged merchandise, export documents, customs clearances, final delivery and, in some cases, payment clearances. For a small direct retailer, such international sales provide new market revenues without a major investment in logistics infrastructure, i.e. a specialized international shipping group. A drawback for the direct retailer is not being known by potential customers in other parts of the country and overseas. Many of us have turned to the phonebook to look for a supplier, but what if you don't have every phonebook in the world? The answer is turn to the World Wide Web and use of search engines. The Internet has given every person with access to the Web an access to every virtual retailer, as testified by the meteoric growth of Amazon (www.amazon.com) from being the seller of books to a few avid readers to becoming one of the largest book and video retailers in the world, and all this exclusively online. Worldwide access to the Web is now so entrenched that successfully established direct retailers such as Lands End (www.landsend.com) established sophisticated order-taking websites and integrate sites into the retailer's marketing and distribution plans as an added retail channel.

Table 10.2 Assessment of retail channels in meeting a retailer's objectives for staff

Retailer's objectives for staff	*Retail channel*		
	Bricks and mortar	*Direct*	*Virtual*
Training: for staff to provide prospective customers with information about the retailer's policies (e.g. returns and privacy)	5	5	5
Training: for staff to respond to the queries of prospective customers about applicability of the retailer's policies and information about the suitability of the merchandise to the customer's needs/applications	5	5	5
Support: provide systems to enable staff to maintain the sales systems (store-based and Web shopping cart procurement systems) which include a 24/7 a week website and data-collection methods	5	5	5
Total score for the retail channel	15	15	15

Scoring the retailer's objectives for staff

The potential for a retail channel to meet the retailer's objectives for staff is assessed on a scale of 1 to 5. A retail channel with little potential scores 1, increasing to 5 for a retail channel with a high potential to meet the individual staff objectives. Using the series of objectives in Table 10.2 and totalling the scores for each retail channel, the maximum potential score is 15.

Why did each retail channel in Table 10.2 receive the same score of 15/15 for staff objectives? It is because that, no matter what retail channels a marketer uses, staff must be prepared to provide the finest service possible within the constraints and advantages of that channel. Consider negative perception of a prospect should they ask a question concerning the exchange policy of the retailer's staff (face-to-face, by mail or through a website) only to receive the reply 'I don't know' and without the follow up 'but I will find out and get back to you by (x period)'. Quality support systems are also essential in all retail channels because it is the retailer's personnel who receive the ire of annoyed prospects when an electronic system (e.g. website or ordering facility) fails.

Table 10.3 *Assessment of retail channels in meeting a retailer's objectives for shareholders*

Retailer's objectives for shareholders	*Retail channel*		
	Bricks and mortar	*Direct*	*Virtual*
The shareholders to have access to the latest financial data pertaining to their retail investment	3	3	5
Keep shareholders informed about upcoming matters that require their attention, i.e. meetings (annual and extraordinary) or changes in payment methods	3	3	5
Advise shareholders of 'news' which may include industry awards, new merchandise lines and responses to media reports	3	3	5
Total score for the retail channel	9	9	15

Scoring the retailer's objectives for shareholders

The potential for a retail channel to meet the retailer's objectives for shareholders is assessed on a scale of 1 to 5. A retail channel with little potential scores 1 increasing to 5 for a retail channel with a high potential to meet the individual shareholder objectives. Using the series of objectives in Table 10.3 and totalling the scores for each retail channel, the maximum potential score is 15.

The immediacy of response and round-the-clock access of the Internet places the virtual retailer in an enviable position for providing shareholders with detailed information as demonstrated by the 15/15 score in Table 10.3. Unlike the brief summaries of financial and business information conventionally available in an annual report, Web-based documents may incorporate interactive graphics and video to display information for more impact upon the shareholders.

Not all shareholders will be retail customers and therefore exposed to the marketing communications provided by both bricks and mortar and direct retailers. To inform their shareholders these retailers traditionally use printed media and call-centre responses to shareholder enquiries, therefore giving both retail channels a score of 9/15 in Table 10.3. Though effective, such methods have high labour costs and are slower to update when compared with information storage and retrieval from Web-based retailing.

Table 10.4 Assessment of retail channels in meeting a retailer's objectives for suppliers, partners and dealers

Retailer's objectives for suppliers, partners and dealers	*Retail channel*		
	Bricks and mortar	*Direct*	*Virtual*
Maintain up-to-date contact information for both the retailer and their third-party providers	2	3	4
Establish an audit trail to track financial transactions and exchanges of information	4	4	5
Fast and accurate recovery of data (for both the retailer and their third-party providers) following a disaster	3	3	4
Total score for the retail channel	9	10	13

Scoring the retailer's objectives for suppliers, partners and dealers

The potential for a retail channel to meet the retailer's objectives for suppliers, partners and dealers is assessed on a scale of 1 to 5. A retail channel with little potential scores 1, increasing to 5 for a retail channel with a high potential to meet the individual supplier, partner and dealer objectives. Using the series of objectives in Table 10.4 and totalling the scores for each retail channel, the maximum potential score is 15.

Synchronizing data records between the retailer and their suppliers, partners and dealers is essential to avoid such errors as:

- missed or duplication of orders;
- misdirected correspondence to personnel or addresses that have changed;
- non-compliance with legislation (e.g. government reporting schedules);
- missed targets (e.g. end of month summaries or sale dates).

Direct retailers have honed their record systems to finalize sales and associated records in the absence of physical customers to score a total of 10/15. When disputes with customers and suppliers do occur, it may take time for the direct retailers to consult and correlate the electronic and manual record systems. Bricks and mortar retailers also pay a great deal of attention to the daily summarizing of financial exchanges. Though important, third-party contact records (e.g. contact names at suppliers or shipping agents) may not be updated as regularly nor carry the same level of priority customer interactions and this lessens the overall score to 9/15. By the nature of their operational environment, virtual retailers depend upon efficient real-time data exchanges through the Internet network, which itself depends upon detailed and automated record-keeping of transmitted information. Such an improved information exchange with the relevant parties gave the virtual retailer a higher score of 13/15, assuming e-retailers and their third-party partners regularly update and utilize the pertinent data over the Internet.

Scoring the retailer's objectives for the community

The potential for a retail channel to meet the stated retailer's objectives for the community is assessed on a scale of 1 to 5. A retail channel with little potential scores 1, increasing to 5 for a retail channel with a high potential to meet the individual community objectives. Using the series of objectives in Table 10.5 and totalling the scores for each retail channel, the maximum potential score is 15.

An integral component of modern marketing plans is keeping the community informed about the direction and intentions of the retailer. For each retail channel, there are alternative communications media to carry messages to the relevant community. The current communications media available to the bricks and mortar and direct retailers include print (e.g. newspapers) and broadcasting (e.g. television). Though extensive, such media may not reach every community person who has a stake in bricks and mortar and direct retailer channels and this restricts the total scores to 8/15 and 9/15 respectively. In communications to the community, the virtual retailers have an interactive advantage over the other two retail channels. The e-retailer's website may incorporate a series of messages to support their objectives for the community in a more convincing manner. Helping

Table 10.5 *Assessment of retail channels in meeting a retailer's objectives for the community*

Retailer's objectives for the community	*Retail channel*		
	Bricks and mortar	*Direct*	*Virtual*
Keep the public informed of improvements in the retailer's social activities, e.g. increased recycling	2	3	5
Promote contributions to charitable institutions	3	3	5
Promote training and employment programmes	3	3	5
Total score for the retail channel	8	9	15

to communicate these messages through the website and achieving a score of 15/15, the retailer may include any of these online facilities:

- hyperlinks to relevant websites
- live footage (webcams streaming video)
- storage of printable documents (e.g. *Adobe Acrobat* format)
- interactive games
- e-mail exchanges.

As shown, each of the retail channels – bricks and mortar, direct and virtual – have varying degrees of suitability to meet organizational objectives. By summing the scores for each objective and each channel, the retailer will identify the retail channel with the greatest opportunity for marketing plan success.

To reiterate, the objectives for the five retail participant groups are *samples* and *not* an exhaustive list for all retailers; the unique environments facing the retailers may require them to add or remove objectives from samples in Tables 10.1, 10.2, 10.3, 10.4 and 10.5. Taking the results for each set of sample objectives, the results are 59/85 for direct retailers, 61/85 for bricks and mortar retailers and 76/85 for virtual retailers, placing the virtual retailer in the most effective position to meet the sample of objectives for the five retail participant groups. This does not restrict the retailer to a single channel. The growing consumer acceptance of electronic shopping is allowing traditional retailers to expand into multiple retailing channels. To do this and provide the greater likelihood of meeting the retailer's multifaceted objectives, the channels chosen should be in order of their scores, which for this set of objectives is virtual retailing, followed by bricks and mortar retailing and finally direct retailing.

Concentrating on the virtual retailer, the next stage is to gauge how suitable merchandise is for this particular retail channel.

ASSESSMENT OF PRODUCT SUITABILITY FOR E-RETAILING USING THE DE KARE-SILVER ELECTRONIC SHOPPING 'ES' TEST

In his book, de Kare-Silver (2000) provided a framework to assess products and services for online retailing suitability. The 'ES' (Electronic Shopping) test simultaneously evaluates fit according to three factors: (1) product characteristics; (2) familiarity and confidence; and (3) consumer attributes as displayed in Figure 10.2.

Product characteristics

Certain products appeal to one or more of the five human senses of sight, sound, smell, taste and touch. The store-based retail environment is most suitable where

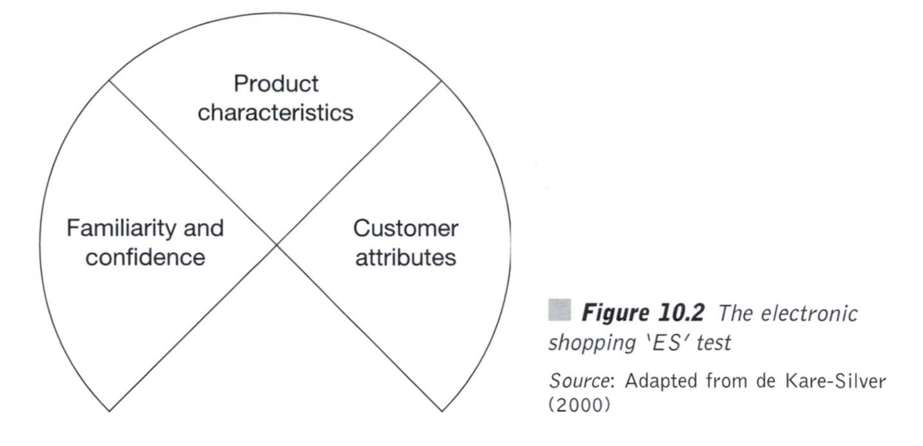

Figure 10.2 *The electronic shopping 'ES' test*

Source: Adapted from de Kare-Silver (2000)

a consumer's purchase behaviour benefits from a physical interaction with a particular product. Conversely, products that primarily activate the sight and sound senses, i.e. music and movies, are most suited for an electronic retailing environment. In addition to the fives senses, people assess certain products and services in an analytical manner using what de Kare-Silver describes as the intellect sense. Figure 10.3 maps the fit between a selection of products and the six noted human senses. Based upon Figure 10.3, very few items are 'pure' touch, taste or smell only products. A large group of products utilize the sight and touch senses, thereby making such products suitable for the store-based retail environment. Encouraging for the electronic retailer is the significant number of products that appeal to the senses of sight and sound and are therefore appropriate for online retailing.

Scoring electronic shopping with product characteristics

Using a score out of 10, the more physical a product's appeal, the closer the result is to zero (0). If a product has an appeal that lends itself to the virtual environment of the Internet, then the product scores closer to the maximum 10. The scoring for product characteristics appears in Figure 10.4.

Familiarity and confidence

The second component of the 'ES' test examines a consumer's feelings of familiarity and confidence towards a product or service considered for purchase. Should a consumer have used or purchased a product-line in the past and therefore be familiar with that product, that consumer is likely to have a higher level of confidence. As portrayed in Figure 10.5, this greater familiarity and confidence reduces the consumer's need to physically handle the products in a future purchase and improves the product's suitability for an online retailing environment.

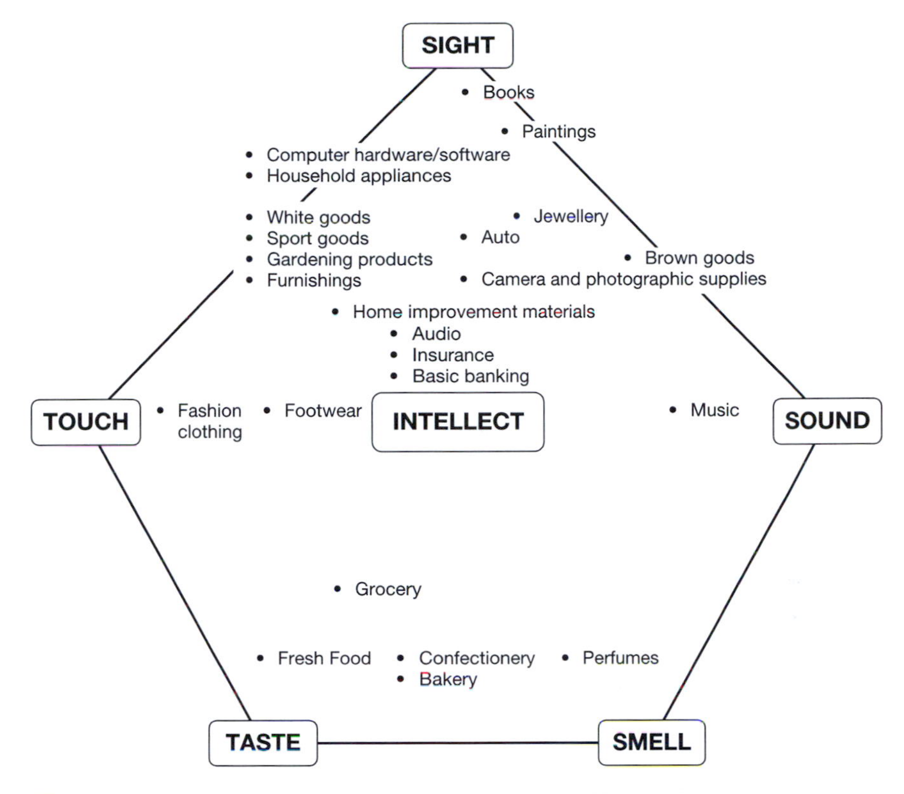

Figure 10.3 *Product characteristics and the five senses*

Source: Adapted from de Kare-Silver (2000)

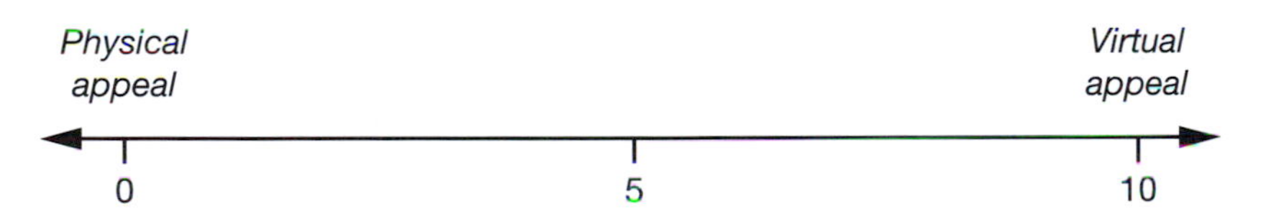

Figure 10.4 *Scoring product characteristics*

Source: Adapted from de Kare-Silver (2000)

The confidence that consumers attribute to a product is not always the result of personal usage. Individuals may develop a positive or negative attitude from communications with family and peer groups or from the reputation associated with a product's brand. On identifying a brand, a consumer will perceive various anticipated value dimensions even if the consumer has not used a particular product from that brand. Depending upon the brand's reputation for social status and quality of finish, a consumer will depend upon a physical inspection that would usually be associated with trying something new. An electronic retailer

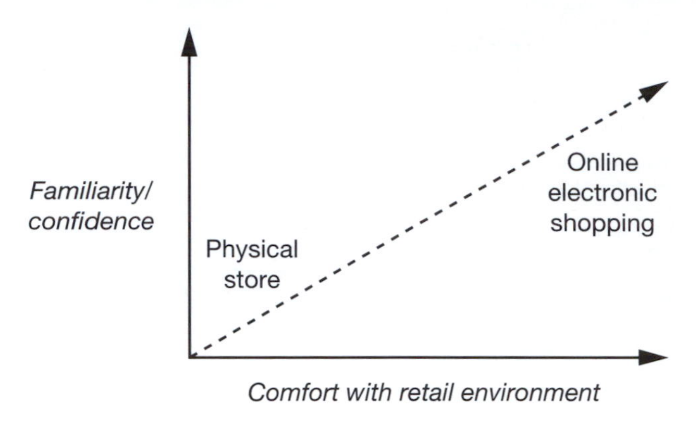

Figure 10.5 *Familiarity/confidence and electronic shopping*

Source: Adapted from de Kare-Silver (2000)

who emphasizes universally recognized brands will not only attract confident online shoppers but individuals that do little or no online shopping.

Scoring electronic shopping with familiarity and confidence

Using a score to a maximum of 10, the individual is given a higher score as their familiarity/confidence with a product environment also increases. This familiarity/confidence is gauged by three components: previous level of product usage; the satisfaction gained from using the product; and the familiarity with the reputation and branding of the organization offering the product. The scoring for familiarity/confidence is displayed in Figure 10.6.

Customer attributes

The influence of and experience with a product or service are themselves not adequate determinants of the retail environment used by a shopper. The failures of many dot.com retailers in the late 1990s resulted from a misconception that being online was itself a sufficient attraction to Internet sites and sales. Just as traditional retailers try to understand their shoppers to secure sales, online retailers also need to identify consumer attributes, shopping motives and shopping triggers.

A number of researchers have attempted to profile and categorize an individual's level of electronic shopping, such as A.C. Nielsen (A.C. Nielsen, Mintel, Henley Centre, Kalchas). Nielsen suggests the following six categories to evaluate an organization's current consumers as electronic shoppers:

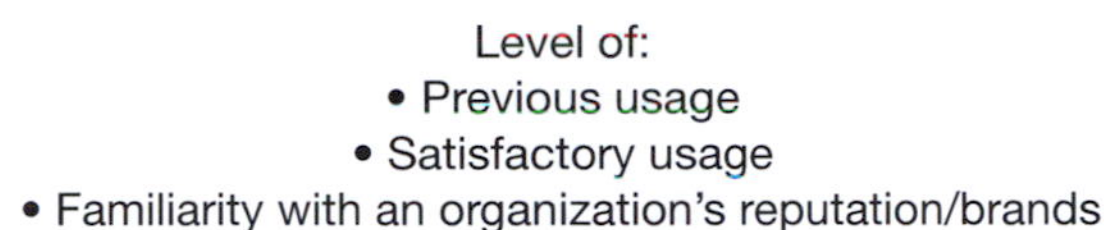

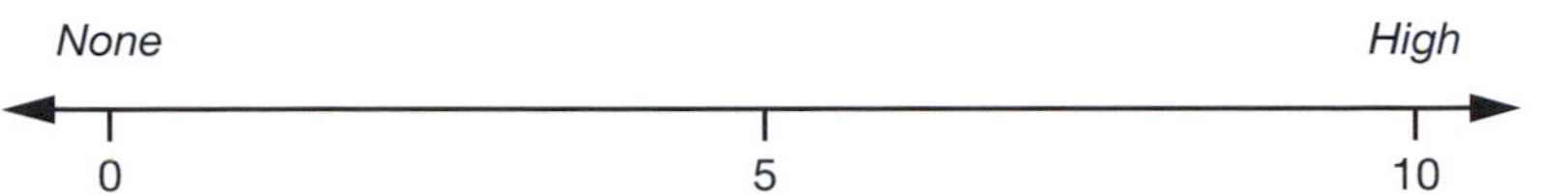

Figure 10.6 *Scoring familiarity and confidence*

Source: Adapted from de Kare-Silver (2000)

- *Social shopper* Such an individual enjoys the shopping experience. This person visits stores for a pleasurable social experience that may include meeting up with friends or family.
- *Experimental shopper* As the name implies, this person is at ease with trying new stores and ways of shopping, e.g. the Internet or mobile phone shopping.
- *Convenience shopper* This shopper seeks opportunities to save time when shopping and avoid the delays associated with traditional store shopping, e.g. finding parking or waiting in checkout lines. This shopper often welcomes retail opportunities such as Internet retailing that can remove these 'inconvenient' steps to shopping.
- *Habit die-hard* Such an individual is entrenched in a routine or system for doing activities and that includes shopping. They may not be a technophobe or dislike the use of computerization but are still not using electronic shopping because it is a departure from their status quo.
- *Value shopper* This is not merely a seeker of cost savings. Such a shopper looks for the combination of product quality, effective service and monetary outlay that in totality equals good value for that person. Should electronic shopping offer cost savings for the same quality of product and provide relatively equal service levels to a store alternative, the value shopper should utilize this new shopping channel.
- *Ethical shopper* A small but growing segment, this shopper is less concerned with the shopping medium than the social and ethical issues associated with shopping. For example, is the seller socially responsible with their waste packaging or sourcing products from child labour employers? Should the electronic retailer establish credibility and ethical procedures, the ethical shopper will become a likely user of this retail channel.

Figure 10.7 demonstrates the potential for each of these consumer categories to use electronic shopping: the social shopper has the lowest electronic shopping potential and the convenience shopper has the greater potential for the new retail channel.

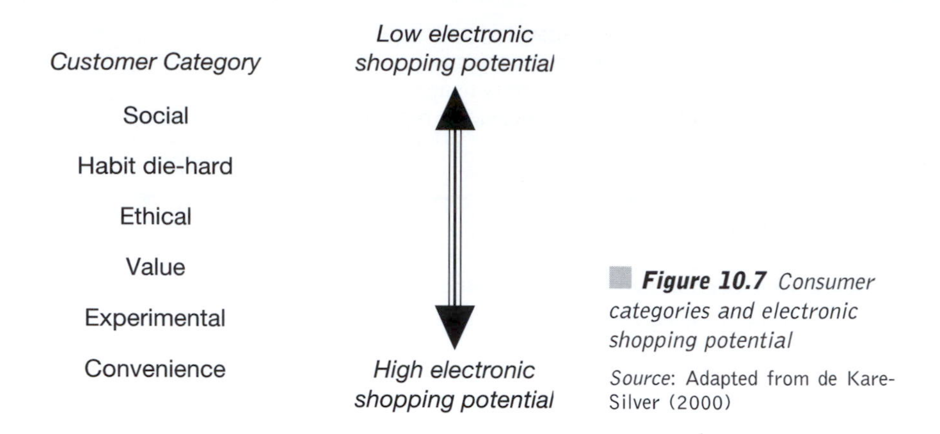

Figure 10.7 *Consumer categories and electronic shopping potential*

Source: Adapted from de Kare-Silver (2000)

Scoring electronic shopping with customer attributes

Owing to the significant influence of this electronic shopping factor, scoring for customer attributes is out of a maximum of 30. This third step in the ES test begins with an assessment of the organization's proportions for each of the customer categories (e.g. social, ethical, convenience). Next comes the evaluation of which customer category dominates (i.e. forms the largest group) in the organization's market for the product in question. Finally, it must be decided if the dominating category is large enough to sustain a targeted marketing effort for electronic shopping; in other words, are the returns from this group worth the expenditure of marketing resources by this organization? The scoring for customer attributes is shown in Figure 10.8.

The three de Kare-Silver tests for electronic shopping are now added together to give a possible maximum ES test score of 50 as shown below.

Scoring product characteristics	10
Scoring familiarity and confidence	10
Scoring customer attributes	30
	50

To further illustrate the ES test, a series of products and services are evaluated and displayed in Table 10.6.

The results in Table 10.6 indicate that certain products and services have a greater potential for electronic shopping. To highlight the process, a distinction is given between a new perfume produced for the youth market and a long-standing/traditional perfume. For both a new/youth-oriented perfume and a long-standing brand of perfume the product characteristics are similar and the sense of smell dominates the human assessment. The confidence with the product and brand will be slightly greater for the long-standing perfume as a result of

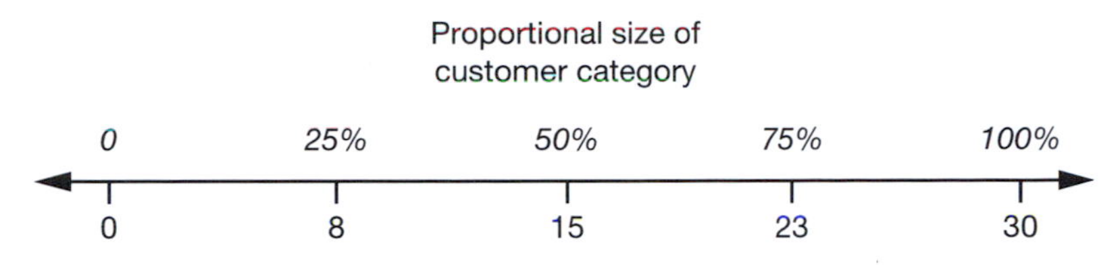

Figure 10.8 *Scoring customer attributes*

Source: Adapted from de Kare-Silver (2000)

Table 10.6 Examples of electronic shopping (ES) tests

Product or service	*Product characteristics (0–10)*	*Familiarity and confidence (0–10)*	*Customer attributes (0–30)*	*Total (0–50)*
Perfume (new/ youth-oriented)	1	8	20	29
Perfume (long-standing)	1	9	5	15
Acer tablet PC	5	6	21	32
Domestic airline booking	10	8	15	33
Groceries	4	8	15	27
Books	8	7	23	38
DVD movies	8	6	25	39
Car insurance	10	6	9	25

longer exposure to the marketing communications for that brand. Nonetheless, the likely media saturation to promote the youth-oriented new perfume is likely to result in a familiarity level for that market that is not far behind the mature perfume. Where the two perfumes will differ significantly in the ES test is in the customer attributes component. The target market for the newer perfume has a higher awareness of computer and Internet usage. This market will not feel a high aversion to the concept of electronic shopping for this new perfume, especially if it means price savings and easy access to stock levels that may be lower in retail stores following media promotions. In contrast, the long-standing perfume will have a more mature (older) market with less hands-on exposure to the Internet and who are not as comfortable with electronic shopping. In addition, while the youth market may congregate with peers at fashion venues, e.g. a mall, for the social interaction, the mature market (female) may enjoy the pampering provided at retail store perfume counters, which again lessens the propensity to shop for such a perfume online. In summary, the new youth-oriented perfume has a greater score (29 vs. 15) in the ES test compared to the long-standing perfume brand.

CHAPTER SUMMARY

Retailing through the Internet requires more sophistication than setting up a website and offering merchandise for sale. The e-retailer needs to consider the business model that will most effectively meet its objectives and the expectations of its prospective customers. Participant groups that will help to determine the e-retailer's business model will include the customers, staff, shareholders, suppliers, partners and dealers, and the community. Categorization of the business model is initially done by the type of distribution channel and then by the revenue stream the model derives. To assess the appropriateness of a particular e-retailing business model one may assign a score to the retailer's customer objectives, staff objectives, shareholder objectives, supplier, partner and dealer objectives, and the objectives for the retailer's community. The suggested technique in this chapter for scoring participant group objectives is the de Kare-Silver electronic shopping (ES) test.

Not every piece of merchandise will be successful in every channel of distribution and this includes the World Wide Web. We can increase the likelihood of achieving sales success in e-retailing by examining the elements that make up the retailer's marketplace and using devices such as the ES test to assign a suitability rating before the merchandise is offered online.

In the next chapter we will venture beyond the desk-computer-based Internet to explore developing issues in shopping via mobile communication devices – m-shopping.

Case study 10.1: EXTRASTOCK PTY LTD (www.extrastock.com.au)

Entrepreneurs have always found an undeveloped or ignored niche in established and developing markets; that's what makes them entrepreneurs. If you were to think of an organization that has truly leveraged the Internet around the world and been profitable from its inception for buying and selling, it would have to be eBay (see Case study 4.1, pp. 104–105). The Australian firm Extrastock has built upon this successful business model by providing an auction environment that commercial operators can utilize to sell excess, refurbished and closeout inventories through the World Wide Web. Unlike the traditional eBay transaction where one consumer presents their item for online auction to many potential consumers (bidders), in effect consumer to consumer (C2C), Extrastock facilitates auction sales through the eBay platform, from business to consumer (B2C).

Extrastock enables commercial operators to achieve the advantages of being a virtual retailer without the software, hardware and administrative overheads that would be necessary to establish an e-retailing presence on the Internet and capture some of the 55 million registered eBay users that generate some US$10 billion in transactions (as at 2001) (Arnold, 2003). Extrastock's objective is to provide strategic, full-service market place management for retailers, distributors and manufacturers. To achieve this, Extrastock offers the required technology to the commercial suppliers that integrates a business's existing technology infrastructures, including inventory databases, payment and fulfilment systems, to reduce time to market and extend profits for online channel sales. Revenue for Extrastock is by way of final auction price commission which means they want the highest possible price in any auction they run. To do this, the service provided by Extrastock must meet the requirements of the supplier and the online auction customer. If not, bidding will be restrained and keep the final price too low. That may be encouraging news for the final bidder but not for Extrastock and the supplier seeking a high return.

Just as the C2C eBay market place, the variety of merchandise that Extrastock has effectively sold for its clients includes watches, wine, minor and major kitchen appliances, home theatre components and systems, wholesale bulk lots, cameras and accessories, computer and office hardware, as well as sports memorabilia. Clients of Extrastock include:

- Pepper Tree Wines – an award-winning Australian wine label
- Scala Leathergoods, a manufacturer of premium leather products.

Extrastock has shown that retailers may adapt a successful e-business model into new markets that had previously been excluded from online sales.

QUESTIONS

Brief feedback to these questions is included at the back of the book.

Question 10.1

How would use of the retail participant groups in a retailer's environment help minimize channel *disintermediation*?

Question 10.2

If catalogues and website pages look the same, i.e. are two-dimensional images, yet the web page can include other features including music and changing graphics, why do many catalogue customers resist buying online?

Question 10.3

Can a customer be in more than one of the A.C. Nielsen electronic shopper categories?

FURTHER READING

Golicic, S.L., Davis, D.F., McCarthy, T.M. and Mentzer, J.T. (2002) 'The impact of e-commerce on supply chain relationships', *International Journal of Physical Distribution & Logistics Management*, 32 (10), 851–871.

Kinder, T. (2002) 'Emerging e-commerce business models: an analysis of case studies from West Lothian, Scotland', *European Journal of Innovation Management*, 5 (3), 130–151.

Osmonbekov, T., Bello, D.C. and Gilliland, D.I. (2002) 'Adoption of electronic commerce tools in business procurement: enhanced buying center structure and processes', *The Journal of Business and Industrial Marketing*, 17 (2), 151–166.

REFERENCES

Arnold, S. (2003) *Extrastock Company Overview*. www.extrastock.com.au/company.htm [accessed November 23 2003].

de Kare-Silver, Michael (2000) *The Electronic Shopping Revolution: Strategies for Retailers and Manufactures* (1st edn), London: Macmillan Press Ltd.

Eduard, T. (2001) 'Adding clicks to bricks', *Consulting to Management*, 12 (4), 10–23.

WEB LINKS

www.avon.com
Web information and ordering facility to support the customers, distributors and investors of this successful door-to-door retailer of cosmetics.

www.dhl.com
Ordering logistics and tracking shipments online.

www.doubleclick.com
A specialized Internet organization that tracks and analyses website visitor traffic. This information is particularly important for the sites that charge others based on the volume of 'clicking through' to their respective sites.

www.ebay.com
The first and most successful Web-based auction facility.

www.fedex.com
Ordering logistics and tracking shipments online; facilities and advice for e-business.

www.landsend.com
A leading catalogue retailer of clothing, luggage and footwear that expanded to use the Web as a customer distribution channel.

www.nytimes.com
Online summary of the famous daily newspaper. The site includes links to shopping sites, affiliated media (such as BBC), charities and daily financial information.

www.qvc.com
The US full-time television shopping channel that provides access to their merchandise lines through the website while keeping clients informed of up-coming events and television programmes.

www.sanity.com.au
Music chain selling recorded music, digital phone themes, music collectibles, and DVD.

www.sears.com
Web information and ordering facility for the original catalogue and then bricks and mortar retailer.

www.yahoo.com
Oldest Web portal that provides customization of user content; search engine facilities; categorized website directory; messenger services; shopping facilities; free mail facilities; employment searches; software links; and much more.

Chapter 11

m-Shopping

LINKS TO OTHER CHAPTERS

- Chapter 2 – e-Retailing in practice
- Chapter 4 – Understanding and communicating with the e-consumer
- Chapter 6 – e-Store design: navigability, interactivity and web atmospherics
- Chapter 7 – e-Service
- Chapter 12 – Multi-channel success and the future of e-retailing

KEY LEARNING POINTS

After completing this chapter you will have an understanding of:

- How to identify shopper motivations for m-shopping
- Classifying products and services into the main m-shopping categories
- How to be aware of the developments in m-shopping

ORDERED LIST OF SUB-TOPICS

- Remote shopping continues to evolve, now into m-shopping
- How has m-shopping come about?
- What is needed to go m-shopping?
- Features that distinguish m-commerce from traditional e-commerce
- Contributors to the growth in m-commerce
- Payments through m-commerce

REMOTE SHOPPING CONTINUES TO EVOLVE, NOW INTO M-SHOPPING

Retailing has seen many incarnations in the last 200 years. As displayed in Figure 11.1, shoppers have accessed retail merchandise through traditional stores, mail order, door-to-door distributors, telephone ordering, television shopping, the World Wide Web and now mobile shopping technology. A key to this evolution is not that the 'new' retail medium is the latest shopping incarnation available to the consumer but more the flexibility of accessing merchandise at a location that is complementary to the needs of the consumer at that time in their lives. If the Internet and Web gave the consumer the facility to shop *anytime* that suited their needs, mobile shopping approaches the added advantage of *anywhere* the consumer feels the need or want for merchandise.

As the early days of the Internet mediated shopping, many new terms were used to describe the emerging wireless electronic shopping environment. Examples

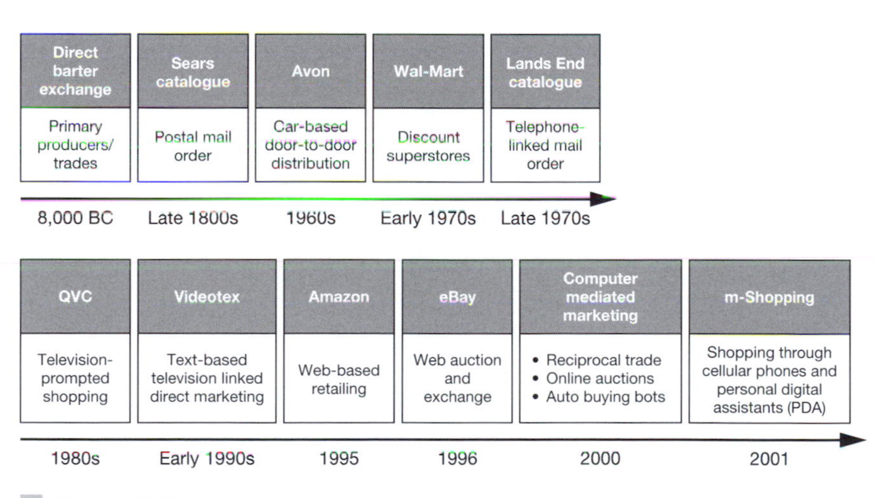

Figure 11.1 *Evolution of retailing*

Source: Adapted from Fenech (2001)

of such terms are mobile commerce, m-commerce, m-business, mobile shopping and m-shopping. For this text we shall use the term m-shopping to define:

> Any retail purchase made from a mobile electronic device, such as a cellular phone through a wireless network; in most cases these transactions are made through an Internet-mediated facility.

Where store retail meant shopping at the store's address and Web shopping means shopping where the computer is wire connected to the Internet, m-shopping provides shopping access where the buyer is geographically located within a wireless network.

HOW HAS M-SHOPPING COME ABOUT?

In less than one decade the Internet has gone from a file transfer facility between academics around the world to a communications and entertainment medium for almost every person with a personal computer. Growth of Internet usage was exponential until recently when signs of a slowdown in the rate of new user uptake of the Internet became apparent (see Figures 11.2 and 11.3).

This slowdown is partly explained by the Rogers (1971) adoption curve; the innovators and early adopters were quickly drawn to the Internet and slowly followed by the early majority. The statistics that indicate this slowing of usage uptake do not reflect usage popularity. As identified by Von der Luehe (2003), hours spent using the Internet have almost doubled between 2001 and 2003 (see Figure 11.4).

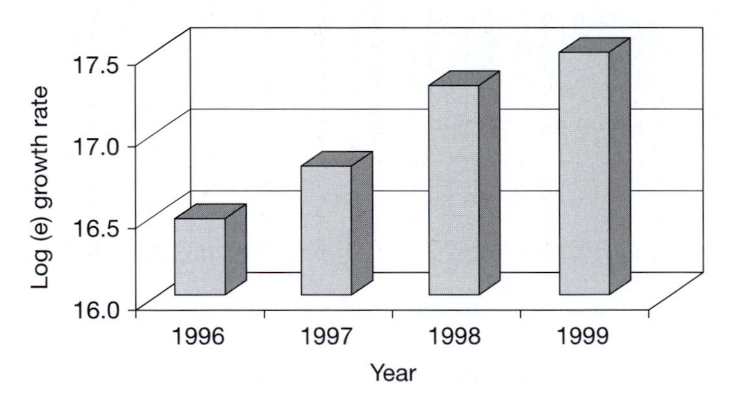

Figure 11.2 *Internet hosts, growth rates 1996–1999*

From e-mail correspondence and looking at news, to conducting banking and online shopping, Internet users are using the Internet longer when the access is readily available, as is the case with growing access to home broadband facilities (see Figures 11.5 and 11.6). Where we access the Internet for personal usage is also changing. While initial private Internet usage was in the home, current Australian research identified that over 40 per cent of Internet usage in the workplace is for personal purposes (Strutt, 2003).

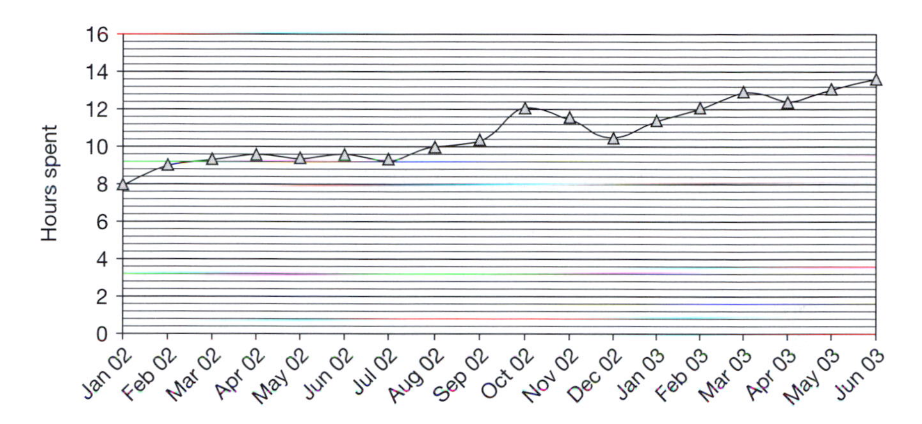

Figure 11.3 *Time spent on the Internet*

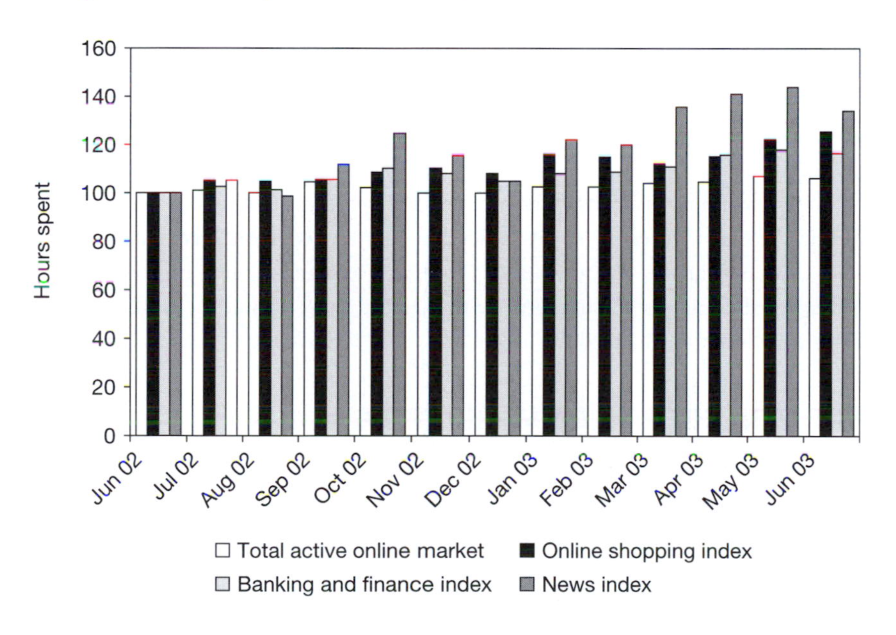

Figure 11.4 *Visitors to a website in each category compared to a baseline of June 2002*

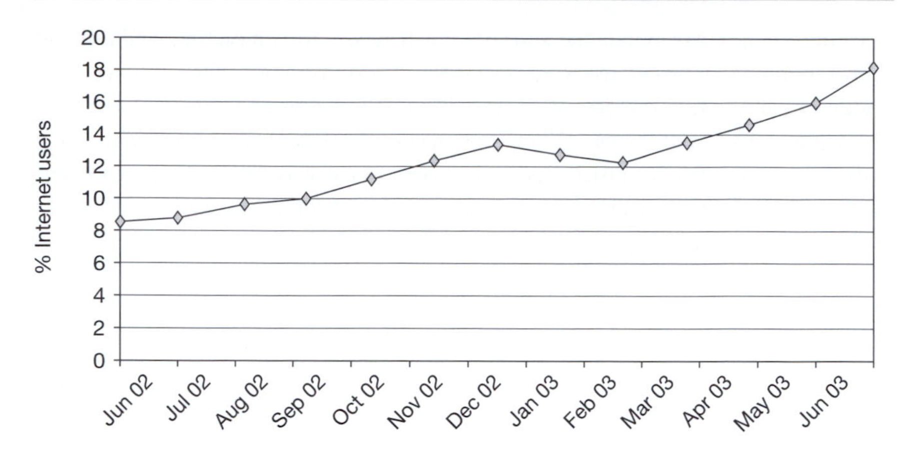

Figure 11.5 *Broadband adoption by Internet users*

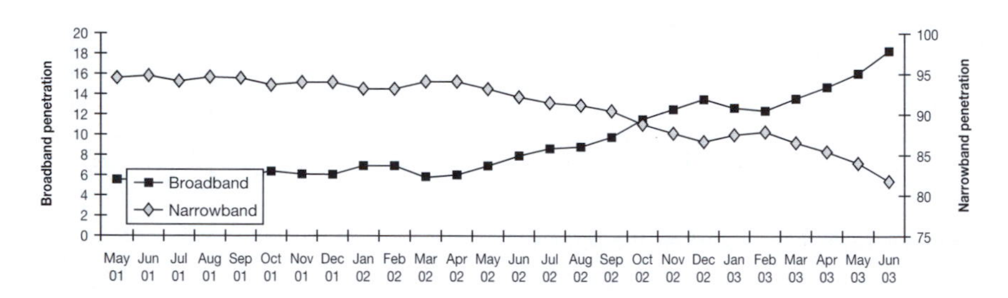

Figure 11.6 *Broadband penetration: recent development in broadband usage (percentages)*

Source: www.nielsen-netratings.com (8 July 2003)

What is clear now is that users are becoming dependent upon the Internet and expect to have access when it is needed and not wait until access becomes available. The solution to 'anywhere' Internet access for any online activity including m-shopping is to supplement the cabled/wired Internet facilities with mobile/wireless Internet facilities.

WHAT IS NEEDED TO GO M-SHOPPING?

In the same context as accessing the Internet for the first time, a potential m-shopper requires certain platform elements. The principle platform elements of the m-shopping environment are a network and telecommunications hardware.

Network

Suppose you were conducting a meeting in a restaurant and subsequently needed to book travel. Certainly, you could book the travel over the Internet but there is no phone to plug in your modem or Ethernet socket for an *LAN* connection. Until recently your alternative was to link your notebook computer to the Internet through a cellular phone on the GPRS or GSM network. Drawbacks to this access method are the slow access speed of between 9,600bps and 68Kbits and the corresponding high telephone charges for the session. A better alternative is the increasingly available wireless fidelity (Wi-Fi) networks.

'Hotspot' locations delivering Wi-Fi in hotels, fast-food chains and airport lounges are being established by major telecommunications carriers in the US, Europe and Asia Pacific, e.g. Telstra (www.telsta.com.au) and Sprint (www.sprint.com). Emulating traditional consumer Internet access, entrée to these Wi-Fi networks is by way of subscription and hourly usage contracts – higher than a cabled Internet network fee. As an alternative to the major carriers, wireless communities grant inexpensive or free Wi-Fi access to the Internet for e-mail, shopping, gaming, etc.

Telecommunications hardware

Establishing yourself within a Wi-Fi network footprint (the area of transmission coverage) will have little benefit if your computing devices are only configured to link to the wired Internet. The options to surf the wireless Internet and fulfil m-shopping needs are noted below:

- Wi-Fi-enabled PC – linked to an Internet service provider (ISP) network:
  - Notebook PCs are now being enabled by the manufacturers to include integrated wireless networking, e.g. Dell Inspiron 500M with Intel Centrino chip.
  - Similar to adding a modem to a PC for Internet access, PC users may purchase a wireless access card for their desktop or notebook computers (see Figure 11.7).
- Wi-Fi- or *Bluetooth*-enabled Personal Digital Assistant (PDA). Bluetooth is a radio transmission service that links cellular phones and computer hardware in a similar manner to Wi-Fi, though over a much shorter distance and with slower transmission times. Such an enabled PDA may access the Internet through either:
  - an ISP network; or
  - Internet-linked PC network; or
  - cellular phone that is linked to GSM network.
- Wi-Fi- or Bluetooth-enabled cellular phone that is linked to the GSM network (see Figure 11.8).

Figure 11.7 *Wireless networking hardware*

Source: D-Link

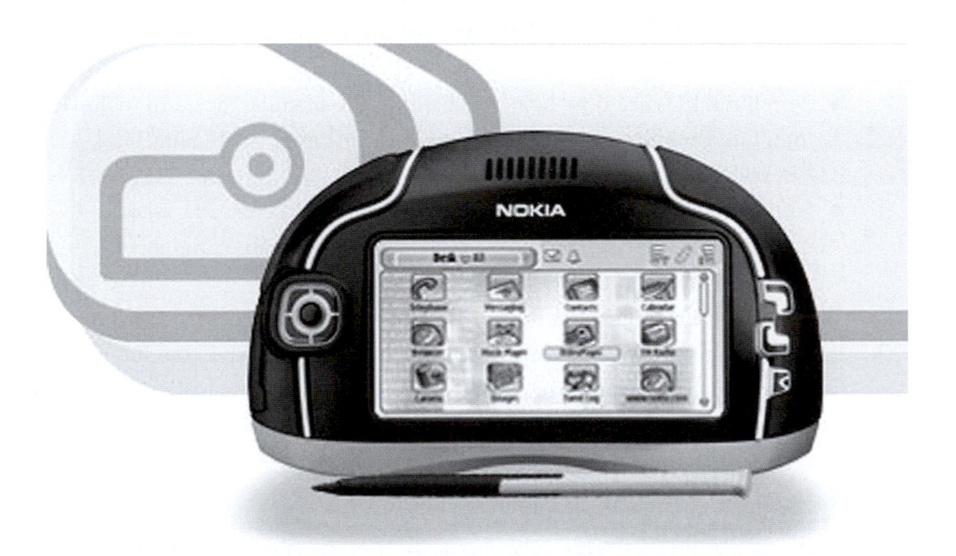

Figure 11.8 *Phones are already under development to include Internet connectivity, music and video playback and minor computer functions (i.e. view spreadsheets and documents)*

Source: www.nokia.com/nokia/0,8764,47563.html (5 November 2003)

THINK POINT

Does all this seem familiar – high Internet access cost, few users and few places to use the service? Sounds as though this is too specialized for general appeal, right? Wrong. This is just what happened in the mid- to late-1990s when the Internet was being promoted and marketed to the general public. As end-user (customer) numbers increased and supplier/e-retailer sites expanded there was a corresponding decline in Internet access fees and the costs of the associated accessing technology (i.e. computers and modems). We may expect the same adoption curve with Wi-Fi.

FEATURES THAT DISTINGUISH M-COMMERCE FROM TRADITIONAL E-COMMERCE

Though a component of e-commerce, m-commerce has its own distinguishing elements which are listed below:

- *Mobile* By its very nature, m-commerce is not restricted to a fixed telecommunications line (hard cable) that is linked to the Internet at a single location – m-commerce users may carry their mobile communications device (including cellular phone or personal digital assistant) and use this device to make a purchase in any region that provides mobile/wireless communication coverage.
- *Ubiquity* Mobile technology enables the user to access information wherever they are assuming the user is, within the mobile communication broadcast region.
- *Personalization* Due to the limited memory capacity of the current mobile hardware, internal software enables a finer degree of information sorting and categorization to meet the mobile user's needs.
- *Flexibility and convenience* The mobility of the mobile hardware delivers the early promise of e-commerce, that is, 'anywhere anytime' shopping. For example, cellular phone handsets and PDAs permit users to conduct transactions and/or receive information even when the user is engaged in another activity such as travelling or working.
- *Dissemination and localization* Originators of information, for example local retailers, may use wireless networks to deliver specific information to some or all m-shopping users who enter the geographic region.

Using these features we can envisage that a local restaurant may broadcast their vegetarian menu (the personalization) lunchtime specials within a few blocks of the restaurant (the dissemination) and this message would reach m-commerce enabled users even if driving (the flexibility) in an unfamiliar geographic region (the ubiquity).

CONTRIBUTORS TO THE GROWTH IN M-COMMERCE

The features of m-commerce are not themselves sufficient to expand its adoption. Other factors that are contributing to the growth of m-commerce include:

- Growth in cellular phone and PDA usage.
  - Improvements in chip technology. Intel has already integrated wireless network connectivity into their Centrino computer chip (www.intal.com/products/mobiletechnology/index.htm). Wireless modems for notebook and desktop computers have significantly dropped in price and are starting to become real alternatives to wired networking.
  - Mobile communication devices are culturally entrenched. Cellular phones have evolved from costly commercial sales tools to personal communication facilities with voice and text (SMS and MMS). To improve the adoption rates, cellular phone companies such as Nokia and Siemens have developed a range of phones that are more fashion accessories than telecommunications hardware.
- Declining costs of connectivity.
  - Competitive pressures between the communications providers and improving production systems have reduced costs of telecommunications hardware and transmissions.
- User incentives provided by telecommunications carriers.
  - Discounted hardware to encourage network usage.
  - Discounted airtime to increase network usage.
- User equity.
  - Potential m-shoppers who have a communication disability may use mobile devices to make a retail purchase using voice prompts, or a voice-navigated site.

Mini case study 11.1: AVANTGO.CO.UK

In the UK, AvantGo is the market-leading content provider for Internet phones and PDAs with a wide range of information and shopping, including: books, CDs/videos, computers, travel, electronics and clothing from over 200 suppliers. Based in

California with over 350 employees, AvantGo has been supplying mobile Internet content since 1999. PDA sales are growing fast, with over seven million units sold per year in Europe. The chief use of AvantGo's content is to provide up-to-the-minute information. Financial information comes from sources such as Bloomberg and the *Financial Times*. News is from live feeds from the BBC and newspapers such as the *Telegraph*. Other important content includes mapping and sports. AvantGo is paid by content providers for hosting the content and also receives a share of the advertising revenue. Consumers pay subscriptions to use the content channels.

Shopping via PDAs is popular in the UK among young, male, educated, affluent shoppers. AvantGo's expertise is in providing Internet content in a suitable form for use on mobile phones and PDAs. Using a PDA, a shopper can prepare orders at any convenient time – providing efficient use of, say, travel time. The orders are then sent automatically the next time the PDA is connected either via land line or mobile. This system provides great flexibility and many of the benefits of m-shopping without always needing the cost of mobile connection. Users of PDAs and mobile Internet are loyal and interactive – click-throughs are 10 to 20 per cent higher than for conventional Internet promotions. According to AvantGo, special offers redeemed by electronic *bar code* are achieving astonishing 5 to 8 per cent response rates. See Figure 11.9 for the most popular shopping categories.

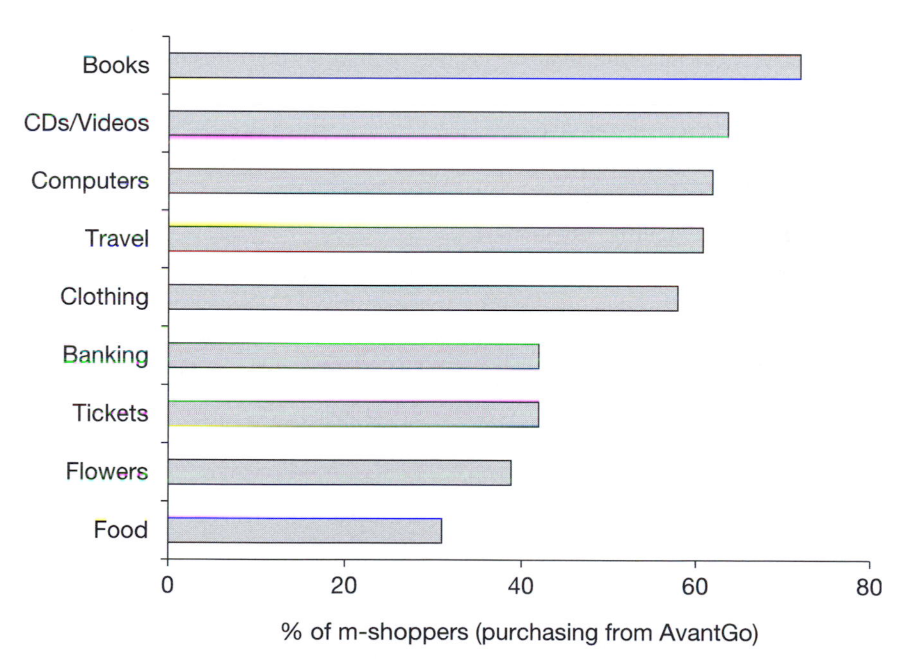

Figure 11.9 *What m-shoppers buy (mobile phone Internet and PDA)*

Source: AvantGo Demographic Survey

PAYMENTS THROUGH M-COMMERCE

Using a mobile network device to make a payment is often referred to as a *micro-payment*. Depending upon the mobile device and available networks in the geographic region, a consumer has the option of making a micropayment in one or all of these modes:

- *Short Message Service (SMS) charges* The consumer keys in the SMS number that is assigned to the merchandise to be purchased and a charge appears on the billing consumer's account where SMS charges are normally listed. For example, some Coca-Cola beverage vending machines accept traditional coin payments and also display the SMS number for the particular machine. The beverage buyers call the SMS number from their own mobile device and, once the vending machine receives the SMS signal, the consumer may select the beverage to be dispensed. The charge for the beverage appears on the consumer's next SMS bill.
- *Direct charge billing to the account linked to the consumer's mobile device* Mobile network devices today are fitted with facilities to transmit data to another computerized device in close proximity without making a telephone call. These data transmission facilities range from inferred (IR) beams, Bluetooth and Wi-Fi transmissions. The owner of the mobile device transacts the purchase sequence as they would do traditionally, that is, select the merchandise to be purchased and take it to the sales counter/checkout for payment. The only difference is that, instead of payment by cash, EFTPoS (Electronic Funds Transfer Point of Sale) or credit card, the mobile device owner transmits the account details using one of the data transmission facilities noted above.

  Similar to the already described Coca-Cola SMS purchases, India's BPL mobile customer may send a message to 2233, which will be displayed on the LCD panel of the vending machine. The vending machine confirms the customer's mobile number, then asks for the choice of chocolate and, once selected, dispenses the chocolate. Finally, the customer receives an SMS confirming the transaction. The vending transaction cost is debited from a pre-paid card or added to the monthly bill of a post-paid customer (Hindu Business Line, 2003).
- *Using a clearing house service* Intermediaries allow for payment authorities on behalf of the customer to pay for merchandise. One group, the Mobile Payment Services Association, is a coalition between Spain's Telefonica Moviles SA, Germany's T-Mobile AG and Britain's Orange SA and Vodafone Group PLC. The system of making payments through a mobile communications device is often referred to as a micropayment.

Micropayments

As seen above, m-shopping-enabled technology permits the shopper to make payments in a variety of situations that may be grouped as:

- *Unmanned point of sale equipment*, i.e. food and beverage vending machines, parking meters, public transport ticketing systems (Editor, 2003b).
- *Manned shopping counters*, i.e. fast food and beverage providers.
- *Full-time cellular phone merchant connections*, i.e. SMS and WAP sites that automatically take payments by way of a cellular phone account rather than needing to enter credit card details.

The benefits of micropayment to retailers include:

- Billing the accounts linked to the mobile devices, e.g. the cellular phone does not carry the charges associated with the transfer of credit card funds.
- Reduced need to provide customers with change for vending machines.
- Bill fraud is reduced. When a mobile device is stolen, the communications carrier usually disables network access for that device and so it cannot be used to make further micropayments.
- Extends the frequency of impulse purchases for items of small value.

The benefits of micropayment to the mobile consumer include:

- Reduced dependence upon carrying cash and credit cards.
- Record of purchase appears on the account attached to the micropayment, e.g. cellular phone account.

PROFILING THE M-SHOPPER

As indicated at the start of this chapter, the mobile shopping environment is still in its emergent stage of retailer development and shopper adoption. For retailers to tailor their market offering to the needs of the mobile shoppers, we should profile the current and intended adopters of m-shopping. As a contributor to this profiling we have incorporated the wireless shopping research of Fenech (2002, 2003).

- *Buying behaviour* Such individuals are frugal, enjoy shopping and take up new shopping facilities when they become available. In summary they are:
  - buying impulsive;
  - highly desirous of shopping convenience;
  - innovative in shopping;
  - positive in their attitude towards non-store marketing;
  - positive in their attitude towards shopping;
  - price conscious;
  - seekers of variety.

- *Use of mobile communication technology* This individual already uses the functionality of their mobile technology; this is demonstrated by:
  - Frequently sending SMSs.
- *Shopping and communication environment* This shopper is confident in the parties that contribute to the shopping process and desires the convenience of m-shopping. In summary they:
  - desire the convenience of mobile phone shopping;
  - enjoy mobile phone shopping;
  - have a low concern of financial risk from visited Web retailer;
  - have a low concern of privacy risk from ISP;
  - are satisfied with mobile phone carrier.

As surprising as the concept of Web-based e-retailing was in 1996, the concept of mobile shopping far from a phone jack or retailer must also be surprising in the beginning of this new millennium. Fortunately, we have already seen the benefits of e-retailing and this should significantly shorten the adoption rate of m-shopping.

CHAPTER SUMMARY

It is often said that there is nothing new in selling, but that is not true for retailing. Retailing has evolved from face-to-face exchanges, to non-store shopping and now shopping on the go with mobile shopping (m-shopping), which requires the availability of a wireless network and a device that the shopper can employ to enter and use the wireless network to browse and shop. The devices are not only used for placing orders for merchandise but may now be used to pay for goods and services that previously required cash or a credit card.

It is unlikely that m-shopping will displace the entrenched and growing cabled/desktop Web shopping experience. Nevertheless, the applications for m-shopping-linked devices do present opportunities to provide existing and non-shoppers with facilities to access services that would have required the establishment of prohibitively expensive individual corporate networked systems to distribute the services and collect fees. Just one example concerns the universal problem of shopping trolleys (carts) being removed and dumped after shopping. Trolley loss could be reduced by linking the trolley to a mobile phone. The shopper keys in a code and the trolley is unlocked for use; if the trolley is not returned to a designated docking bay the same day, the cost of the trolley is passed on to the mobile phone account. Retailers continually find ways to use existing technology to adapt to the way people shop and to save waste.

In the final chapter we will continue the theme by exploring the possible future shape of (e-)retailing.

Case study 11.1: MCDONALD'S 'WOULD YOU LIKE WI-FI WITH YOUR MEAL?' OFFERING

The story of McDonald's Corporation is a marketing success envied by many industries; it has even become a benchmark for growth, franchising and consumer sales. The story began with a single restaurant established in 1940 by the two McDonald brothers and first franchised in 1954, coincidentally to the future owner of the McDonald's name and concept, Ray Kroc. Kroc bought out the brothers, later taking the company public in 1965 and continued its growth to become a global restaurant chain that is in more than 100 countries with over 30,000 restaurants (www.mcdonalds.com).

Surprising many, McDonald's reported its first-ever quarterly loss in 2002 after costs incurred in closing hundreds of its restaurants. The giant restaurant chain lost US$344m for the third quarter of 2002, compared with a profit of US$272m in 2001 (Editor, 2003a). The situation was not helped by a recession, increased competitive pressures, beef safety scares in Europe and increased complaints about poor service (Comitex, 2002). Difficulties were not only from outside the corporation but began to emerge from McDonald's own franchisees. A few franchisees across the globe were unsettled over practices by the McDonald's company and took the chain to court on many occasions (Smith, 2001). While the organization did respond to the issues with innovations that embraced a revised menu for the new millennium customer, there would need to be further advancements to turn McDonald's reputation and profits around.

One method being used to improve customer marketing is the adoption of Wi-Fi Internet accessibility in the McDonald's restaurants. At these locations, all the McDonald's visitor needs is a laptop computer or a handheld communication device (e.g. mobile phone or PDA) configured for Wi-Fi as well as a credit card to pay the hourly fee. Cost for a two-hour wireless Internet connection at these locations is around

Figure 11.10 *Many new phones are Wi-Fi enabled, needing only browsing software and a hotspot to use the Web.*

Source: www.nokia.com/nokia/0,8764,47563,00.html (5 November 2003)

US$5.00 per hour. Customers will be able to identify participating restaurants by signage that displays the Golden Arches in the universal Internet @ symbol.

The McDonald's food chain is testing Wi-Fi hotspots in 25 countries around the world (TechWeb News, 2003). Why? Phil Gray, McDonald's central division vice president says, 'this is a high-tech blend of innovation and convenience that will tell our customers McDonald's is going to be a part of their world' (Kewney, 2003; McDonald's, 2003). McDonald's CEO Guy Russo believes that many of his customers are business people on the road or high users of mobile data: 'there is a McDonald's restaurant in virtually every community and by making this service available to so many we are taking a leadership position and anticipating the future communication needs of our customers' (Russo, 2003). The company will select a single hotspot service provider in each of its markets, such as Toshiba's SurfHere high-speed wireless Internet access service in Chicago, to provide uniform easy Wi-Fi access for franchisees. This uniformity also means that restaurant goers do not have to search for an available local hotspot if they want Internet access (Shim, 2003). Just as many think of McDonald's when hunger pangs strike, McDonald's may become an initial thought when there is a need to use the Internet away from the office or home. According to Jupiter Research analyst Julie Ask:

> I think it's as much about McDonald's and incremental money from food as it is about how McDonald's is ubiquitous. They are everywhere. And if they are everywhere, and they put hotspots in their restaurants, then there's a great footprint of Wi-Fi access points. So it's less about public hotspots than it is about piping information out of McDonald's.
>
> (Singer, 2003)

Outside the US, McDonald's is planning up to 4,000 hotspots in the company's Japanese outlets and is also negotiating with Australia's largest telecommunications carrier, Telstra, to use Telstra's existing wireless network, which already covers many of the country's airport lounges and a hotel chain (Russo, 2003; Singer, 2003).

In the short term, the incorporation of Wi-Fi at McDonald's may not cover its costs considering nearly all Wi-Fi services in the US are losing money and several have already gone out of business (Kessler, 2003). Also, is this service consistent with what people have come to expect under the golden arches? McDonald's grew on a culture of attracting patrons, feeding patrons, exiting patrons, and all these fast. The concept of patrons staying around or drawing out the meal is a far cry from what the chain's mentor Ray Kroc envisaged (Silicon.com, 2003). Detractors think that computing work and eating a quick meal are a less than perfect match (Mohney, 2003). In his article Mohney writes 'Don't get me wrong, I love the Egg McMuffin and the sausage biscuit, but like many 'mericans I've stopped going in there to eat unless it's a real, real emergency' (Mohney, 2003).

McDonald's as a retailer has grown up and so too have the facilities. Initially, Ray Kroc was impressed by the speed of service and volume of milk shakes available at McDonald's. Kroc was able to extend the service offering to produce simple and inexpensive burgers and meals for the family to eat out. In the same vein as introducing drive-through (Anonymous, 1996) and even ski-through facilities, McDonald's has tried to meet the lifestyles of its patrons. The offer of Wi-Fi hotspots is another way in which McDonald's is trying to contribute to the changing lifestyles of its patrons who want to stay in contact with the Internet for e-mail, chat, research, document accessing and, of course, m-shopping.

QUESTIONS

Brief feedback to these questions is included at the back of the book.

Question 11.1

It took half a decade to get a critical mass of computer users to adopt the Internet as an information and shopping environment. Will retailers need to have specialized Internet sites to display the e-retailers' offerings on the compact screens of PDA or mobile phones?

Question 11.2

Many people use cafés and restaurants to get away from the work environment. Will providing restaurant Wi-Fi hotspots like McDonald's and Starbucks alienate these people?

FURTHER READING

Balasubramanian, S., Peterson, R.A. and Jarvenpaa, S.L. (2002) 'Exploring the implications of m-commerce for markets and marketing', *Journal of the Academy of Marketing Science*, 30 (4), 348–361.

Gordon, C. Bruner II and Kumar, A. (in press) 'Explaining consumer acceptance of handheld Internet devices', *Journal of Business Research*.

Irvine, Clarke III (2001) 'Emerging value propositions for M-commerce', *Journal of Business Strategies*, 18 (2): 133–149.

REFERENCES

Anonymous (1996) *A Brief History of McDonald's*. 2003, mcspotlight. www.mcspotlight.org/company/company_history.html [accessed 26 November 2003]

Comitex (2002) *McDonald's CEO Defends Revival Plan*, Associated Press, www.licenseenews.com/news/news79.html [accessed 25 November 2003].

Editor (2003a) *McDonald's Posts First-ever Loss*, BBC, www.news.bbc.co.uk/2/hi/business/2688665.stm [accessed 25 November 2003].

Editor (2003b) *'Park and Ring' Scheme Launched*, BBC, www.news.bbc.co.uk/1/hi/scotland/3229217.stm [accessed 20 November 2003].

Fenech, T. (2002) 'Exploratory study into WAP (Wireless Application Protocol) shopping', *International Journal of Retail and Distribution Management*, 30 (10), 482–497.

Fenech, T. (2003) 'Factors Influencing Intention to Adopt Wireless Shopping', in J.E. Lewin (ed.) *Proceedings of World Marketing Congress*, Perth, Western Australia: Academy of Marketing Science, pp. 729–734.

Hindu Business Line (2003) *Now You Can SMS For A Chocolate: Cadbury, BPL Mobile, E Cube Tie-up for Venture*, www.allaboutvending.com [accessed 20 November 2003].

Kessler, M. (2003) *Small Firms Get in Position for Wi-Fi Boom, USA Today*, www.usatoday.com/tech/news/2003–07–07–wifi-quirky_x.htm [accessed 26 November 2003].

Kewney, G. (2003) *News – Burger-surfing: McDonald's Announces 'Biggest WiFi Move Yet' in Chicago*, Newswireless, www.newswireless.net/articles/030813-burger.html [accessed 25 November 2003].

McDonald's (2003) *McDonald's Announces Largest Wi-Fi Launch to Date*, www.McDonald's.com/countries/usa/whatsnew/pressrelease/2003/08122003/.

Mohney, D. (2003) *McDonald's Wi-Fi Overcooked?*, Breakthrough Publishing, www.theinquirer.net/default.aspx?article=8283 [accessed 25 November 2003].

Russo, G. (2003) *McDonald's Nets Telstra Wireless*, Hospitality Magazine, www.hospitalitymagazine.com.au/articles/aa/0c0154aa.asp [accessed 26 November 2003].

Shim, R. (2003) *McDonald's Shakes Out Wi-Fi*, Silicon.com, www.silicon.com/networks/wifi/0,39024669,39116639,00.htm [accessed 25 November 2003].

Silicon.com (2003) *Leader: Wi-Fi: Right Time, Wrong Place?*, www.silicon.com/comment/0,39024711,39116650,00.htm [accessed 25 November 2003].

Singer, M. (2003) *McDonald's Serves Up Wi-Fi in SF*, Jupitermedia Corporation [accessed 25 November 2003].

Smith, T. (2001) *Brazil Franchisees Sue McDonald's*, Associated Press, www.mcspotlight.org/media/press/meds/associatedpress0712011.html [accessed 25 November 2003].

Strutt, S. (2003) 'Fun on the net . . . at the boss's expense', *Australian Financial Review*, 18 July: 5.

TechWeb News (2003) *Race for McDonald's Wi-Fi Business*, United Business Media, www.techweb.com/wire/story/TWB20031028S0009 [accessed 25 November 2003].

Von der Luehe, M. (2003) *Overall Growth is Steady in Internet Connections, but Broadband Increases by 36% in Past 6 Months*, Nielson-netratings, www.nielsen-netratings.com [accessed 18 August 2003].

WEB LINKS

www.csd.toshiba.com/cgi-bin/tais/hs/hs_home.jsp
SurfHere is a high-speed public wireless network provided by Toshiba using Wi-Fi 802.11b technology.

www.intel.com/products/mobiletechnology/index.htm
The Centrino chip was developed by Intel to provide personal computer manufacturers with integrated wireless LAN capability, improved mobile performance and extended battery life, with thinner and lighter designs.

www.mcdwireless.com
McDonald's provides high-speed wireless Internet access at over 100 restaurants in Chicago, New York, San Francisco Bay and Canada. In September 2003 McDonald's conducted online promotions and provided prize giveaways including Toshiba notebook computers and Pocket PCs.

www.sprint.com
Large US telecommunications organization providing long distance telephony services, dial-up and broadband Internet services, and mobile telephony facilities.

www.telstra.com.au
The largest telecommunications carrier in Australia, which carries the majority of the Internet and mobile phone traffic.

www.weca.net
A non-profit association formed in 1999 to certify interoperability of wireless Local Area Network products based on IEEE 802.11 specification.

Chapter 12

Multi-channel success and the future of e-retailing

LINKS TO OTHER CHAPTERS

- Chapter 4 – Understanding and communicating with the e-consumer
- Chapter 6 – e-Store design: navigability, interactivity and web atmospherics
- Chapter 10 – e-Retailing models
- Chapter 11 – m-Shopping

KEY LEARNING POINTS

After completing this chapter you will have an understanding of:

- How successful retailing principles are consistent across physical and virtual market places
- How shoppers will develop their own service exchange situations with the aid of new technological developments in e-retailing

ORDERED LIST OF SUB-TOPICS

- Consumer buying decision process
- The hybrid retailer – the most likely winner in the future of retailing
- What can you expect to see and hear in e-retailing?
- Chapter summary
- Case study
- Questions

INTRODUCTION

To the students at the University of Capetown, South Africa, on 6 June 1966, Senator Robert F. Kennedy said, 'There is a Chinese curse which says, "May he live in interesting times". Like it or not, we live in interesting times.' Despite serious questions as to the origin of the phrase, that is, that the phrase is more likely to be of Western origin than Chinese (Editor, 2002), the sentiment 'living in interesting times' holds true now and will continue to do so for e-retailing. Changes in the retailing service exchange medium from bricks and mortar to an electronic medium have not endowed retailers with magical insights into the needs and buying processes of potential customers. This lack of consumer understanding was confirmed by the collapse of so many would-be Web e-retailers in the dot.com crash. What is needed is to consider the demands upon e-retailing from the point of view of the potential interaction between the website and shopping browser. Huarng and Christopher (2003) suggested examining the issues that come into play during such interactions through the traditional consumer buying decision process.

CONSUMER BUYING DECISION PROCESS

A potential e-consumers buying decision process will follow the established stages of need recognition, information search, information evaluation, purchase decision and post-purchase behaviour.

Need recognition

An e-retail website is a combination of the traditional store display window, information desk, stocked display shelving, mood lighting/sound, promotional material that shout out specials, and the time-honoured *barker/spruiker* used to stimulate shopping interest. Such an e-retail site ought to elicit a need recognition response from any visitor to the site. A new or returning visitor should be treated to a combination of the four basic marketing elements – *price* (e.g. specials, discounts, interest free periods), *product* (e.g. new lines, clearance items, seasonal products, fashion and fad limited ranges), *promotion* (e.g. sales, seasonal specials, select shopper campaigns) and *distribution* (e.g. free delivery, lay-away, home installation) that accentuate the visitor's own need identification. Technology within the website, for example cookie files, captures data about the visitor's responses and what information was accessed. Such information then enables e-retailers to improve the rapport with the online customer by tailoring the site content to consumer demand. One positive application from such data collection is the inclusion of customer loyalty programs that encourage return visitation to the e-retailer site and increased purchases.

THINK POINT

Since we often choose to go to an e-retailing website rather than finding the site by accident or clicking through to the site, are we not already in a need recognition state at that point?

Information search

Improved telecommunications technology and general population access to the Internet have transformed user availability to customization of, and digestion of, large information volumes. Unlike the bricks and mortar retailer, an e-retail site has the facilities to make available such large volumes of information in a customized format to meet the immediate and potential queries of site visitors following the need recognition stage. Without personal embarrassment or the self-consciousness of asking a stranger (e.g. a shopkeeper) what may be an obvious or foolish product-related question, the e-retail site visitor can access online product brochures, price comparisons, frequently asked questions (FAQs), suggested product applications, cleaning and repair information, and an efficient search engine technology, as well as asking for specialized information via the e-retailer's e-mail system.

Information evaluation

When seeking to evaluate the collected information on products and services, the potential shopper will often turn to the experiences and advice of family, friends and persons who have already experienced use of such merchandise. Also, e-retailing gives the user added facilities to access evaluative experts and previous users of the merchandise in question to aid in the digestion and customization of all this information. Many consumer groups act as such reference experts through the testing and personal evaluations of retailed products and then make these findings available to others. Experienced e-retailers encourage interactions between previous, current and future shoppers by way of:

1 Online discussion groups.
2 Suggesting site visitors rate the available merchandise.
3 Suggesting site visitors express comments about this merchandise and the service exchange experiences.

Monitoring of the online discussions and visitor comments endows the retailer with invaluable knowledge regarding merchandise features and limitations that may be incorporated into promotional materials. To conclude, apart from all the benefits mentioned above, the e-retailer gains all this free information that would normally require expensive market research.

Purchase decision

After a visitor to an e-retailer site has determined the merchandise to be appropriate for their needs, it is still not a certainty that this visitor will finalize a purchase. Commonly, an online customer nominates particular merchandise from an e-retail website and places those items in the online *shopping cart* (also known as a *shopping trolley*) for the checkout, but later the customer discontinues the purchase process and leaves the e-retailer's site. This action of discontinuing an online purchase is termed 'abandoned cart syndrome' (Davis, 2001; Berry *et al.*, 2002; Fenech, 2002). From his research into abandoned cart syndrome, Fenech (2002) identified the principal contributors, as (in order of highest to lowest):

1 A lower level of education.
2 Higher frequency of Web purchases.
3 Greater concern of online data risk and fraud.
4 Greater frequency of website service problems.
5 The use of shopping as a facility to see family and friends.
6 High levels of concern about online retailers' tracking data.
7 Younger buying groups.
8 Shopping causing little arousal.
9 Higher frequency of browsing for a later purchase.
10 Higher fashion consciousness.
11 Higher frequency of Web search for product information.

Although the e-retailer cannot yet duplicate the human interactions possible in a physical store setting, e-retailers may still empower customers in an attempt to reduce the incidence of online cart abandonment. One positive step to improve the e-retailer's customer interactions is streamlining the order process by:

- Making improvements in the e-retailer's site navigation.
- Incorporation of help links and interactive facilities to stimulate the shopper's arousal and fashion consciousness.
- Supplying the relevant merchandise information as needed.

- Greater use of online help facilities and screen prompts.
- Establishing chat rooms and customer discussion opportunities to share experience with family, friends and new acquaintances.
- Improved guarantees (including deliveries, data security, 30-day trials).
- Offline contact details (phone number, fax number, street address).

Post-purchase behaviour

The key to a retailer's survival and success whether offline or online is to generate repeat purchase behaviour. For a customer to return to a retailer that customer needs to have confidence in the retailer, but e-retailer confidence is often difficult to establish in light of online issues that have caused customers to make complaints and/or never return to the e-retailer. According to Cho *et al.* (2002), the online issues that often alienate customers and lead to complaints are the failure to meet customer *expectations* in relation to:

- Merchandise offerings.
- The e-retailer's store-front technology (this includes, but is not limited to, the website) that integrates:
  - usability of the technology;
  - the technology failing to carry out a function.
- The e-retailer's information sources (the policies).
- Payment/settlement issues;
  - agreed conditions (including delivery timing).

To reduce the chance of customer expectations being unfulfilled, e-retailers will compensate for the lack of a face-to-face exchange by making available more information details than would otherwise be considered in a bricks and mortar environment. Dealing with each of the Cho *et al.* (2002) points, we suggest the following responses:

- Merchandise offerings –
  - Define all dimensions of the size options, colour variations, and accessories provided. One suggestion is to include the supply of actual colour swatches to reduce the colour errors often attributed to variations on computer colour monitors.

- The e-retailer's store-front technology (this includes, but is not limited to the website) –
  - Provide sufficient technology to cope with peak buying periods such as St Valentine's Day and Mother's Day.
  - Keep redundant backup to take over when systems fail.

- Offer facilities to store (file) partial orders for future use should the customer be interrupted and/or wish to continue the shopping process in the near future.
- Provide improved access facilities for the disabled/impaired computer user. Facilities may consist of:
  - selectable larger display fonts;
  - voice recognition commands;
  - spoken responses embedded in the web pages;
  - written descriptions of displayed images (these can be read out to the non-sighted user even if they can't see the picture).
- Alerts given by the e-retailer's site to advise users:
  - pending specials;
  - replenishment of merchandise that was out of stock;
  - arrival of special orders.
- Such alerts can reach the user through e-mail, phone short message service (SMS), automated faxing or other communications technologies.

■ The e-retailer's information sources (the policies) –

- Information is to be detailed (even exhaustive), accurate and timely (not noticeably out of date).
- Information is to be easy to find on the e-retailer site.
- Links to relevant or 'just interesting' sites shall establish the e-retail not only as an appropriate purchasing site but as a point of reference or portal for future enquiries in this area; thereby achieving a great milestone: being bookmarked as a favourite site in the user's Web browsing software.
- A continued customer relationship should be maintained after a purchase by:
  - continued updates on the relevant and near-relevant issues by e-mail or newsgroup (for example, a customer purchases an electric grill and then receives a monthly recipe; the e-retailer keeps the contact and the customer's satisfaction in the purchase is supported);
  - space may also be sold to sponsors seeking to promote their products.

■ Payment/settlement issues –

- Not all customers want to reveal their personal details and movements to online parties. To aid these potential customers, e-retailers can now provide alternatives for the customer in the shopping cycle to minimize risk. In Australia, a purchaser using the Wishlist retailer (www.wishlist.com.au) may opt to have their online purchases delivered to a participating BP petrol service station rather than to their home address. In this way the customer picks up the merchandise at a time that suits and conceals their personal address details while still gaining the advantages of shopping online.

- Most courier organizations (i.e. DHL and FedEx) used by e-retailers have facilities for the purchaser to trace and track the merchandise while it is in transit. The e-retailer receives proof the item is 'on its way' and the client achieves the peace of mind of 'seeing' where the item is any time they go online.

THINK POINT

For a retailer, traditional advertising communications devices cover such things as printed brochures, display signs and shelf display signs. New retailer advertising communication devices cover SMS and the company website. If it takes effort by a retailer to update all these advertising communication devices, why do we consider that Web information is more up-to-date than the more traditional advertising devices?

THE HYBRID RETAILER: THE MOST LIKELY WINNER IN THE FUTURE OF RETAILING

As discussed in Chapter 10, retailers today are not restricted to just bricks and mortar, direct and virtual categories of retailing but often opt for a hybrid business model. Hybrid retailers, sometimes referred to as 'multi-channel retailers', appear to be taking the greatest advantage of e-retailing opportunities.

In a study by Haeberle (2003) multi-channel retailers were identified as generating 72 per cent of Web-based sales in 2002, 5 per cent up from 2001, and 18 per cent up from the Web sales of 2000. Using profitability as a success measure, multi-channel retailers and particularly those established in the market as catalogue brands, made the greater impact as e-retailers. The Haeberle (2003) study found that, in 2002, 92 per cent of those retailers for whom catalogue was the primary sales channel were profitable. That compares with 80 per cent of bricks and mortar-based retailers and 50 per cent of Web-based retailers in the study.

When John Lewis bought the UK arm of Buy.com, the takeover gave Buy.com financial credibility while Buy.com gave one of the 'Old Men' of UK retailing street credibility (Editor, 2001). Though the purchase of a virtual retailer by a bricks and mortar retailer was nothing new, it was an early example of a continuing trend as virtual retailers ran out of operating capital. These new players in the retailing arena are faced on one side by the downwards pressure on prices to stay competitive and on the other by fearful investors who remember all too clearly the dot.com crash at the end of the first millennium.

Retailer adaptation: a key to survival and growth

Long-standing bricks and mortar retailers are not only looking at a Web presence as the means to becoming e-retailers. To improve the relationship with their customers, retailers are adopting new electronic systems that complement their physical store presence. Sears in the US (www.sears.com) uses a system termed 'buy online, pick up at the store', where the customer places and pays for an order with a credit card at the Sears website, Sears.com, but, departing from other Web stores' procedures, picks up the merchandise from a local Sears store. An e-mail is then used to advise the customer about stock availability at the time of the order and when the merchandise is ready for store collection.

Misunderstanding or ignoring a market position of strength is a failing that leads to the demise of some retailers. The availability of a new distribution channel is not an automatic indication of future success. Consider the US retailer Egghead (was www.egghead.com), which in the early 1990s had strong market presence with around 250 stores across the country. The retailer was well respected by its consumer market, had a solid brand image and was profitable. Long before most other retailers, Egghead created an online presence for its technology-minded customers in 1994. Effectively, this entry into a new distribution channel made Egghead one of the first multi-channel retailers. But, as Lightfoot (2003) described, Egghead did not leverage its unique multi-channel position; rather, it decided to abandon all of its offline stores in 1998 and exclusively sell online, evolving into a virtual retailer. Regrettably, following a series of problems, e.g. much-publicized hacking attacks on Egghead's website, technical failures in the e-commerce technology, failing customer loyalty and internal management problems, Egghead went the way of many dot.coms and exhausted its cash reserves and filed for bankruptcy in 2001 (Thornton and Marche, 2003). On the positive side for customers, the Egghead assets (including brand name and customer base) were sold to Amazon in 2001. To Amazon's credit, the new owner honoured the privacy policy of the previous Egghead clients as noted in the statement:

> Please note that if you are a returning Egghead.com customer, Egghead.com will not disclose any existing account information to Amazon.com, so you will need to re-enter all information necessary to complete a transaction. For information about how Amazon.com treats the information you give us, see Amazon.com's Privacy Notice.
>
> (Amazon, 2003)

WHAT CAN YOU EXPECT TO SEE AND HEAR IN E-RETAILING?

Improved customer education, availability of information and increasing legislation have given rise to a new type of customer for this new millennium. Our new customers are more demanding, have a higher expectation and are increasingly adversarial in their service exchanges with retailers. Part of the retailer response will be to empower the customer to tailor their own service exchange in the physical store and online. Metro, an organization that already markets hardware systems to retailers, has suggested a series of scenarios in a future retail store to provide technologies that make shopping encapsulate greater individualization, reliability and convenience (Metro Group, 2003a).

Greater individualization

Just as Web browsing technology learns and recalls a user's preferences for colour, fonts and items for inclusion, future stores will match their offering to learned customer experiences. Once the customer is identified to the store through a loyalty card or personal *radio frequency identification* (RFID) tag (see the Merchandise tracking section on p. 254 for details), the store's 'electronic personal shopping assistant' (EPSA) technology will record the shopper's preferences for merchandise, delivery (i.e. home delivery, parcel pick-up) and method of payment. To save the customer time, the store system would forewarn the customer of difficulties (including stock outages) and then make suggestions for alternative merchandise that is either in stock or pending (e.g. new season's stock).

Figure 12.1 *Future customers will identify themselves to the retailer with a loyalty card*

Source: www.future-store.org

Greater reliability and convenience

New store technology will improve reliability for both customer and retailers. When a customer selects an item and adds this to their shopping trolley, the EPSA will read the merchandise's RFID tag and present the details to the shopper via shopping trolley mounted visual display. No longer will the customer be disadvantaged by the omission of shelf pricing or getting to the checkout only to be told that the product is 'not on the system' and needs a delaying price check. Through the use of the unique RFID tag being identified by EPSA, the customer will be advised of these details at the point of merchandise access – the shelf or bin stocking the merchandise. Once the price information absence is detected, the retailer's system can search or calculate the price before the checkout is reached.

Aiding the retailer, this technology will indicate low- or out-of-stock situations at the shelf as customers place the item into their trolley, long before the item is removed from the inventory system at the checkouts. Staff will have a perpetual inventory rather than depending upon physical stock updates.

Retailers use a *planogram* to determine what merchandise is displayed where and in what quantities throughout a store. Shoppers become familiar with their favourite stores but what do they do when a new merchandise line is added to

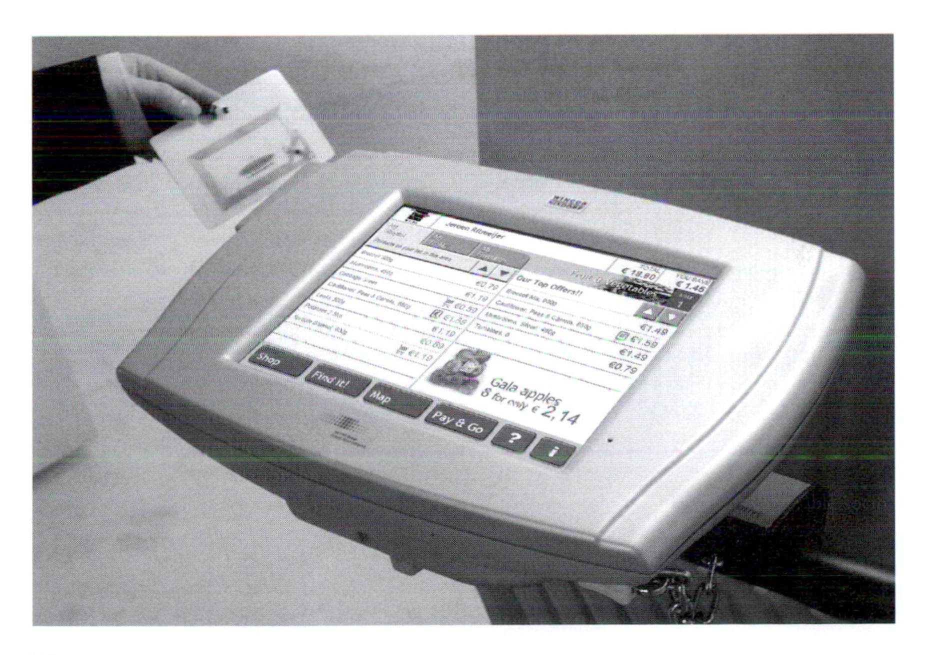

Figure 12.2 *The new shopping trolley will record the selected merchandise and advise the customer of the details, including price and running total expenditure*

Source: www.future-store.org

the store and they are unsure where it is located? What is needed is a personal guide or in the future an EPSA to direct customers through the store like a global positioning system (GPS) directs a car through traffic.

Merchandise tracking

With delivery problems representing one of the main elements holding back the growth of e-shopping (see Chapter 7), merchandise tracking may be one of the essential development areas for the future. Early developments in bricks retailing followed research by Bernard Silver and Norman Woodland in the early 1950s. As a result, the bar code became a world standard for tracking and recording the movements of retail stock (Anonymous, 2003). A standard bar code is made up of dark (predominantly black) vertical bars broken up with light (predominantly white) spaces. To read the bar code a beam of light is passed over the code where the dark bars absorb the light and the spaces reflect it. The scanner (also known as a reader or detector) then turns the reflected light into electrical pulses that may be recorded on a data file.

While an excellent product identification system, bar codes have a significant and obvious limitation, that is, they need to be scanned to register stock movement. Stock may enter or be removed from the retailer's premises and if the bar code is not scanned with a reading laser, the stock is not identified and recorded so its movement is unknown. The solution is to have the stock *speak* up and identify *itself* to the retailer's electronic inventory management system. The stock speak? How? By adding to, or replacing the bar code with a miniature RFID tag.

Figure 12.3 *A sample of a bar code*

Figure 12.4 *Sample alternative broadcasts from RFID tags*

Source: Taken from www.rsasecurity.com/rsalabs/staff/bios/ajuels/publications/blocker/RFID privacy.ppt

RFID tags are tiny (about one quarter of a square millimetre), carry between 64 and 96 bits of information and have a life of at least ten years. They are inexpensive (as low as one cent per unit) and can be energized and activated by radio waves from a scanner/receiver in close proximity, or can be hooked up to a battery. After being activated by the transmitter's power, the RFID tag then passes the information to the retailer's stock system. RFID tags have already been trailed and applied in a variety of applications. McDonald's (www.mcdonalds.com) and KFC (kfc.com) are trialling RFID tags; the US Department of Defense will be incorporating RFID tags to improve the management of inventory through hands-off processing; Nokia is incorporating the tags in some of its mobile phones; theme parks are providing them on wristbands to identify the positions of children; and the European Central Bank is considering incorporating the tags on new Euro notes to reduce counterfeiting and track illicit monetary flows.

Some bricks retailers have already piloted RFID tags. Privacy concerns have since led to Wal-Mart (www.walmart.com) and Benetton (www.benetton.com) dropping trials and orders of the tags (Gengler, 2003). Privacy becomes an issue when you consider that although the RFID receivers were conceived to detect the movements of the tagged merchandise, they are in effect able to track the movements of the customer carrying the tagged merchandise within a shopping district that contains multiple RFID scanners/receivers. Consider that, if an organization has more than one member store in the company's group (e.g. a supermarket, a bottle shop and a variety store all owned by one organization) in the same shopping mall, radio triangulation by the RFID receivers triggered by the merchandise's RFID radio signal could detect the move of merchandise

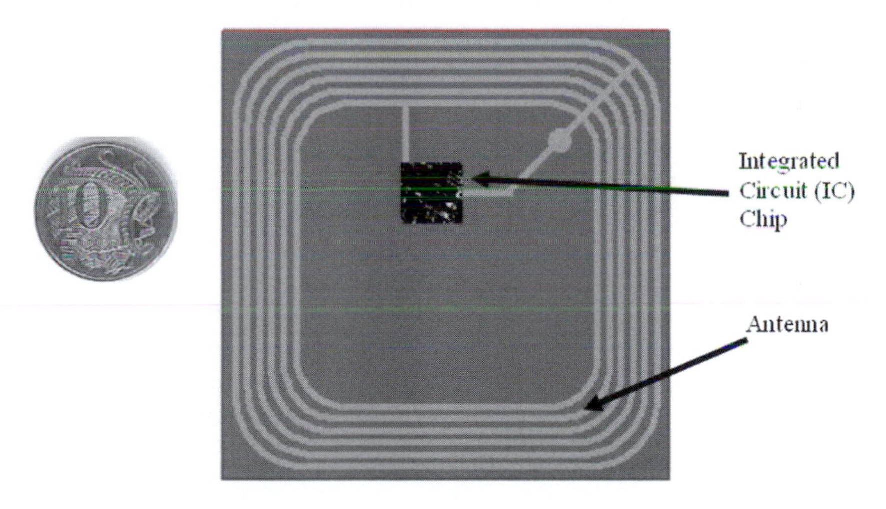

Figure 12.5 *RFID tag*

Source: Taken from www.rsasecurity.com/rsalabs/staff/bios/ajuels/publications/blocker/RFID privacy.ppt

Figure 12.6 *Sample alternative broadcasts from RFID tags*

Source: Taken from Dr Ari Juels' document at www.rsasecurity.com/rsalabs/staff/bios/ajuels/publications/blocker/RFIDprivacy.ppt

and, therefore, the shopper from one store to another and so on. The data from these movements could also interpret how long the shopper spent at various spots in the mall and all this data is collected *without* the shopper having given their permission. It is an *ethical* dilemma that will be debated for some time. Despite the debate, bricks retailers such as Tesco (www.tesco.com) are pushing ahead with RFID tags for tracking supply-chain movements and for further trials in-store. As we argue below, the potential benefits are substantial, so we expect the development to diffuse into e-retail tracking as shoppers become more accustomed to it.

As the number of applications for RFID tags increases retailers may expect to fulfil management and marketing objectives, including:

1 *Reduced retail fraud and theft*
RFID tags will track products for clothing, grocery items, electrical merchandise and recorded music to reduce shrinkage.
2 *Asset supply-chain control*
RFID tags will track the movement of goods from one process centre to another, e.g. delivery dock and warehouse. This is not limited to the selling inventory but includes organizational assets that have in the past left the premises without authorization or without being entered in a log book, e.g. storage pallets and shopping trolleys.
3 *Inventory control*
RFID tags will transmit inventory relevant information, e.g. batch number, unit code, number of items on the property and consumer-related merchandise information such as product category, size and colour.

4 *Intelligent packaging*
RFID tags can be linked to a sensor that recognizes any tampering or deterioration of the merchandise while in transit and when that damage behaviour occurred. This damage may relate to a non-deliberate deterioration error, e.g. food storage temperature being outside the recommended range. Equally, the sensor would detect malicious actions of third parties upon the merchandise, e.g. when a sealed lid on a container is removed and a subsequent replacement is made to disguise the tampering activity.

For customers, the expected benefits from a retailer using RFID tags are:

1 *Speedier checkout process*
In combination with intelligent shopping carts/trolleys, shoppers would have all their purchases totalled automatically as the individual product RFID tags are read by the shopping cart and the totals provided at the checkout point for payment.
2 *Security*
Manufacturers will introduce RFID tags into the components of final products so that if the components are removed they can be tracked. Consider the theft of car parts from a whole vehicle; in the past the panels would be almost impossible to detect and trace once removed from the original car.
3 *Tracking*
'Where are the b——y car keys?' Consumer RFID tag readers will become available to learn the tag codes of products that the consumer wishes to inventory. An immediate benefit is being able to locate the proximity of individual RFID tagged items, such as the ever-elusive car keys.
4 *Preparation and care*
RFID tags provide the opportunity to include preparation and care information that will be understood by future appliances. Potential applications in this vein are:
   - For allergens – home health systems that are programmed for the individual's health requirements will 'listen' to the RFID tags of grocery items. The tags may contain all the ingredients of the grocery items, even the complicated chemical codes, and notify the home health system of potential allergens that could be harmful to the customer/householder.
   - For clothing – RFID tags would alert the washing machine that the fabric is not machine washable or should be dry cleaned only.

- For frozen foods – RFID tags would alert the freezer display panel that the food is near or at its expiration date.
- For frozen foods – RFID tags would pass cooking instructions to the microwave or convection oven to avoid over- or under-cooking.

In-store interactive electronic kiosks

Multi-channel e-retailers are not restricted to the sale of physical merchandise in bricks and mortar establishments, but may also market digital products and services that were previously limited to virtual retailers. Through the use of interactive kiosks, retailers will be able to offer such services as:

- detailed product information;
- price checks;
- recipes and product application suggestions;
- tickets for events;
- reservations for events and activities;
- self-checkout to make purchases;
- personalized and targeted promotions;
- photo-finishing – this is a growing segment as customers bring in their digital camera cards and have the kiosks transfer the images to final photos;
- Internet access;
- customer loyalty programmes;
- banking and financial services;
- maps and direction services;
- human resource services, e.g. recruitment.

Interactive kiosks generate extra revenue and, because the customer is self-servicing, the variety of service exchanges is increased without added staff and subsequent drains on profits.

Greater use of electronic payments

The advent of the cheque made it possible for consumers to make purchases for items that cost more than the cash funds they carried on their person. A cheque could only be written up to the amount of funds the customer had in, or could deposit into, the financial institution issuing the cheque prior to the cheque being cashed by the retailer. To improve on the flexibility of the cheque and to make purchases using the financial institution's funds (up to a predetermined limit) the store and bank credit card became a popular alternative to the cheque.

Figure 12.7 *Interactive kiosks come in a variety of styles*
Source: www.meridiankiosks.com/Kiosks.asp

To make a payment by credit card necessitates the retailer obtaining a payment authorization from a financial clearance centre and the customer's identification being validated by a signature or personal identification number (PIN). All this takes time and depends upon the retailer's authorization equipment being operational. Now that consumers are carrying their own mobile technology (see Chapter 11), e.g. cellular mobile phones, there is an opportunity for the consumer to contribute to the transaction verification process. As described in Chapter 11, in its basic form, the consumer may pay for the goods by sending an SMS message to a specific phone number that verifies that a payment should be made to the retailer for the specific merchandise. Other mobile phones permit the transmission of an inferred (IR) transmission to the retailer's equipment to again verify that this payment is to be passed to the customer's charge or mobile phone account.

Widening the application of wireless device payments, Royal Philips Electronics and Visa announced an alliance to encourage and develop chip technology that does not require any physical contact with other devices. With this technology consumers will be able to pay for merchandise by waving the new smart card in front of a sensor in the retailer's store (Shim, 2003). For both retailer and customer it means reduced payment delays and improved customer satisfaction.

A further development in progress by the major credit card companies at the time of writing is 'pay-as-you-go', which should enable consumers who do not have access to credit to e-shop.

Audio visual shopping trolley

As seen in the section Greater reliability and convenience (pp. 253–254), the electronic personal shopping assistant will increasingly support shoppers as they negotiate a bricks store, and we argue below that the development should lead to future benefits for e-retailers and e-shoppers. Linked to a future shopping trolley-mounted touch screen, an EPSA will provide shoppers information on current store merchandise, in-store events, specialized product demonstrations/taste testing and, of course, store specials.

The audio visual shopping trolley will act as a two-way shopping data vehicle presenting benefits to customers and retailers. Benefits to customers from using the EPSA-linked shopping trolleys are:

- A quicker shopping trip for those customers who do *not* enjoy the shopping experience.
- Personalization of the product offering and related information.
- Recall of frequently purchased items to reduce the chance of forgetting items.
- Reduced embarrassment in asking for item locations.
- Reduced delays by transmitting special orders to specific departments before arriving at those sections, e.g. special cuts of meat from the meat department.
- Suggested recipes for a grocery item on special or in bulk.

Figure 12.8 *Audio-visual shopping trolley with EPSA technology*

Source: www.future-store.org

Management equally receives benefits from EPSA-linked shopping trolleys through greater control over their operations resulting from improved knowledge and awareness of stock issues. Advantages to the future e-retailer will be:

- Real time inventory levels.
- Better understanding of customer shopping habits and profiling.
- Promotion of specialized or seasonal merchandise direct to the customers with the greater likelihood of making a purchase.
- Shelving that recommends cross-sells and up-sells to increase sales volumes.
- Improved feedback to suppliers on what sells and daily traffic patterns for demonstrations and gondola-end displays.
- Alerts for corrective action being needed in dramatic situations, e.g. staffing issues with long queues of customers at checkouts or other sections of the store.

The future of e-retailing is, as is the case for most estimates of the future, encouraging, but the format is uncertain. What can be said with certainty is that success and profitability will revolve around an historical truism: when the retailer knows the customer, the customer will continue to know the retailer and that translates into repeat sales and profits. The solution is in adopting the appropriate technology to meet the needs of customers.

CHAPTER SUMMARY

The dynamic nature of technology in the future will lead to costly investment decisions for retailers. To reduce the possibility of selecting inappropriate technology the e-retailer must keep in mind the buying decision process that follows the established stages of need recognition, information search, information evaluation, purchase decision and post-purchase behaviour. Not understanding the online customer's buying process has contributed to abandoned cart syndrome and e-retailer closures (for example in the dot.com crash). To overcome the lack of a physical store, e-retailers need to assist the online shopper's buying decision process through improved informational exchanges, e.g. newsgroups and FAQ web pages. The technology is not restricted to e-retailers but is being adopted by bricks and mortar retailers in the form of improved payment systems and merchandise identification through RFID tagging. Bricks retailers are making great strides in modernization. As a result, bricks and clicks retailers are increasingly making the running as opposed to pureplay dot.coms.

In the introductory pages to this book, we quoted the personal experiences of Matthew Wall (*Sunday Times* (UK) journalist) of life as an e-shopper. Matthew concluded that e-retailing is coming of age, but recognized his need to 'get out more'. Even the most committed e-shoppers still like bricks shopping and trust bricks brands and malls. Such shopper loyalty is likely to ensure that the high street will not be replaced by e-retail, but will more and more represent the physical presence of the successful multi-channel bricks and clicks retailers.

Case study 12.1: METRO AG EXTRA FUTURE STORE

In April 2003 the Dusseldorf-based Metro Group opened what they called the 'Extra Future Store' to test a range of retail technologies. Metro is the fifth largest retailer in the world, with 2,300 stores in 26 countries and sales of €51.5bn in 2002. The systems include radio frequency identification, smart shelves, intelligent scales, electronic shelf labels, kiosks, personal shopping assistants, anti-theft portals, portable self-scanning and self-checkout lanes. The 33,000-square-foot Extra Future Store is covered by a wireless LAN (*WLAN*) based on the Wi-Fi 802.11b standard to link this new shopping technology.

Attending the grand opening of the Extra Future Store were officials from the German Government and retailing industry, with German model Claudia Schiffer dubbed the first customer. Metro's partners in the initiative incorporated 40 separate partners including Chep, Cisco, Coca-Cola, Gillette, Hewlett Packard, Kraft Foods, IBM, Intel, Mettler Toledo, NCR, Oracle, Procter and Gamble, Symbol technologies and Wincor Nixdorf.

According to Zygmunt Mierdorf of the Metro Group, the expected outcome of the retailing technology adoption would be higher sales levels and lower costs following improved customer satisfaction from goods being more readily available, the service becoming more individualized and the increase in shopping convenience. The RFID applications in the Extra Future Store represent an ambitious test of the technology developed by the Auto-ID Center at MIT, Cambridge, Massachusetts. This Auto-ID technology uses the EPC (electronic product code) – a 96-bit chip identifier of an individual item or packaged group of items. 'Anti-theft portals' linked to the RFID tags were set up at Extra Future Store exits and 'checkout lanes' were equipped with RFID readers. Checkouts also use bar code scanners for merchandise not yet RFID tagged. As part of the 'smart-shelf application', RFID tag readers recognize the removal of the tagged merchandise from the shelf. An alert may then be passed by Wi-Fi to the store's distribution centre and to store staff via PDAs (currently Hewlett-

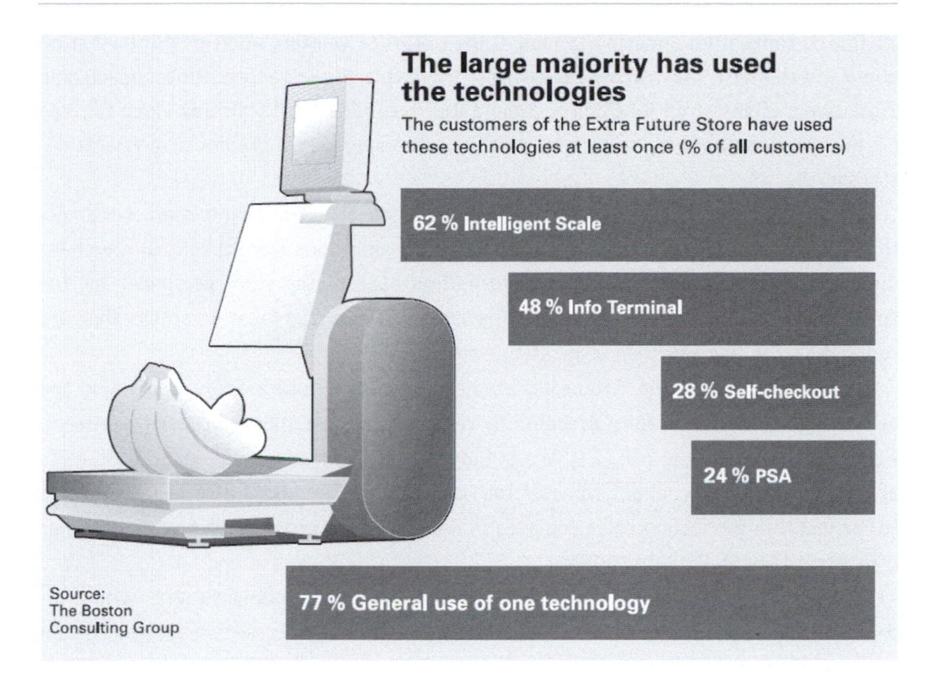

Figure 12.9 *Assessment of the technology usage in the Extra Future Store*

Source: www.future-store.org

Packard's iPaq 5450 and 3970 models as well as Symbol Technologies' PDT-8100) advising that a shelf is low in stock and requires replenishment before embarrassing and loss-causing out-of-stock situations. Through the WLAN-linked PDAs, employees are able to check the inventory and, if necessary, reorder goods by directly linking into Metro's merchandise management system from any area in the store. A future extension of the PDA functionality will be to add telephony features that will allow staff to make calls, send messages or download data.

The next significant Extra Future Store device is the personal shopping assistant (PSA), a mini-computer with a touch-screen video display attached to a shopping cart. Manufactured by Wincor Nixdorf International, a PSA enables the customer to enter their shopping list or download it to the screen from the Internet. PSA computer software then directs the customer to the store positions that hold the merchandise on the shopping list. As an information support to the customer or as an advertising medium, the PSA screen has the facility to display a video about merchandise taken off a shelf or for merchandise in proximity to the PSA shopping cart. Linked to the store checkout system, the PSA empowers the customer to scan bar coded and/or RFID-tagged merchandise prior to arriving at the checkouts and wirelessly transmit the merchandise details and price data to the checkouts and so reduce the payment stage of the shopping experience. Should the customer choose, they have the option of self-checkout machines that avoid the need to interact with checkout staff.

For customers not choosing to look at their PSA or wanting additional information about merchandise taken from the shelves, the Extra Future Store utilizes electronic kiosk applications at various points around the store. The kiosks display video footage on the merchandise with such information as the supplier, ingredients, preparation, storage, etc.

Metro's electronic shelf labelling and advertising displays permit store personnel to wirelessly update merchandise prices and any promotions from a central merchandise management system. Providing information back to the store personnel are the smart shelves with shelf-mounted RFID readers to impart updates on stocks that are running low or nearing their expiration dates.

The Boston Consulting Group has studied the Extra Future Store and found the new technologies are readily accepted by most of the customers. Dr Gerd Wolfram, Project Manager of the METRO Group Future Store Initiative explained, 'customers are really enthusiastic about some of the innovations. The study also bears evidence to the fact that the technologies deployed in the store have prompted a higher customer frequency' (Metro Group, 2003b).

Of the specialized Extra Future Store technologies, especially popular with two-thirds of the customers was the Intelligent Scale containing the so-called VeggieVision camera, which automatically recognizes the fruit or vegetable being weighed and then

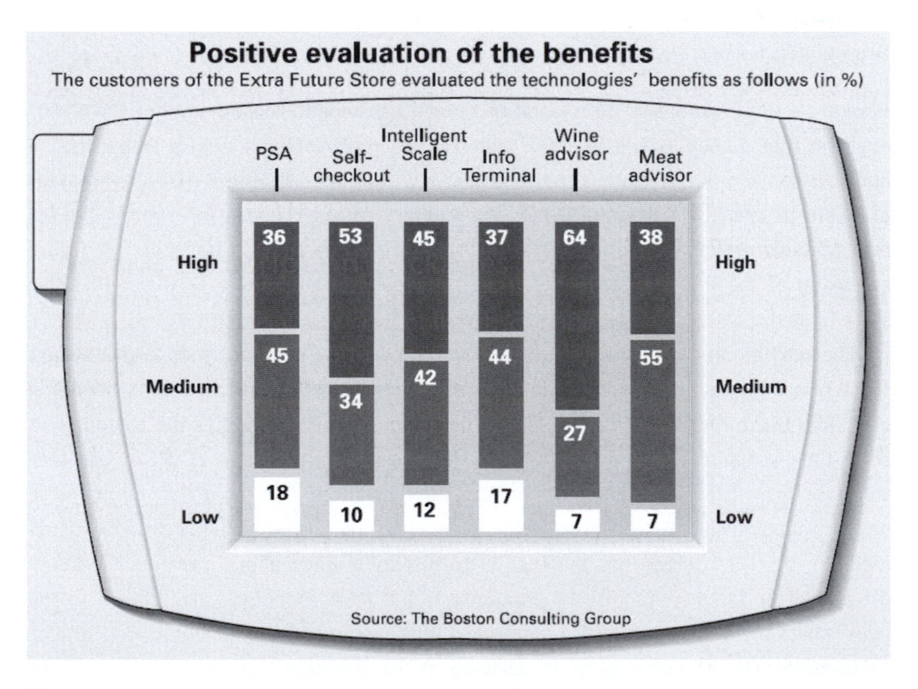

Figure 12.10 *Positive evaluation of the benefits of technology in the Extra Future Store*

Source: www.future-store.org

prints out the appropriate price labels. Dispelling the long-held view that technology adoption is inversely related to age, elderly people using the Extra Future Store also made regular use of the new technologies offered. As an example, 56 per cent of the customers over 60 years old were using the Intelligent Scale. Figures 12.9 and 12.10 show the level of information adoption.

Although it is a working experiment in future retailing and customer interactions, the Metro Extra Future Store is a strong indicator of how e-retailing will look in the near future and traditional retailers had better take note.

Sources: Blau (2003); Mathieson (2003); Metro Group (2003b); SN (2003)

QUESTIONS

Brief feedback to these questions is included at the back of the book.

Question 12.1

Some workplaces are restricting Internet access due to high levels of online personal activities. How should e-retailers respond to this limited access threat?

Question 12.2

If a consumer can buy goods online to save money and then pick up from the retailer's bricks and mortar store, isn't this cannibalizing the bricks and mortar store sales?

FURTHER READING

Kaufman-Scarborough, C. and Lindquist, J.D. (2002) 'e-Shopping in a multiple channel environment', *Journal of Consumer Marketing*, 19 (4): 333–350.

Omwand, H.K., Favier, J., van Tongeren, T. and Méndez, M.Á. (2003) *Smart Multi-channel Grocery Retail Strategies*, Forrester Research, www.forrester.com/ER/Research/Report/Summary/0,1338,16718,FF.html.

Reh, F.J. (2003) *Pareto's Principle: The 80–20 Rule*, Abiut Inc., www.management.about.com/library/weekly/aa081202.htm [accessed 2 December 2003].

Schoenbachler, D.D. and Gordon, G.L. (2002) 'Multi-channel shopping: understanding what drives channel choice', *Journal of Consumer Marketing*, 19 (1): 42–53.

REFERENCES

Amazon (2003) *Egghead Orders and Policy Info*, Amazon.com, www.amazon.com/exec/obidos/tg/browse/-/776128/102-7635508-9796126 [accessed 19 November 2003].

Anonymous (2003) *A Brief History of Barcodes*, www.geocities.com/SiliconValley/Campus/8351/page1.htm [accessed 19 October 2003].

Berry, L.L., Seiders, K. and Grewal, D. (2002) 'Understanding service convenience', *Journal of Marketing*, 66 (3): 1–17.

Blau, J. (2003) *Supermarket Tunes into Wireless*, IDG, www.computerweekly.com/Article124242.htm [accessed 29 November 2003].

Cho, Y., Im, I., Hiltz, R. and Fjermestad, J. (2002) 'An analysis of online customer complaints: implications for web complaint management', *Proceedings of 35th Hawaii International Conference on System Sciences*, IEEE: Hawaii, pp. 1–10.

Davis, G. (2001) *Just Windows Shopping*, The Standard, www.europe.thestandard.com/articles/display/0,1151,15414,00.html [accessed 16 May 2001].

Editor (2001) *Traditional Retailers Eye Online Future*, BBC News, www.news.bbc.co.uk/2/hi/business/1155860.stm [accessed 26 September 2003].

Editor (2002) *The Quote 'May You Live in Interesting Times'*, BBC, www.bbc.co.uk/dna/h2g2/alabaster/A807374 [accessed 26 September 2003].

Fenech, T. (2002) 'Antecedents to web cart abandonment', *Proceedings of Australian and New Zealand Marketing Academy Conference (ANZMAC 2002)*, Gold Coast, Queensland/Melbourne, Victoria.

Gengler, B. (2003) 'Privacy problems for RFID', *The Australian*, 22 July.

Huarng, A.S. and Christopher, D. (2003) 'Planning an effective Internet retail store', *Marketing Intelligence & Planning*, 21 (4), 230–238.

Kennedy, R.F. (1966) *May You Live in Interesting Times*, Cape Town, SA: University of Cape Town.

Lightfoot, W. (2003) 'Multi-channel mistake: the demise of a successful retailer', *International Journal of Retail and Distribution Management*, 34 (4), 220–229.

Mathieson, R. (2003) *Shopping for Insights at 'The Store of the Future'*, HP – mpulse Magazine, www.cooltown.com/mpulse/0803-supermarket.asp?print=yes [accessed 27 November 2003].

Metro Group (2003a) *Future Store Initiative*, METRO Group, www/future-store.org/servlet/PB/menu/1000372_12/1066514206871.html [accessed 19 October 2003].

Metro Group (2003b) *Store of the Future Passes First Field Test*, www.future-store.org/servlet/PB/menu/1000456_12/1064707754311.html#7 [accessed 29 November 2003].

Shim, R. (2003) *Wireless Credit Card in Development*, CNET, www.news.zdnet.co.uk/software/developer/0,39020387,2135361,00.htm [accessed 27 November 2003].

SN (2003) 'Metro AG Future Store', *Supermarket News*, 12 May.

Thornton, J. and Marche, S. (2003) 'Sorting through the dot bomb rubble: how did the high-profile e-tailers fail?' *International Journal of Information Management*, 23 (2), 121–138.

WEB LINKS

www.benetton.com
An innovator in many fields, Benetton were one of the first major manufacturers to consider the application of the RFID tags to track stock.

www.dhl.com
Ordering logistics and tracking shipments online.

www.egghead.com
Now part of Amazon.com at www.amazon.com/exec/obidos/tg/browse/-/776128/102-7635508-9796126 (19/11/2003).

www.fedex.com
Ordering logistics and tracking shipments online; and facilities and advice for e-business.

www.kfc.com
Originally called Kentucky Fried Chicken, KFC is trialling RFID tags to monitor inventory items.

www.mcdwireless.com
McDonald's provides high speed wireless Internet access at over 100 restaurants in Chicago, New York, San Francisco Bay and Canada. In September 2003 McDonald's conducted online promotions and provided prize giveaways including Toshiba notebook computers and Pocket PCs.

www.sears.com
Web information and ordering facility for the original catalogue and then bricks and mortar retailer.

www.walmart.com
The world's largest retailer has tested a number of techniques to monitor its inventory, one of these techniques being the RFID tags.

www.wishlist.com.au
Web shopping site where buyers may arrange to have the purchased items delivered to a nominated and participating BP Service Station for collection.

Answers

Preliminary feedback is given to each question, but this should be seen merely as a guide. It is up to the reader to elaborate on the answer and in some cases maybe take quite a different tack to that provided by the authors. We do not imply that there is only one correct answer.

CHAPTER 1: THE WORLD OF E-RETAILING

Question 1.1
What do you think would be disadvantages of e-retailing for an independent baker like Botham's?
Feedback – May be put off by high set-up investment and ongoing costs plus level of know-how and technology needed.

Question 1.2
What do you consider are the main advantages of e-retailing for a small independent baker like Botham's?
Feedback – Location is unimportant; size does not matter; and it reaches a larger audience.

Question 1.3
Why do you think Abbey National's e-bank is separately branded as 'Cahoot'?
Feedback – High street customers might consider they were being unfairly treated if e-customers of the same bank received a better deal.

Question 1.4
Why do you think that the 7Cs of the e-retail mix represent a superior model to the traditional 4Ps and other versions of the retail mix?
Feedback – More customer-orientated than the 4Ps, emphasizing *C1 Convenience for the customer* rather than a company's distribution network; *C2 Customer value*

and benefits rather than a product a company sells; *C3 Cost to the customer* rather than the price set by the company; and *C4 Communication and customer relationships* rather than promoting products with a hard sell. More specific to (e-)retail than the 4Ps, also including the essential elements of success and customer satisfaction: *C5 Computer and category management issues* needed to provide slick, reliable delivery without high stocks; *C6 Customer franchise*, i.e. the vital brand image and customer trust; and *C7 Customer care and service*, giving priority to looking after the customers' interests. Easier to remember than the traditional less standardized versions of the retail mix.

CHAPTER 2: E-RETAILING IN PRACTICE

Question 2.1

Why are books, CDs and DVD movies particularly suitable e-shopping categories?

Feedback – High on all three aspects of the de Kare-Silver ES test.

Product characteristics: low touch products, simple to deliver by post.

Familiarity and confidence: customers usually know exactly what they are ordering.

Consumer attributes: the typical buyers tend to be younger, better educated and of a higher socio-economic group than the general population.

Question 2.2

Why is it surprising that groceries are among the biggest-selling e-retail products in the UK?

Feedback – Low on all three aspects of the de Kare-Silver ES test.

Product characteristics: high sensory input in selection (visual, touch and smell), perishable, cannot be delivered by post.

Familiarity and confidence: non-packaged products like fruit and vegetables can be variable in characteristics and quality.

Consumer attributes: on average, older and less educated than typical shoppers for products such as CDs.

Question 2.3

Why are groceries one of the main UK e-shopping categories?

Feedback – One of the first UK e-retail products, pursued by Tesco with single-minded determination to provide customer satisfaction, using an easy-entry, cost-effective e-retailing system.

Question 2.4

How might mass-market clothing e-retailers increase business?

Feedback – Improve web atmospherics, e.g. more attractive, interactive site design and layout, more personalization and customization.

CHAPTER 3: INTEGRATION OF E-RETAILING INTO AN ORGANIZATION

Question 3.1

What do you consider to be the advantages and disadvantages that traditional retailers have in comparison with Internet pureplays, in terms of online trading?
Feedback – This chapter outlines several advantages and disadvantages for traditional retailers integrating e-retail; for example, they may have experience in the given product sector but often lack experience in the e-commerce dimension. Further advantages and disadvantages are given in Boxes 1.1 and 1.2 (pp. 3 and 4).

Question 3.2

Why do you think online customers may not be loyal to a particular company?
Feedback – Where online shopping is price-driven, it is much easier to compare prices online and move from website to website, than it is to do the same with physical shops. Also, many aspects of the normal retail shopping experience, such as face-to-face interaction, are missing from the online shopping experience, which can increase the homogeneity among outlets.

Question 3.3

What are the dangers of multi-channel operations from a company's perspective?
Feedback – A company must maintain a consistent brand, not just concerning, for instance, standards for logos, colours and fonts, etc., but regarding values and message. Other factors include having consistent terms of business so that there is no conflict in pricing or returns policy, for example.

CHAPTER 4: UNDERSTANDING AND COMMUNICATING WITH THE E-CONSUMER

Question 4.1

Why do people shop?
Feedback – To obtain useful benefits, but also for many other reasons. For example, to enjoy the process or to socialize with others.

Question 4.2

Can e-shopping satisfy shoppers as much as bricks shopping does?
Feedback – Bricks shopping and e-shopping are different and there is some evidence that e-shopping does not satisfy recreational motives as well as bricks shopping does. Even so, successful e-retailers can provide satisfaction for enjoyment and social motives.

Question 4.3

How can the mechanistic process of e-shopping satisfy shoppers' social motives?
Feedback – For example, by providing social experiences, communication with others having a similar interest, and membership of virtual communities.

Question 4.4

What can e-retailers do to provide enjoyment and social benefits for e-shoppers?

Feedback – For example, provide chat rooms and bulletin boards; provide facilities for product reviews and suggestion boxes; and personalize offers.

CHAPTER 5: INFORMATION SEARCH ON THE WEB

Question 5.1

What is the *one* thing I can do to get my website noticed?

Feedback – Build a good home page, with a title, meta-information, no frames and with content pointing to what goods and services you are offering.

Question 5.2

I put up a good web page some months ago, but nobody is accessing it much nowadays.

Feedback – Change the content! People get bored by the same old thing. Put something relevant and timely for people to read.

CHAPTER 6: E-STORE DESIGN: NAVIGABILITY, INTERACTIVITY AND WEB ATMOSPHERICS

Question 6.1

Why do you think design issues are more important for e-retailers than for offline (bricks) retailers?

Feedback – Whereas design issues have some importance for offline retailers, they are just one of many components of the retail mix. In contrast, design issues affect just about everything in an e-retail context, including navigation, interactivity, relationships and atmospherics.

Question 6.2

Two checklists have been presented in this chapter (a three-point list and a six-point list – see pp. 132 and 133) to assist in the evaluation of the navigability of an e-retail site. How would you develop these two lists into a 'metric' that quantifies these points?

Feedback – A metric requires us to give numbers to the various aspects of navigability. So we have to develop numbers such as a scale of 1 to 10 if you think the site performs either well or badly on that particular attribute. So a site might make it very clear where you are at the moment and you might give it 9 out of 10, but if it is very confusing about how to go forward to a particular location you might only give it 4 out of 10.

Question 6.3

How could an e-retailer use the metrics developed in Question 6.2 to help improve its navigability performance?

Feedback – Providing you can work out a consistent way of measuring each aspect, then you can do this over time and get a good handle on which things are working and which things are not. The bad things identified by the metrics can be fixed through redesign of the website (for example, better directions on how to find a particular location, if it had only scored 4 out of 10). This should then lead to more satisfied customers.

Question 6.4

What is e-interactivity and how would you measure it?

Feedback – Interactivity occurs between the user of a website and the site itself. The site is an ongoing entity, with a capacity to provide service, sell goods, transact money, be cheerful or grumpy, be there tomorrow for you, and so on. Chapter 6 includes a seven-item scale of interactivity, including, for example, 'site helps the viewer participate, learn and act' and 'the site develops a close, personalized relationship with the viewer'. Metrics can be applied to these items in the same way that you used metrics to measure navigability.

Question 6.5

How does interactivity help an e-retailer build a stronger relationship with its customers?

Feedback – Communication is seen as an important part of building any relationship. Given that e-interactivity is a communication-based interface, it seems likely that it could be important for developing e-relationships.

Question 6.6

Consider two different types of e-retailers. Name them. What sort of web atmospherics would be best for each of them (not necessarily what they are currently using)?

Feedback – The answer to this will depend on the examples chosen by the reader. No doubt some retail categories lend themselves more to the use of web atmospherics – e-grocery shopping, for example, is primarily information driven, whereas online fashion buying has more need and potential for the use of atmospherics.

CHAPTER 7: E-SERVICE

Question 7.1

What is the difference between the macro and the micro view of e-service?

Feedback – Basically, the macro view is a very broad view about what constitutes e-service and more or less equates e-service and e-commerce. The micro perspective sees it in terms of the provision of particular and varied detailed customer services within a site as part of the website-to-user interface.

Question 7.2

Why do Moon and Frei (2000) prefer the co-production model of e-service rather than the self-service model?

Feedback – Moon and Frei (2000) are concerned that self-service may be construed as a laissez-faire free-for-all, in which the e-retailer takes a lazy approach and lets the user/consumer do all the work through self-service. This would prove frustrating for many (but not all) consumers, so instead they advocate a more cooperative or co-production type of approach to the provision of e-services.

Question 7.3

Do you agree that the factors that contribute to *good* e-service are different from the factors that contribute to *bad* e-service? Why?

Feedback – The factors presented from the critical incident study in Chapter 7 (pp. 157–162) are that they are quite different. Interactivity and information were seen as useful ways of developing higher levels of e-service, whereas the traps or negative service were seen as often coming from things such as poor delivery or a poor returns service. One can see these in terms of 'motivators', to get people positively motivated towards a site, and 'hygiene factors' for the negatives – things that may not get people really excited about a site, but make them mad if they do not work well.

Question 7.4

Explain how e-service metrics can help an e-retailer better manage their business.

Feedback – Recall our answers to questions 6.2 and 6.3, because a similar approach is needed. There is no single best way of measuring these things. Numbers on a 1 to 10 scale could be used. Equally, a critical incident is either a yes or a no – if the incident occurs (yes), otherwise (no). This is a simpler approach. Which one do you prefer? Two sections of Chapter 7 are devoted to e-service metrics as a performance tool (see pp. 162–163).

CHAPTER 8: BRANDING ON THE WEB

Question 8.1

A common mistake in branding or the understanding of branding is to treat it very narrowly as a sign, symbol or slogan. What is wrong or limiting with this approach?

Feedback – First, lots of people make this mistake, so you should not feel too bad if you are one of them. Second, the use of a sign or slogan is a good start to branding, so it should be seen as part of a total branding approach. However, it misses opportunities to use branding in a more powerful way. This will happen when we think of the brand in terms of its substance and essence and start to develop these ideas further.

Question 8.2

Briefly summarize the three-stage approach for e-brand development outlined in Chapter 8 (pp. 173–175).

Feedback – The three stages include brand concept (what is the basic idea of the brand?) as a start, followed by building the brand platform (including personality, purpose, point of difference and brand back-up) and finally implementation through the brand elements (elements are all the points of contact between the e-retailer and their customers). More details are in Chapter 8.

Question 8.3

The brand platform stage of e-brand development includes the need to develop the personality of the e-brand. Select a particular e-retailer and show how you would use web atmospherics to develop the brand of this particular e-retailer.

Feedback – Clearly the answer here depends on which e-retailer you have chosen. Chapter 6 gives you more ideas about the options for web atmospherics. The key thing is to choose the right type of atmospherics to suit a specific brand. The matching process between the atmospherics and the brand is a critical branding principle, so be prepared to justify your choice of atmospherics.

Question 8.4

Chapter 8 has really highlighted the importance of interactivity and trust as necessary for building strong e-brands. Why have these two aspects been highlighted in this role?

Feedback – Chapter 8 gives more details, but a key answer is that e-retailers have *experiential* brands, thus interactivity is bound to be important. Trust is important for all brands, but is likely to be especially important because it takes a lot of faith that, by clicking a mouse, money will be transmitted and goods will be delivered!

Question 8.5

Why are Amazon and eBay regarded as such strong e-brands?

Feedback – Both of these e-retailers have had major financial (especially traffic and sales; less so profit) success and stand above most of the remaining field. Several books and many papers have been written about them. They have played pioneering roles in their categories, though neither was the absolute (first) pioneer. They have each displayed leadership qualities in innovating and adopting progressive e-retailing practices. We will leave it to the reader to discover what they see as the best features of each of these two e-retail legends.

CHAPTER 9: E-MALLS

Question 9.1

What is important in managing conventional malls?

Feedback – It is important to manage the tenant relationship and the basics, such as quality (through the tenant mix), service, atmosphere and infrastructure, as well as achieve the right overall image and position in the market. More details are given in the chapter.

Question 9.2

How do you *translate* the principles in managing conventional malls to e-malls?
Feedback – The same principles apply, with just a slight change in the translation. The tenant mix remains critical, with a danger of having too many unknown pure (cyberspace) e-retailers. Big well-known clicks e-retailers are not a problem, but there should not be too many of the www.clickandtrustme.com type.

A major finding of our original research in this chapter is that interactivity and trust, especially the latter, are extremely important for developing and building an e-mall.

Question 9.3

Do you regard a shopping bot as an intelligent agent or a virtual mall? Why?
Feedback – The paper from Rowley (2000), discussed in Chapter 9 (pp. 191–192), indicates that you can interpret shopping bots either way. The chapter primarily views them from the perspective of a virtual mall because its topic is e-malls, but you may wish to reconsider them as intelligent agents, that is, like intelligent shopping assistants. This alternative interpretation would require us to relocate the notion to Chapter 6, where we considered issues such as navigation and information search.

Question 9.4

Why are e-malls less dominant in cyberspace than bricks malls are in physical space?
Feedback – This is an important question and gets to the bottom of the entire rationale for e-retailing. A number of the authors' views are canvassed in the conclusion section of Chapter 9. Perhaps e-malls are late starters at the beginning of their lifecycles. This was also the case with conventional malls. There were very few conventional malls in the 1950s, with rapid growth since then. One view that we do favour is that most online shopping trips are very focused on a particular category and therefore it would suffice to visit a particular e-retailer or a narrowly focused e-mall, whereas multi-purpose shopping trips are common and more desirable offline and, therefore, suit conventional malls.

CHAPTER 10: E-RETAILING MODELS

Question 10.1

How would use of the retail participant groups in a retailer's environment help minimize channel disintermediation?

Feedback – By consulting with suppliers, partners and dealers the e-retailer will identify those distribution issues that may damage the relationship between the channel members before they occur.

Question 10.2

If catalogues and website pages look the same, i.e. are two-dimensional images, yet the web page can include other features including music and changing graphics, why do many catalogue customers resist buying online?
Feedback – Part of the reason is habit, that is, the old adage 'if it ain't broke don't fix it'. The catalogue users are comfortable with what they have used for so long and see no great benefit from the Web's technology. Another often quoted reason given by catalogue users is that the catalogue comes to them regularly without being requested and can be read any time that is convenient to the user. In addition, no PC is needed to view the merchandise.

Question 10.3

Can a customer be in more than one of the A.C. Nielsen electronic shopper categories?
Feedback – As no person is ever a perfect fit for clothing, neither are they for categorization – as helpful as the fit would be for the retailer. A person could be a *habit die-hard* but, because of their employment, they cannot get to the mall for a special purchase and so have to consider the convenience of a non-store retailing channel, such as the Web.

CHAPTER 11: M-SHOPPING

Question 11.1

It took half a decade to get a critical mass of computer users to adopt the Internet as an information and shopping environment. Will retailers need to have specialized Internet sites to display the e-retailers' offerings on the compact screens of PDA or mobile phones?
Feedback – This has already been attempted for WAP-enabled cellular phones and the results received limited success for the suppliers. Using *middleware*, online suppliers packaged the content sought by the end-user and fitted this content to the phone displays. This meant removing much of the visual detail that gives traditional web pages information richness. Fortunately, mobile communication technology is improving with clearer display screens and polyphonic sound quality to emulate and almost duplicate the Web experience of using large computer displays.

Question 11.2

Many people use cafés and restaurants to get away from the work environment. Will providing restaurant Wi-Fi hotspots like McDonald's and Starbucks alienate these people?

Feedback – The Wi-Fi facility is not exclusively the domain of the business person on the road. The Internet provides many distractions through chat rooms and e-mail that would enhance the feeling of getting away from the office. Similarly, Wi-Fi permits the business person to do that last-minute check of documents and calendar appointments while having a meal or a cuppa.

CHAPTER 12: MULTI-CHANNEL SUCCESS AND THE FUTURE OF E-RETAILING

Question 12.1

Some workplaces are restricting Internet access due to high levels of online personal activities. How should e-retailers respond to this limited access threat?
Feedback – Work with the non-associated workplaces. This is not a new concept; social clubs at workplaces have often received preferred customer treatment from retailer groups to encourage purchases at those associated retailers. Employers and their staff could be offered incentives by e-retailers (e.g. discounts or delivery specials) for using the e-retailer at specific times that limit interference with work operations.

Question 12.2

If a consumer can buy goods online to save money and then pick up from the retailer's bricks and mortar store, isn't this cannibalizing the bricks and mortar store sales?
Feedback – Some cannibalization is possible; however, the service is intended and likely to generate sales that would not be made at the bricks and mortar store, for example to busy people who do not get time to browse in a physical store and want to avoid crowds.

Glossary

Adobe Acrobat The PDF (Portable Document Format) developed by Adobe is a format for electronic document exchange that preserves document integrity so files can be viewed and printed on a variety of computer platforms such as MS Windows, Linux, Apple Mac and Palm personal digital assistant handheld devices.

Atmospherics In the bricks retail store, the deliberate design of sensory stimuli for sight, sound, touch and smell, to produce subconscious emotional effects in shoppers, aimed at increasing sales. See also *Web atmospherics.*

Bar code This is a widely used graphic identification tag for merchandise using dark vertical bars for scanning and recording purposes.

Barkers/spruikers Announcers who 'bark' out the specials and retailer offerings to catch the attention of potential shoppers.

Bluetooth Chip technology that links voice and data connections between a wide range of devices over a short range. This includes mobile phones, computers and PDAs. Bluetooth's founding members include Ericsson, IBM, Intel, Nokia and Toshiba.

Brand development A three-stage process that moves from brand identity to the brand platform and is then implemented through the brand elements.

Bricks see *High street.*

Bricks and clicks see *Multi-channel retailing.*

Broadband Connection to the Internet that is considerably faster than the standard telephone dial-up. Broadband saves time in downloading large files such as audio and video and is necessary to obtain quality streamed material. There is no accepted definition of speed.

B2B Business-to-business e-commerce.

B2C Business-to-consumer e-commerce.

Category management (CM) A retailer/supplier process of managing categories as strategic business units, aiming to enhance results by focusing on delivering consumer value.

Clicks see *e-Shopping.*

Click-through A measure of effectiveness of links to one site from another. For example, the 'marketing' site for students, pages.britishlibrary/net/~cdennis, has links to marketing textbooks available from www.amazon.co.uk, and the monthly report from Amazon will list the number of times the link has been used, i.e. clicked through.

Cookie A file containing a unique user identifier that is placed in a user's browser by a website's server, allowing the user's interactions with the site to be tracked. Subject to the user's consent, e-retailers can use cookies to personalize communications with e-shoppers in order to improve online sales/services; enable subscribers to access a site without a password; record popular links; record demographics; and track visitor search preferences.

Customer franchise An (e-)retailer's standing in the assessments of its customers: image, trust and branding.

Customer relationship management (CRM) Techniques and systems for retaining existing customers rather than attracting new ones. The term is often used more narrowly to refer to computer-based systems that integrate information about customers with uses of that information.

Directory Web page with a list of website URLs, usually arranged in some hierarchical manner, e.g. by subject matter. An example would be Yahoo!

Disintermediation The elimination of supply chain members.

Dot.com crash Loss of investor confidence and fall in share prices affecting the technology sector, particularly Internet start-up companies, in the year 2000.

Double-opt-in After a customer has opted in to a mailing list, a message is sent asking them to confirm that that is what they want. This ensures the correct identity of the recipient.

DVD Digital video disc. A type of CD format for greater storage of digital data. DVD movies play video and audio close to cinema quality (but need a good amplifier and speakers). You can burn your own home movie discs through a PC.

e-Branding The application of branding principles to projecting a brand image of an e-retailer. See also *Model of e-branding*.

Efficient customer response (ECR) The retail equivalent of *Just in Time (JIT)*. Focusing on the efficiency of the total supply system rather than individual components, ECR aims to reduce total system costs, inventories and physical assets, while improving consumers' choice. Elements of ECR include efficient 'replenishment', e.g. *EDI* or web links to shorten order cycles; and 'store assortment', e.g. *Category management (CM)* and space allocation.

Electronic data interchange (EDI) Computer systems (usually operated by a third-party contractor and pre-dating the Internet) designed to exchange large quantities of data between computers.

Electronic Point of Sale (EPoS) Retail till systems that operate electronically, currently from bar codes. The data can be fed directly into e.g. *EDI* or *ECR* systems to control stocks and reordering. (Electronic Funds Transfer Point of Sale – EFTPoS – also enables payment via debit or credit cards.)

e-Mall Sometimes referred to as a cyber-mall or a virtual mall or an e-shopping centre. It brings together a number of separately owned e-retail sites to a single virtual location, with the individual e-retailers paying rent to the centre management, as in an offline mall.

e-Retail The sale of goods and services via Internet or other electronic channels, for personal or household use by consumers.

e-Retail mix (or Retail mix) (7Cs) Shorthand term for the blend of tools and techniques that e-retailers (or retailers) use to provide value for customers. Based on the 4Ps or 4Cs of the marketing mix, the key elements of e-retail success can be summarized as the 7Cs: C1 Convenience for the customer; C2 Customer value and benefits; C3 Cost to the customer; C4 Communication and customer relationships; C5 Computer and category management issues; C6 Customer franchise; and C7 Customer care and service.

e-Service The micro perspective involves the provision of particular and varied detailed customer services within a site as part of the website-to-user interface.

e-Shopping (Clicks) The purchase of goods and services by consumers using *e-retail* channels.

e-Store design Refers to the purposeful design of the e-retailer's site. This covers text, graphics and audio. It includes listing products, product information including price, method of payment, navigation, policies, interaction and web atmospherics. See also *Model of e-store design.*

e-Zine A magazine published only in electronic format.

Frequently asked questions (FAQs) A series of questions submitted by previous Internet users. The website owners then provide responses to these questions. The objective is to reduce the resources required to respond to the 20 per cent of questions that are asked 80 per cent of the time (the Pareto Principle 80/20 rule).

High street (bricks) The sale of goods and services from real shops in streets and shopping centres.

Hotspot A geographic area that receives a wireless network signal that may be accessed by hardware with the appropriate Wi-Fi transmission specification.

Hyperlink Where a graphic, image or text has an inbuilt link to another graphic, image, piece or text, document name or website. The user need only click on the hyperlink to move to the linked target.

Hypertext A term first presented by Ted Nelson in a paper for a conference of the Association of Computing Machinery (ACM) in the mid-1960s, hypertext refers to a collection of documents (or 'nodes') containing cross-references or cross-links to move from one document to another.

Initial Public Offering (IPO) In an IPO, shares of a company are offered for the first time on the stock market, and a company obtains a stock market listing. The new issue provides the company with capital for the financing of its future development.

Interactivity Refers to the interactivity between the user of an e-site and the site itself. The site is not simply a machine but rather an ongoing entity, with a capacity to provide service, sell goods, transact money, be cheerful or grumpy, be there tomorrow for you and so on. Interactive software programs on computing and gaming devices take input from the user to adapt to the user's requirements while running the program operation. Interactive input is made by way of an input device, e.g. keyboard commands, mouse clicks, joystick movements, voice commands, etc.

Just in Time (JIT) An IT-based system requiring flexible, efficient processes for ensuring that goods are produced so as to be available where and when wanted, with minimum order quantities and stock levels. The retailers' equivalent is *Efficient customer response (ECR).*

LAN The acronym for Local Area Network, which links computers within a small geographic area.

Mass customization Producing individually designed products and communications to order on a large scale.

Metacrawler (engine) A search engine that submits search terms or words to several other search engines, produces a web page that combines the results and sends this to the e-shopper.

Micropayment A methodology to generate revenue by offering pay-per-view web pages, web links, or web services for small amounts of money called 'microcents'.

Middleware Software that enables a user to request data from a database using the forms on the web browser and then displays the web pages in a configuration based on the user's requests and profile.

Model of e-branding An integrated approach linking key concepts that eventually lead to brand value being created by the e-retailer. Figure 8.1 (p. 177) is a six-component model, including navigability, web atmospherics, interactivity, trust, brand attitudes and brand loyalty.

Model of e-store design A model integrating the main components of design, recognizing that one component might be an influence (causation) on another. Figure 6.4 (p. 142) is a three-component model of e-store design that reflects navigability influencing web atmospherics, while both web atmospherics and navigability combine to influence e-interactivity.

m-Shopping The purchase of goods and services via mobile communications channels such as WAP or 3G, for personal or household use by consumers.

Multi-channel retailing Retailing via more than one channel, e.g. *high street* and Internet *e-retail* (*bricks and clicks*). Multichannel Retail Ltd (MCRL) is a software company that creates innovative solutions for multi-channel retailing.

Multimedia Messaging Services (MMSs) Message services for 3G mobile devices, incorporating graphics and/or sound.

Navigability The ability of the user to move around the site easily, efficiently and effectively, that is, without getting lost. A key objective of good navigation design is to minimize travel, depth and redundancy when travelling within a site.

Opt-in Opt-in lists are based on obtaining permission for future mailing, e.g. by checking a box for 'yes, please send me future communications'. A potential problem is that people can sign others up for services that they do not want (see *double-opt-in*).

Opt-out Opt-out lists assume permission by requiring the recipient to take action to remove themselves from mailings. An individual may be automatically added to a mailing list if they fail to notice the 'Check here if you do not want to receive future mailings'.

PDA (Personal Digital Assistant) First developed by Apple Computers as their Newton hand-held device and later by the 3Com's as the Palm Pilot, the PDA is a mobile computing device that incorporates diary facilities, word processing, e-mail and Internet access. For m-shopping, PDAs are loaded with catalogues such as, for example, Tesco's, usually via a content provider such as AvantGo. An order written out on the move will be automatically placed the next time the PDA is connected to the Internet (unlike shopping from a mobile device such as 3G or WAP where orders are placed immediately). PDAs are also called pocket PCs.

Permission marketing Marketing addressed only to individuals who have specifically requested contact, and limited to the extent of the permission granted by the customer. It is designed to build up trust.

Personal Digital Assistant (PDA) see *PDA*.

Planogram Refers to the placement of merchandise in a store in a specific arrangement to achieve a stated objective.

P2P Peer-to-peer e-commerce between individual users, where individual users connect to each other rather than through a central server, e.g. swapping music files. This is frequently carried out by means of file-swapping software that can be downloaded.

Radio frequency identification (RFID) A miniature electronic device that can track the location of an item and perform many other tasks. The Association for the Automatic Identification and Data Capture (AIDC) gives a description of these electronic identification devices and their usage.

Retail The sale of goods and services for personal, family or household use by consumers using any distribution channel or combination of channels.

Retail mix (*7Cs*) see *e-Retail mix.*

Search engine System used by an e-shopper to obtain lists of URLs related to search terms or words they input.

Search term/word Something that describes what an e-shopper might be interested in and which is to be submitted to a search engine, such as 'shampoo' or 'dendrobium orchids'.

Service component for an e-retailer The sum total of the ancillary support mechanisms provided by the e-retailer and channel intermediaries to aid the prospective buyer in selecting, paying for and receiving the merchandise.

7Cs see *e-Retail mix.*

Shopbot (shopping bot) Amazon may stock the CD that you want – but is the price the lowest possible? What about delivery charges? Shopbots address these questions. These are software agents that automate traditional Web surfing and search the Internet for the best prices or shortest delivery times. For example, for CDs try www.comparebeforeyoubuy.com. The bots can be considered from either a consumer/ shopper perspective or an e-retailer one.

Shopping cart (trolley) An electronic representation of the bricks and mortar shopping cart (or shopping trolley) into which online shoppers place their prospective purchases before the sale is finalized.

Short message systems (SMSs) An increasingly popular text messaging system.

Snake diagram A market-positioning map suitable for multi-attributes. That is, we can use the snake diagram to compare e-retailers across more than two dimensions, which is the limit of the traditional market position maps. In Figure 8.2 (p. 184) we are able to compare three e-retailers across seven attributes.

Spam (sending persistent annoying messages) Unsolicited junk e-mail, or, as a verb, the sending of such messages. Spamming is the opposite of permission marketing, as it refers to unsolicited messages being sent out in bulk to an entire database of addresses. The word is usually said to originate from a Monty Python sketch about a lodging house where you get Spam (processed meat) whether you like it or not.

Start-up A start-up company is one that is formed from scratch, often using private or borrowed funds. By definition, start-ups are new businesses, and may have the advantages as well as the risks of first-to-market innovators, or, in other cases, perhaps lack of experience when compared to businesses already operating in the same sector.

Streaming Playing audio or video live via the Internet (like radio or TV) as opposed to downloading files to be played later.

T-commerce e-Commerce facilitated by interactive TV, or instigated by TV commercials.

3G Third generation mobile phone technology that allows fast data transmission, e.g. for Internet connections. 3G and WAP m-shopping orders are placed immediately (unlike PDAs, where the order is delayed until the device is next connected to the Internet).

24/7 Used for activities (such as retailing) that run 24 hours a day, 7 days a week. In other words, they are operating all the time (as opposed to 9.00 a.m. to 5.30 p.m., say) and usually every day of the year.

VAT (Value Added Tax) A tax payable on purchases in the UK.

Videotex An early, television-based, data transmission system. While its use has diminished, its legacy is the ability of television sets to be able to show closed captions for the hearing impaired. France's videotex industry came to be called Minitel under the marketing umbrella of the nation's telecommunications organization.

Viral marketing Taking advantage of the network effects of the Internet to spread messages widely by customer endorsement.

Virus A computer code that attaches itself to another program, replicating by using that program's resources to make copies of itself and attach them to other programs, causing damage to the operation of networked computers.

WAP (Wireless Application Protocol) A standard used in cellular phones and other mobile devices for accessing Internet content in a concise manner that fits the phones' very small screens. The system enables access to information via a wireless service platform. WAP and 3G m-shopping orders are placed immediately (unlike PDAs where the order is delayed until the device is next connected to the Internet).

Web atmospherics Refers to the sum of the cues used to stimulate the senses of the online user or consumer. Graphics, visuals, audio, colour, product presentation at different levels of resolution and 3-D displays are among the more common examples. The creation of the virtual environment of the e-retail store includes structural design (e.g. frames, pop-ups, 1-click checkout); media (video, audio, graphics and colour management); layout and usability (search facilities, organization and grouping of merchandise); and sound and music. In theory, atmospherics can also include: touch and smell (which might be incorporated by offering to send samples); personalization/customization; visuals and video clips; text; and navigation and usability of the website.

Web crawler A program used to set up the database used by a search engine.

Wi-Fi Short form of the term wireless fidelity (Wi-Fi) and is another name for IEEE 802.l lb transmission specification. It refers to a non-wired connection between a wireless client and a base station or between two wireless clients. The term is most often linked to the Wireless Ethernet Compatibility Alliance (WECA). Wi-Fi is used in place of 802.11b just as we have come to know the term Ethernet in place of the IEEE 802.3 transmission specification.

WLAN (Wireless Local Area Network) Links computers within a geographic area covered by a Wi-Fi network.

Worm A self-replicating program that exists on its own, travelling through and damaging computer networks.

Index